DISCARD

JONSON'S MAGIC HOUSES

Jonson's Magic Houses

Essays in Interpretation

IAN DONALDSON

CLARENDON PRESS · OXFORD
1997

Oxford University Press, Great Clarendon Street, Oxford OX2 6DP

Oxford New York

Athens Auckland Bangkok Bogota Bombay
Buenos Aires Calcutta Cape Town Dar es Salaam
Delhi Florence Hong Kong Istanbul Karachi
Kuala Lumpur Madras Madrid Melbourne
Mexico City Nairobi Paris Singapore
Taipei Tokyo Toronto
and associated companies in
Berlin Ibadan

Oxford is a trade mark of Oxford University Press

Published in the United States
by Oxford University Press Inc., New York

British Library Cataloguing in Publication Data
Data available

Library of Congress Cataloging in Publication Data
Data available
ISBN 0–19–818394–1

1 3 5 7 9 10 8 6 4 2

Typeset by Alliance Phototypesetters
Printed in Great Britain
on acid-free paper by
Biddles Ltd,
Guildford and King's Lynn

FOR GRAZIA

Acknowledgements

SEVERAL of the essays in this book were originally delivered as invited lectures, and many have been published elsewhere in an earlier form; all have been revised for present publication. I am grateful to those who originally commissioned and published these pieces, and to those who have commented on them: in particular to those many friends in the Australian National University's Humanities Research Centre who patiently heard and helpfully criticized some of the earliest drafts. For a period of leave and relief from teaching that enabled me to complete this book, I am indebted to the Dean of the Faculty of Arts at Edinburgh University, Professor J. S. Richardson, and the Research Fund of Edinburgh's Faculty Group of Arts, Music, and Divinity.

'Jonson and the Tother Youth', the C. A. Patrides Lecture at the University of York for 1995, has been published in R. B. Parker and S. P. Zitner (eds.), *Elizabethan Theater: Essays in Honor of S. Schoenbaum* (Newark, 1996), 111–29. 'Gathering and Losing the Self' was presented at a Humanities Research Centre conference on Literary Biography, 'Self and Text', in 1990, and subsequently published in Ian Donaldson, Peter Read, and James Walter (eds.) *Shaping Lives: Reflections on Biography* (Canberra, 1992), 1–20. 'Jonson's Magic Houses' first appeared in *Essays & Studies* (1986), 39–61, and 'Clockwork Comedy' in the *Glasgow Review*, 1 (Spring 1993), 23–38. 'Unknown Ends', the David Novarr Memorial Lecture at Cornell University in 1988, was first published in *Sydney Studies in English*, 18 (1992–3), 48–71. 'The Story of Charis' and 'Politic Picklocks', written with the encouragement of James Tulip and G. A. Wilkes, appeared in the same journal, volume 13 (1987–8), 3–20, and volume 19 (1993–4), 3–20. 'Fathers and Sons' was written for a meeting of the American Society for Eighteenth-Century Studies at Victoria University, British Columbia, in 1977, and appeared in *Southern Review* (Adelaide), 18 (1985), 314–27. ' "Not of an Age" ', presented at the University of Melbourne's 1991 seminar on History and Literature, is published in James Hirsch (ed.), *New*

Perspectives on Ben Jonson (Cranbury, NJ, 1996). 'Jonson, Shakespeare, and the Destruction of the Book' (an early version of which was read at the Folger Shakespeare Library in 1988) and 'Jonson's Duplicity' (delivered at the Ben Jonson conference at Leeds University, 1995) are here published for the first time. I am grateful to Martin Butler for his characteristically helpful reading of this last essay, and for the wider stimulus of his own Jonsonian work; and to Kim Scott Walwyn and Jason Freeman for their good counsel and unfailing support.

King's College, Cambridge

Contents

I
Twice a Man

EARLY in 1638, six months after the death of Ben Jonson, a volume of verses to his memory was published in London under the editorship of his old friend Bryan Duppa, then Bishop of Chichester. The volume bore a suitably learned title: *Jonsonus Virbius, Or, The Memorie of* Ben: Johnson *Revived by the Friends of the Muses*. Virbius was the name given to Theseus' son Hippolytus, who was torn to pieces by his own stampeding horses on the seashore after rejecting the advances of his stepmother Phaedra, and then miraculously restored to life by Aesculapius, god of medicine, at the request of the goddess Diana. The name means literally 'twice a man'. According to John Aubrey, the title was the brainwave of Lucius Cary, Lord Falkland, who was himself (oddly enough) to be trampled to death by horses at the Battle of Newbury just a few years later.[1] Though Jonson had met his end in an altogether less dramatic style than either Hippolytus or Lucius Cary, expiring gently at an advanced age after many years of illness, the title suggested that he somehow needed now to be put together again, *Revived by the Friends of the Muses*. Like the many scholars and critics that were to follow them down the centuries, this pioneer band of Jonsonian admirers set out to collect the literary pieces, to reconstruct the biographical subject, to give Ben Jonson another life, making him in some mysterious manner *twice a man*.

It is a central feature of the classical legend that the second man does not resemble the first: that Virbius is always unlike Hippolytus. For Diana, it is said, took such pains to protect her protégé from

[1] MS Aubrey 6, fo. 93, cit. *Ben Jonson*, ed. C. H. Herford and Percy and Evelyn Simpson, 11 vols. (Oxford, 1925–52), xi. 428, cited below as Herford and Simpson. All quotations are from this edition unless otherwise specified; u/v and i/j spellings have been regularized. Falkland died in a suicidal charge at Newbury. 'The next day, when they went to bury the dead, they could not find his Lordship's body; it was stript and trod-upon and mangled, so there was one that wayted on him in his chamber would undertake to know it from all other bodyes, by a certain Mole his Lordship had in his Neck, and by that marke did finde it': *Aubrey's Brief Lives*, ed. O. L. Dick (Harmondsworth, 1962), 154.

further danger that she changed not merely his name but also his appearance, turning him from a youth to an elderly man, hiding him in the woods of Aricia where he served as her priest or as one of her minor gods. Commentators on the story sometimes wondered if the second man was not in fact a fraud. 'This *virbius*', wrote George Sandys darkly, 'who boasted to have beene *Hipolytus* was according to some authors a cunning Imposter, suborned by the Preists of *Diana Aricina*, to draw a greater concourse to that Grove, that their gaine might increase by more frequent devotion.'[2] Virbius was, moreover, not a single but a recurrent figure, whose significance Sir James Frazer begins to unravel in the masterly opening chapter of *The Golden Bough*, seeing Virbius as the archetype or forerunner of the anxious priest of Nemi, the King of the Woods who traditionally gained office by murdering his predecessor, and constantly prowled the sacred groves with a drawn sword in his hand, waiting for an attack by some would-be successor.

The entire history of Jonsonian scholarship and performance, one might almost say, is prefigured in the suggestive title of this memorial volume. For all scholars and interpreters are in some sense resurrectionists, who produce a secondary creation that is, and is not, like the object of their study; all are (moreover) priests of the wood, who will eventually be succeeded by others; and there are many Jonsons, fraudulent or otherwise, that interpretation has created, and might in turn consider. This book sets out to examine that multiple and recurrent figure, looking at some of the many ways in which Jonson in his own lifetime chose to present himself, and in which he has been understood and represented in different historical periods.

I begin with a belief that Jonson's own character was altogether more diverse and complex than his repeated pronouncements might suggest, and an earlier generation of scholars tended to assume. Chapters 3 to 5 explore fissures and contradictions within Jonson's personality and moral position, generally favouring social, over psychological, explanations for this dividedness. But Jonson was a multiple figure in another sense, too, that is strikingly (if unwittingly) suggested by the title of his own memorial volume. For throughout his career he attempted repeatedly to make and remake himself as a professional author, acting as his own best Aesculapius: editor, interpreter, and resurrection man. When his tragedy *Sejanus*

---

[2] G[eorge] S[andys], *Ovid's Metamorphosis* [sic] *Englished, Mythologiz'd, and Represented in Figures* (Oxford, 1632), 524; roman/italic reversed, u/v regularized.

was rowdily dismissed from the stage, Jonson's response was to publish a much revised and 'Romanized' version of the play in a quarto edition, shifting the piece from the hazardous realm of the playhouse to the relative safety of the library in an evident attempt to secure it from further popular attack and government suspicion. Jonson's tragedy concludes with an account of the physical dismemberment of Sejanus at the hands of the Roman mob. Dedicating the folio text of the play to his patron Lord Aubigny, Jonson remarked that his tragedy had 'suffer'd no lesse violence from our people here, then the subject of it did from the rage of the people of *Rome*; but with a different fate, as (I hope) merit'.[3] In piecing the violated tragedy together for publication, Jonson aimed to give his play a second life, to make the rejected *Sejanus*—as his own memorialists would later attempt to make Jonson himself—'twice a man'. My final chapter ('Jonson, Shakespeare, and the Destruction of the Book') looks at the great confidence Jonson placed in publication and in the power of books, and at his contrary fear—spectacularly fulfilled in the fire of 1623 that burnt his library—that books were fragile objects which, like their authors, could all too easily be dismembered and destroyed.

In the centuries following their deaths, the linked and contrasted 'characters' of Jonson and Shakespeare were reinvented through a variety of biographical legends that importantly affected the way in which their works were read, and their modern reputations established. The curiously interdependent reputations of Jonson and Shakespeare are examined in Chapter 2 ('Jonson and the Tother Youth') and again in Chapter 11 (' "Not of an Age" '). Jonson was replicated in another way during the seventeenth century, through the work of his various imitators, and the adulation of the so-called Tribe of Ben. Chapter 10 ('Fathers and Sons') looks at John Dryden's mockery of one of these imitators, Thomas Shadwell, arguing that in *Mac Flecknoe* Dryden demonstrates not (as is sometimes thought) a contempt for Jonson, but a deep acquaintance with his literary standards and satirical techniques.

Most of the essays in this volume have been previously published; details of their earlier appearances are given in the Acknowledgements. In gathering them together, I have revised them in various

---

[3] Herford and Simpson, iv. 349. For a discussion of the significance of the quarto text, see Philip Ayres's introduction to his edition of *Sejanus* in The Revels Plays (Manchester, 1990), and John Jowett's ' "Fall Before this Booke": The 1605 Quarto of *Sejanus*', in *TEXT: Transactions of the Society for Textual Scholarship*, 4 (1988), 279–95.

ways and brought them up to date where necessary with more recent scholarship. While they do not aim to present a single, consecutive argument, the essays as collected will, I hope, reveal certain recurrent beliefs and preoccupations. Many were written in an attempt to think about various theoretical and practical problems besetting a larger task on which I have been engaged over the past several years, a life of Ben Jonson, and to reflect more generally on the challenges of literary biography. A central assumption of the present volume, as of the work in progress, is that biographers and critics face similar and intimately related problems of interpretation, which need to be pondered together; that lives must be read with the same subtlety that in recent years has been shown in the reading of texts, and with an equal awareness of the interpretative limits; and that—contrary to common belief—both criticism and biography are likely to be deficient without the other's aid.

The concerns of this book are thus by turns historical, biographical, and critical. The study of Jonson's Catholic years and his period of residence with his patron Lord Aubigny in Blackfriars in Chapter 4 leads naturally, for example, to a larger enquiry into Jonson's development of the house as a complex symbol of domestic life, and thence to an examination of the settings of his plays: in particular, of his Blackfriars comedy, *The Alchemist*, and of other, temporal, boundaries in Jonson's comic writing (Chapters 6 and 7). Chapter 9, on 'A Celebration of Charis', begins with a historical account of the many ways in which these poems have been regarded down the centuries, and discusses the various temptations the sequence offers to literal-minded biographical interpretation, that are in turn reviewed through a close reading of the lyrics themselves.

Several chapters examine the methodologies and consequences of historical scholarship, ancient and modern. 'Politic Picklocks' looks at the kind of historical reading of which Jonson in his own lifetime appears to have been most nervous: the practice of 'application', or finding parallels between historical and contemporary, fictional and real-life, events; and goes on to consider more recent styles of historical interpretation to which Jonson's texts have been subjected. About the immense power of history to set the record ultimately right, to vindicate past wrongs, Jonson was strongly optimistic. History, he imagined, would be the true Aesculapius, preserving and reviving his own work and that of his most gifted contemporaries, ensuring its continuing life in future times:

From Death, and darke oblivion, neere the same,
   The Mistresse of Mans life, grave Historie,
Raising the World to good or evil fame,
   Doth vindicate it to eternitie.[4]

Chapter 11 explores the ironies which history itself has inflicted upon Jonson's firm belief. By the late eighteenth century, Jonson was commonly regarded as a writer whose work could not easily be revived, so time-bound was it, so heavily dependent upon topical and local allusions, so deeply immersed in the customs and practices of a bygone age, so unlike the seemingly transhistorical writings of his greatest contemporary. Jonson had placed his faith in the ultimate verdict of posterity, but posterity, it seemed, was to let him down.

But that verdict is currently undergoing revision. Over the past generation Jonson has found more sympathetic and intelligent readers than he has had for many centuries. Recent scholarship has aroused new interest in his work, and a number of the plays that had not been professionally performed since his lifetime have found their way triumphantly back into the commercial theatre. This book has been greatly stimulated by the recent Jonson revival, to which I hope it will in turn contribute.

[4] 'The Mind of the Frontispice to a Booke', *The Underwood*, 24. 1–4, first printed opposite the engraved frontispiece of Sir Walter Ralegh's *The History of the World* (1614). On the significance of this poem in its historical context, see Annabel Patterson, *Censorship and Interpretation: The Conditions of Writing and Reading in Early Modern England* (Madison, Wis., 1984), 134 ff.

2

Jonson and the Tother Youth

IN a short play for puppets written towards the end of his life, George Bernard Shaw addressed a question that had exercised him on and off throughout much of his career: was his genius equal, or perhaps superior, to that of Shakespeare? Throughout the play two very talkative and opinionated puppets named Shakes and Shav vigorously debate this issue, which Shakes at the outset proposes might be settled by means of a fist-fight. As a young man, Shaw had rather fancied himself as a boxer, having taken instruction from the celebrated Ned Donnelly, Professor of Boxing at the London Athletic Club; yet his puppet-self, Shav, proves rather less competent than his creator, being felled in the opening seconds of the play by a straight left from the untutored Shakes. By the count of nine, however, Shav is on his feet again, talking powerfully, scoring a number of mean body-blows, until the play, like a dialectical issue that can never be fully resolved, ends in an exhausted draw. Shaw was entranced by boxing, which he regarded as a sort of paradigm of capitalist enterprise. In *Shakes versus Shav* he appears to offer boxing also as a sort of paradigm of literary history, in which famous pairs of writers, challengers and defenders, may be ranked in contest against each other, and watched vying for supremacy, thwacking each other to the canvas. In his preface to the play Shaw was at pains, however, to point out that his contest with Shakespeare was entirely a friendly fight, in no way tainted by 'mere professional jealousy'.[1]

Shaw's persistent wondering whether he might not be (as he liked to put it) 'better than Shakespear' seems to modern readers a preposterous speculation. Since the early Romantic period no one has been seriously regarded as 'better than Shakespear', nor has the

---

[1] *The Complete Prefaces of Bernard Shaw* (1965), 917; Michael Holroyd, *Bernard Shaw*, 5 vols. (1988–92), vol. i, *The Search for Love* (1988), 104–5. In his resistance to Shakespearian bardolatry—the term was his invention—Shaw acknowledged the precedent of Jonson ('for I lov'd the man, and doe honour his memory (on this side Idolatry) as much as any', *Discoveries*, 654–5): *Prefaces*, 749, 759–60.

question been seriously regarded as worth putting. Not only is the
ring empty of challengers: it is, as a symbol, empty of significance.
Shakespeare is viewed instead as a unique figure, whose genius is in
some way beyond comparison and beyond contestation, 'Out-
topping knowledge', as Matthew Arnold put it (in a significantly different figure), 'Making the heaven of heavens his dwelling place'.[2] Yet
Shaw's view of literary history being determined through a series of
one-to-one combats has in fact a long ancestry, and the view he invites us to take of Shakespeare might not have seemed so surprising
in earlier times. For throughout the seventeenth and much of the
eighteenth centuries Shakespeare was frequently seen not as a solitary genius but as one of a group, or, more pointedly, one of a *pair* of
celebrated English writers, whose qualities came gradually to be
defined through a series of formal and, eventually, much-repeated
contrasts. It was indeed, as I want to argue, through this very process
of comparison that Shakespeare's modern reputation was established. The writer with whom Shakespeare was regularly compared
was Ben Jonson, who was regarded by many good judges in the
seventeenth century as the supreme genius of his age. The comparisons began early, in the lifetime of the writers themselves, being encouraged at first by Jonson himself, who was, however, destined in
due course to fall victim to a process he had, ironically, helped to
initiate. The formal opposition of the two writers encouraged an
imaginative reconstruction of their lives, which in turn affected the
reading and interpretation of their texts. This circular and incre-
mental process might fairly be called the *invention* of Shakespeare
and Jonson.[3]

⟪❧⟫

Ben Jonson's comedy *Epicoene, or The Silent Woman* is about a man
who hates noise and women yet marries a supposedly silent wife in
order to beget an heir and disinherit his troublesome nephew. In the
second act of the play this disagreeable character is visited on the eve
of his wedding by one of his nephew's friends, who, in a lengthy

---

[2] 'Shakespeare', in *The Poems of Matthew Arnold*, ed. Kenneth Allott (1965), 49.
[3] This essay builds on the arguments of Samuel Schoenbaum in *Shakespeare's Lives*
(Oxford, 1970), and 'Shakespeare and Jonson: Fact and Myth', in David Galloway (ed.),
The Elizabethan Theatre, vol. v (Hamden, Conn., 1970), 1–19.

tirade fulfilling and exceeding Morose's wildest nightmares, warns him of the many perils of marriage. All women, argues Truewit, bring noise, terror, and tribulation to a household, but one kind of woman is to be avoided above all others, and that is the female critic: the sort who will 'censure poets, and authors, and stiles, and compare 'hem, DANIEL with SPENSER, JONSON with the tother youth, and so foorth' (II. ii. 115–19).

Scholars have long wondered who this 'tother youth' could be. Upton in the eighteenth century suggested he was Thomas Dekker; Gifford in the nineteenth century proposed John Marston; Herford and Simpson in this century confidently declared him to be Samuel Daniel, an identification accepted by most modern editors of the play.[4] Mulling over the significance of the phrase, Gifford conceded that it was 'more easy to say who is not meant than who is'; and who in his opinion the tother youth most definitely was *not* was William Shakespeare. Gifford was determined to head off an unwelcome identification proposed by his old adversary, Edmond Malone, who had incautiously written, 'In the *Silent Woman* the author perhaps pointed at Shakespeare, as one whom he viewed with fearful, yet with jealous eyes.' Gifford was scornful: 'A more improbable conceit . . . has rarely been hazarded.' Eager to dispose once and for all of the myth of Jonson's supposed malignity towards Shakespeare, Gifford could not contemplate the possibility of Jonson's making even a light-hearted allusion to the existence of his great rival or the possibility of public debate concerning their respective merits. 'With what propriety', laboured Gifford, 'could Shakespeare be called "the t'other *youth*"? He was now in his 46th year, a time of life to which such an expression can scarcely be applied.'[5]

I believe Jonson's reference in *The Silent Woman* is indeed to Shakespeare, who (it is certainly true) was scarcely a youth in 1609. But then neither was Jonson himself, who was by then a highly successful writer in his late thirties: and that of course is the humorous point. 'The tother youth', with its Falstaffian casualness, wittily rejuvenates both men, while dispatching the older, more celebrated dramatist, young what's-his-name, to anonymous obscurity. 'Jealousy', 'malignity', 'fearfulness' seem hardly the appropriate

---

4   *The Works of Ben Jonson*, ed. William Gifford and Francis Cunningham, 3 vols. (1904), i. 415; Herford and Simpson, x. 17. The best modern edition of *Epicoene*, by R. V. Holdsworth, New Mermaids (1979), identifies 'the tother youth' as Shakespeare.

5   *Works*, ed. Gifford and Cunningham, i. 415.

terms to invoke in relation to such a quip, but some sort of friendly contestation between the two men is (we might think) afoot.

Truewit's catalogue of the perils of marriage in *The Silent Woman* is freely adapted from Juvenal's even more deeply misogynistic sixth satire. Juvenal's female critic, the moment she sits down to dinner, 'commends Virgil, pardons the dying Dido, and pits the poets against each other, putting Virgil in one scale and Homer in the other': 'committit vates et comparat, inde Maronem / atque alia parte in trutina suspendit Homerum' (436–7). If Homer and Virgil are balanced in one set of classical scales, Jonson would surely have been choosy about the poet measured against him in the English heavyweight contest; and in 1609 Shakespeare was the obvious choice. *Committit vates et comparat*: to 'commit' poets against each other, bringing them together like gladiators or fighting cocks, was a well-established classical exercise. Homer and Virgil were regularly paired in this manner for formal comparison, a habit encouraged by Virgil's own contestive practice. Juvenal himself compares Homer and Virgil in his eleventh satire (180–1), and Juvenal was to find himself in turn matched against Martial, who wrote an indignant epigram (VII. xxiv) against the impertinent critic who attempted this feat, beginning 'Cum Iuvenale meo quae me committere temptas'. 'When you try to commit me against my Juvenal', says Martial, you might as well suggest that Orestes and Pylades, Castor and Pollux, were not devoted friends and brothers, but envious and jealous rivals. 'Iuvenale meo', 'my Juvenal', writes Martial affectionately, staving off the very notion of possible envy existing between himself and his fellow poet.[6]

This habit of assessing authors (or people) comparatively in pairs formed the basis of a rhetorical exercise known to the ancient Greeks as *syncrisis*. This was an exercise in persuasion, intended to demonstrate the superiority of one author or one individual over another; it was widely practised in classical times, by Longinus, Quintilian, and Cicero, for example, and even indeed by Homer himself.[7] Syncrisis

---

[6] *Juvenal and Persius*, trans. G. G. Ramsay, Loeb Classical Library (1930); Martial, *Epigrams*, trans. Walter C. A. Ker, Loeb Classical Library, 2 vols. (1968) (translation varied). On the verb 'commit', used in its Latin sense, see *OED* 9.

[7] *'Longinus' on the Sublime*, ed. D. A. Russell (Oxford, 1964), 12. 2–13 (Plato and Demosthenes, Demosthenes and Cicero), 32. 8 (Lysias and Plato); Quintilian, *Institutio Oratoria*, trans. H. E. Butler, Loeb Classical Library, 4 vols. (1920–2), x. i. 93, 98, 101, 105; Cicero, *Brutus*, trans. G. L. Hendrickson, Loeb Classical Library (1962), 36 ff. At Christ's Hospital the young Coleridge was taught by the Reverend James Bowyer to discriminate

was also practised by critics in England from the Renaissance period well into the eighteenth century: Dryden's comparative evaluation of Horace and Juvenal in his *Discourse Concerning the Original and Progress of Satire* and Dr Johnson's extended analysis of the merits of Dryden himself in relation to those of Pope in *The Lives of the Poets* are obvious examples of the art.[8]

One needs no special rhetorical training, however, to grasp the basic point in Jonson's comedy, which I have seen conveyed in one modern production of *The Silent Woman* by a pair of familiar Jacobean portraits of bearded men—one bald, the other plump— hung on either side of the stage; at the line 'the tother youth', the actor gestured absent-mindedly towards the man with the big bald head. This is a device which, interestingly enough, was actually used on the Elizabethan stage, in the final act of Thomas Dekker's *Satiromastix*. Wanting to deflate Ben Jonson's pretensions in identifying himself with the Roman poet Horace, Dekker has his character Captain Tucca produce two portraits, one of Horace, the other of Ben Jonson; and triumphantly demonstrate the superiority of the Roman poet over his presumptuous English imitator.[9] Shakespeare allowed Hamlet to practise the art of syncrisis in a similar manner and with similar visual aids in conversation with his mother.

> Look here upon this picture, and on this,
> The counterfeit presentment of two brothers.
> See what a grace was seated on this brow . . .
> This was your husband. Look you now what follows;
>
> (*Hamlet*, III. iv. 53–5, 63).[10]

---

in this way: 'He early moulded my taste to the preference of Demosthenes to Cicero, of Homer and Theocritus to Virgil, and again of Virgil to Ovid': *Biographia Literaria* (1817; Everyman, edn. 1906), ch. 1. Plutarch's 'Parallel Lives' of Greeks and Romans further encouraged the comparative habit. See Friedrich Focke, 'Synkrisis', *Hermes*, 58 (1923), 327–68. (I am grateful to Dr Gordon Howie and Professor Peter France for advice about this figure.)

[8]   John Dryden, *Of Dramatic Poesy and Other Critical Essays*, ed. George Watson, 2 vols. (1962), ii. 71–155; Samuel Johnson, 'Pope', in *The Lives of the English Poets*, ed. George Birkbeck Hill, 3 vols. (Oxford, 1905), iii. 220–3. Pope himself was to reflect shrewdly on the critical custom of matching Shakespeare against Jonson in the preface to his edition of *The Works of Shakespeare*, 6 vols. (1725), vol. i, p. xi.

[9]   *Satiromastix*, in *The Dramatic Works of Thomas Dekker*, ed. Fredson Bowers, 4 vols. (Cambridge, 1953), vol. i.

[10]   All Shakespeare quotations are taken from Peter Alexander's 1951 edition, unless otherwise specified.

To 'commit' poets formally against each other is to imply—and it is precisely this implication that Martial in the epigram just quoted is determined to resist—that they are somehow naturally at enmity with each other, or mutually envious, or engaged in some kind of bitter flyting in the manner of Kennedy and Dunbar; and it is not therefore surprising to find a legend developing in the seventeenth century about a war that existed between Jonson and Shakespeare—a merry war, perhaps, but a war none the less. Thomas Fuller was to give this legend its classic shape in his *History of the Worthies of England* in 1662, when he wrote about Shakespeare as follows:

Many were the *wit-combats* between him and *Ben Johnson*, which two I behold like a Spanish great Gallion, and an *English man o' War*; Master *Johnson* (like the former) was built far higher in Learning; *Solid*, but *Slow*, in his performances. Shake-spear, with the *English man of War*, lesser in *Bulk*, but lighter in *sailing*, could turn with all tides, tack about and take advantage of all winds, by the quickness of his Wit and Invention.[11]

Fuller presents these celebrated wit-combats as a replay of the Spanish Armada, in which the heavy Spanish galleons were repeatedly outmanœuvred by the lighter, faster English vessels. Shakespeare is thus cast as a national hero, a Sir Francis Drake of the realm of letters, while Jonson's role is that of the bungling foreign invader. This vivid and seemingly first-hand account was to have a powerful effect on subsequent perceptions of the entire relationship between Shakespeare and Jonson. Well into the nineteenth century, it continued to shape (for example) Carlyle's view of the two writers:

And there are Ben and William Shakespeare in wit-combat, sure enough: Ben bearing down like a mighty Spanish War-ship, fraught with all learning and artillery; Shakespeare whisking away from him,—whisking right through him, athwart the big bulk and timbers of him; like a miraculous Celestial Light-ship, woven all of sheet-lightning and sunbeams![12]

Fuller's account is the starting-point and seeming validation of such indefatigable works of Victorian scholarship as Robert Cartwright's *Shakespere and Jonson: Dramatic, versus Wit-Combats* (1864), a book that sets out to demonstrate the existence of a long-standing feud whose progress (so Cartwright believes) can be clearly read in almost every play which the two dramatists wrote.

[11] *The History of the Worthies of England* (1662), 'Warwickshire', 126.
[12] *Historical Sketches of Notable Persons and Events in the Reigns of James I and Charles I* (1898), 76.

But, as Samuel Schoenbaum has pointed out, Fuller's *History of the Worthies of England* was written a quarter of a century after Jonson's death and nearly half a century after the death of Shakespeare. Fuller himself was 8 years of age and living in Northamptonshire when Shakespeare died in Stratford-upon-Avon, where he had been living in retirement for several years. When Fuller says that he *beholds* the wit-combats of Jonson and Shakespeare at the Mermaid tavern in London he is not speaking as an old drinking companion who once witnessed such scenes; he beholds them, rather, in his mind's eye; he makes them up. There is in fact no evidence that Shakespeare ever drank at the Mermaid tavern, or that these wit-combats ever occurred.[13] They are invented, I believe, in the spirit of the rhetorical exercise of formal comparison that I have just described.

Dryden's *Essay of Dramatic Poesy*, written six years after the publication of *The History of the Worthies of England*, begins with the invocation of another sea battle, not this time from England's glorious past but from the historical present: Dryden sets his literary debate on 'that memorable day, in the first summer of the late war, when our navy engaged the Dutch: a day wherein the two most mighty and best appointed fleets which any age had ever seen disputed the command of the greater half of the globe, the commerce of nations, and the riches of the universe'. The sea battle of 3 June 1665 forms the fitting background of a debate in which the two great English dramatists, Shakespeare and Jonson, are also brought into comparison. 'If I would compare him with Shakespeare', says Neander of Ben Jonson, 'I must acknowledge him the more correct poet, but Shakespeare the greater wit. Shakespeare was the Homer, or father of our dramatic poets; Jonson was the Virgil, the pattern of elaborate writing; I admire him, but I love Shakespeare.' Skilled in the art of syncrisis—the comparison of Homer and Virgil is one which he develops more fully elsewhere, along with the comparison between Horace and Juvenal—Dryden formalizes the contrast of Shakespeare and Jonson, tipping his thumb finally on the balance in favour of Shakespeare. Dryden extends this comparison in other essays and prologues over a period of years; and, as G. E. Bentley has shown in detail, it was through Dryden's decisive influence that

---

[13] Schoenbaum, *Shakespeare's Lives*, 294–6; I. A. Shapiro, 'The Mermaid Club', *Modern Language Review*, 45 (1950), 6–17.

Shakespeare's literary reputation began in the last decade of the seventeenth century finally to outstrip that of Jonson.[14]

While Dryden was attempting these serious exercises in literary assessment, another, more frivolous, kind of comparative narrative involving Shakespeare and Ben Jonson was developing, namely, the popular anecdote. Most of the anecdotes about Shakespeare and Jonson that survive from the late seventeenth century are set in taverns, and most turn upon strikingly feeble pieces of wordplay. They memorialize Jonson's remarks on tumbling downstairs at the Feathers tavern after a bout of drinking ('Gentlemen, since I am so luckily fallen into your company, I will drink with you before I go'), and on finding a familiar entry to the Half-Moon tavern unexpectedly closed: 'Since that the *Moon* was so unkind to make me go about, / The *Sun* henceforth shall take my coin, the *Moon* shall go without.' One persistent story is that of Shakespeare standing as godfather to one of Jonson's children, and resolving to give the child 'a dozen good latten [i.e. brass] spoons', quipping to Jonson as he does so, 'and thou shalt translate them'.[15] Many of these distressing anecdotes are solemnly recorded in a recent biography of Ben Jonson on the grounds that they accord with 'Jonson's own precept and practice in following the principle of classical historians that the gossip, rumour, and anecdote surrounding a great life are as informative as the facts about him'.[16] Yet unless some effort is made to sift such stories it is not easy to see in what sense they can ever be regarded as 'informative'. Jonson and Shakespeare appear in them as pedantic buffoons, trading laboured jokes in the manner of Holofernes and Sir Nathaniel in *Love's Labour's Lost*, or a couple of characters from the Elizabethan jest books. And it is indeed from the

[14] Dryden, *Of Dramatic Poesy*, i. 18, 70. For the comparison between Homer and Virgil see ibid. ii. 36, 144, 166–7, 186, 204, 274–7; between Virgil and Ovid, ibid. ii. 21 f.; between Horace and Juvenal (and Persius), *Discourse Concerning the Original and Progress of Satire*, ibid. ii. 71–155 *passim*. The methodology of G. E. Bentley, *Shakespeare and Jonson: Their Reputations in the Seventeenth Century Compared*, 2 vols. (Chicago, 1945) has been challenged, most notably by David L. Frost in *The School of Shakespeare* (Cambridge, 1968), but the broad picture he gives of Jonson's commanding reputation throughout the seventeenth century and of Dryden's critical role seems indisputable. See also D. H. Craig (ed.), *Ben Jonson: The Critical Heritage* (1990), and E. A. J. Honigmann, *Shakespeare's Impact on his Contemporaries* (1982).

[15] J. F. Bradley and J. Q. Adams, *The Jonson Allusion-Book* (New Haven, 1922; repr. New York, 1971), 412, 415, 91; Sir Nicholas Le Strange, *Merry Passages and Jeasts: A Manuscript Jestbook*, ed. H. F. Lippincott (Salzburg, 1974), 19.

[16] Rosalind Miles, *Ben Jonson: His Life and Work* (1986), p. x.

jest books, as one scholar has pointed out, that many of these anecdotes derive.[17] They are pre-existing stories about a pair of clowns,
to which in the course of the seventeenth century the names of
Jonson and Shakespeare are simply attached. The stories are 'informative', then, not on account of their content, but in what they
imply about the semi-legendary status of Jonson and Shakespeare in
the period, considered as a famous pair; and about the wider process
of folkloric transmission, adaptation, and attribution.

Towards the end of the seventeenth century, at the very time when
the oral tradition to which an appeal is made can no longer reliably
be verified, another and more interesting kind of biographical narrative about Jonson and Shakespeare begins to show itself. In this
narrative, the focus is no longer upon the witty quips of the two
dramatists, but upon their inner character, their basic temperament
and disposition. This new curiosity about the inner life of Shakespeare and Jonson develops at much the same time that critics begin
to interest themselves in the interior life of Shakespeare's dramatic
characters, and to speculate imaginatively about those aspects of
their existence which the dramatist chose not to describe. A loosely
ruminative, quasi-fictionalizing approach to Shakespeare's dramatic
characters was to develop particular momentum throughout the
eighteenth and nineteenth centuries, giving rise to such studies as
The Girlhood of Shakespeare's Heroines, and meeting its Waterloo
only in the 1930s (if then) with L. C. Knights's influential essay, 'How
Many Children Had Lady Macbeth?'[18] During the same long period
literary biography perfected much the same loosely ruminative,
quasi-fictionalizing mode which might enable a novelistic scholar (or
scholarly novelist) to write, for example, a three-volume work entitled *Judith Shakespeare*. (Not a great deal is known about
Shakespeare's daughter, but this did not deter William Black, who
published such a work in 1884.)[19]

From the late seventeenth century onwards, biographical and literary interpretations of Shakespeare and Jonson became intriguingly
confused, as writers attempted to deduce the personal characters of

---

[17] Thornton S. Graves, 'Jonson in the Jest Books', in *The Manly Anniversary Studies in
Language and Literature* (Chicago, 1923), 127–39.

[18] *Explorations* (1946), 1–39.

[19] For different rhetorical purposes Virginia Woolf was later to wonder 'what would
have happened had Shakespeare had a wonderfully gifted sister, called Judith, let us say':
A Room of One's Own (1928), ch. 3.

both men from the dramatic characters they created. As both Shakespeare and Jonson created a very large number of dramatic characters, the choice is clearly crucial. Which of Shakespeare's characters could be said to typify the author's temperament and genius? By the mid-eighteenth century there was a measure of agreement on this question: it was Falstaff.[20] Not the Falstaff whom Hal describes as a 'bolting-hutch of beastliness', or whom Jeremy Collier declared had been 'thrown out of favour as being a *Rake*' to die 'like a Rat behind the Hangings',[21] but an altogether more benign and well-behaved character who was carefully laundered and presented through the writings of such scholars as Corbyn Morris, William Guthrie, and Maurice Morgann. Sir John Falstaff, wrote Corbyn Morris in 1744,

possesses Generosity, Chearfulness, Alacrity, Invention, Frolic and Fancy superior to all other Men;—The *Figure* of his *Person* is the Picture of Jollity, Mirth, and Good-nature, and banishes at once all other Ideas from your Breast; He is happy himself, and makes you happy.—If you examine him further, he has no Fierceness, Reserve, Malice or Peevishness lurking in his Heart; his Intentions are all pointed at innocent Riot and Merriment; nor has the Knight any inveterate Design, except against *Sack*, and that too he *loves*.[22]

Notice the variations Morris plays on Shakespeare's language: Falstaff's 'I am not only witty in myself, but the cause that wit is in other men' (2 *Henry IV*, I, ii. 10–12) becomes 'he is happy himself, and makes you happy'. Happiness replaces wit as the cardinal comic virtue, and Falstaff's amiability is thought to derive more or less directly from the good-natured temperament of the author who created him. It is hardly necessary to point out that the character of Falstaff is open to other constructions, and that a very different picture of Shakespeare's temperament might in any case have been drawn if the concentration had been upon other dramatic characters, such as Edmund, or Titus Andronicus, or Lady Macbeth.

Ben Jonson's personality, it was agreed, was quite contrary to that of Shakespeare, and was not amiable at all. The contrast was sometimes expressed in relation to the two dramatists' characteristic

[20] Stuart Tave, *The Amiable Humorist* (Chicago, 1960), ch. 6; R. W. Babcock, *The Genesis of Shakespeare Idolatry, 1766–1799* (Chapel Hill, 1931).

[21] *1 Henry IV*, II. iv. 436–7; Jeremy Collier, *A Short View of the Immorality and Profaneness of the English Stage* (1698), 154.

[22] *An Essay Towards Fixing the True Standards of Wit, Humour, Raillery, Satire, and Ridicule* (1744), 26–7.

comic techniques, which were explained by reference not primarily to dramatic or generic convention but rather to authorial temperament. Here again is Corbyn Morris:

Johnson by pursuing the most useful Intention of *Comedy*, is in Justice oblig'd to *hunt down* and *demolish* his own Characters. Upon this Plan he must necessarily expose them to your *Hatred*, and of course can never bring out an amiable Person. . . . But *Shakespear*, with happier Insight, always supports his Characters in your *Favour*.[23]

Jonson's compulsion to hunt down and demolish his own dramatic characters seems, in this analysis, attributable as much to authorial temperament as to the demands of dramatic convention. Shakespeare is perceived as having quite another nature, happily sustaining his dramatic characters as he no doubt in real life sustained his friends and colleagues. 'One exalted, the other debased, the human species', declared 'Horatio' (significantly so called) in the *Gentleman's Magazine* in 1772, speaking of the qualities of Shakespeare and Jonson. 'You despise Bobadil, though he makes you laugh. You wish to spend a jolly evening with Falstaff, tho' you cannot esteem him.'[24]

The character and disposition of the two playwrights themselves had long been the subject of confident speculation. 'He was a Man of very free Temper, and withal blunt, and somewhat haughty to those, that were either Rivals in *Fame*, or Enemies to his Writings. . .', wrote Gerard Langbaine of Ben Jonson in 1691, 'otherwise of good Sociable Humour, when amongst his Sons and Friends in the *Apollo*.'[25] The adjectives favoured by Langbaine are worth pondering. 'Haughty': none of Jonson's contemporaries, so far as I am aware, ever used this word (at least in print) to describe him, but from the 1690s 'haughty' is used repeatedly in relation to Jonson's character, being joined before long by another tenacious adjective, 'morose'. Sir Thomas Blount liked Langbaine's description of Jonson well enough to repeat it verbatim in 1694.[26] Now Jonson has a female character called Haughty in his comedy *The Silent Woman*, whose protagonist is named, of course, Morose. Dryden's Neander in the *Essay of Dramatic Poesy* declares that he has been assured 'from divers persons that Ben Jonson was actually acquainted with such a

[23] Morris, *An Essay* 33–4.   [24] *Gentleman's Magazine*, 42 (1772), 522.
[25] *An Account of the English Dramatic Poets* (Oxford, 1691); see Bradley and Adams, *The Jonson Allusion-Book*, 431.
[26] *De Re Poetica* (1694): Bradley and Adams, *The Jonson Allusion-Book*, 444.

man' as Morose, 'one altogether as ridiculous as he is here represented'. By the 1750s this story has changed: W. R. Chetwood now
affirmed that Jonson had modelled the character of Morose on himself, and had actually played the part in the theatre. This identification of the temperament of the author with that of his own dramatic
creation survives into modern times in Edmund Wilson's Freudian
essay of 1948 entitled 'Morose Ben Jonson'.[27]

By the eighteenth century the contrastive epithets are well in place:
Jonson is not merely haughty and morose, but crabbed, pedantic,
slow, grudging, sour, saturnine, envious, and splenetic. Shakespeare
is regularly seen as generous, loving, open, quick, and amiable: not
merely as a national genius, but also as a thoroughly nice man. 'It is
highly gratifying to an Englishman', declared a writer in the *European Magazine* in 1793, 'to observe, that every new discovery tends
to confirm the opinion that Shakespeare was as estimable for the
goodness of his private life, as he was superior in genius to every one
of his contemporaries.'[28] The two portraits were mutually dependent and mutually sustaining, the view of Shakespeare's character
being elaborated in contradistinction to that of Jonson, like Henry
Fielding's contrastive portraits of Tom Jones and Blifil, or Sheridan's
of Charles and Joseph Surface in *The School for Scandal*. How did
these largely fictitious portraits of Shakespeare and Jonson ever develop, and how were they made plausible?

Part of the answer lies in the remarkable publishing history of that
enigmatic text which came to be known as Jonson's *Conversations
with William Drummond of Hawthornden*.[29] These are the notes
made by the Scottish poet William Drummond of remarks which
Ben Jonson had made when he stayed with Drummond in Scotland
over the winter of 1618/19. These frequently cryptic, telegrammatic,
asyntactical jottings were quite clearly not intended for publication,
but as rudimentary *aides-mémoire*, to remind Drummond of some
of the gossip and literary opinions which his famous and at times
perturbing house-guest had voiced in his cups at Hawthornden. We
cannot judge the tone, we do not know the context, of Jonson's

---

[27] Dryden, 'Of Dramatic Poesy', i. 71; [W. R. Chetwood], *The British Theatre* (Dublin,
1750), 26; Edmund Wilson, *The Triple Thinkers* (Harmondsworth, 1962), 240–61. On
Wilson's essay, see Ch. 3 below.

[28] *European Magazine*, 24 (1793), 185.

[29] Part, but not all. The contrasts are already apparent in Nicholas Rowe's 'Some
Account of the Life &c. of Mr William Shakespear' in his edition of *The Works of William
Shakespear*, 6 vols. (1709), vol. i.

seemingly laconic verdicts upon Shakespeare which Drummond scribbled down—'That Shakesperr wanted Arte' (50); 'Sheakspear in a play brought in a number of men saying they had suffered Shipwrack in Bohemia, wher yr is no Sea neer by some 100 Miles' (208–10)—but for eighteenth-century readers they were sufficient to establish the fact of Jonson's malevolence towards his great contemporary. It is important to realize that Drummond appears to have made no attempt to publish these notes, which did not see the light of day until 1711, nearly a century after Jonson's walk to Scotland. Drummond's editor, Bishop Sage, took some liberties with the text he chose to publish, running together for example the two quite separate comments about Shakespeare just quoted, and adding a few words of his own: 'He said, Shakespear wanted Art, *and sometimes Sense*; for in one of his Plays he brought in a Number of Men, saying they had suffered Ship-wrack in Bohemia, where is no Sea near by 100 Miles.'[30]

This, however, was a trifling amendment compared with that which was made in 1753 in a volume entitled *The Lives of the Poets of Great Britain and Ireland*, attributed to Theophilus Cibber but actually the work of a literary hack named Robert Shiels, who had worked as an amanuensis for Dr Johnson in the preparation of his *Dictionary*. In composing *The Lives of the Poets* Shiels simply took over material from wherever he could find it, plundering the work of earlier literary historians, and adding certain flourishes of his own. In his chapter on Ben Jonson, Shiels quotes the passage which Drummond writes towards the end of the *Conversations*, after Jonson has finally left Hawthornden and is heading back to London.

'He is a great lover and praiser of himself, a contemner and Scorner of others, given rather to lose a friend, than a Jest, jealous of every word and action of those about him (especiallie after drink which is one of the Elements in which he liveth) a dissembler of ill parts which raigne in him, a bragger of some good that he wanteth, thinketh nothing well bot what either he himself, or some of his friends and Countrymen hath said or done. he is passionately kynde and angry, carelesse either to gaine or keepe, Vindicative, but if he be well answered, at himself.'[31]

This is the most detailed and suggestive account of Ben Jonson's personality that has come down to us. To interpret the passage one

[30] William Drummond of Hawthornden, *Works* [ed. J. Sage and T. Ruddiman] (Edinburgh, 1711), 225 (emphasis mine).
[31] *Conversations with Drummond*, 680–9.

needs to remember the somewhat prim character of William Drum-mond himself, and the occasion of the two men's encounter; it is necessary also to observe the fine balance of Drummond's reckon-ing, what is reluctantly admired, not merely deplored, in that ' "pas-sionately kynde and angry, carelesse either to gaine or keepe, Vindicative, but if he be well answered, at himself." ' Overriding this balance, Shiels chooses to add a few words of his own, keeping the passage still within quotation-marks as though he were still simply relaying Drummond's first-hand observations: ' "In short, he was in his personal character the very reverse of Shakespear, as surly, ill-natured, proud and disagreeable, as Shakespear with ten times his merit was gentle, good-natured, easy and amiable." '[32]

How did Shiels know, or imagine he knew, that Shakespeare had these qualities? Why is Shakespeare invented after this fashion in the eighteenth century? Very little in fact is known about the personality of William Shakespeare, and it is precisely this absence of informa-tion which has traditionally prompted conjecture of every variety, from the radically sceptical to the waywardly anecdotal and the romantically novelistic. It is one of the more curious ironies of liter-ary history that the fullest, most plausible, and most heavily relied upon references to Shakespeare's personality are made by Ben Jonson himself; and that the greatest stumbling-block to those who wish to argue that 'Shakespeare' was not really Shakespeare but Bacon or Oxford has always been the clear and unambiguous testi-mony of his friend and colleague Ben Jonson.[33] One clue to the eighteenth-century interpretation of Shakespeare may lie in that passage from Jonson's *Discoveries* which, for its incidentally critical remarks, was often quoted as evidence of Jonson's malevolence to-wards Shakespeare: 'He was (indeed) honest, and of an open, and free nature: had an excellent *Phantasie*; brave notions, and gentle ex-pressions: wherein hee flow'd with that facility, that sometime it was

[32] Theophilus Cibber [Robert Shiels], *The Lives of the Poets of Great Britain and Ireland*, 5 vols. (London, 1753), i. 241.

[33] For some characteristic wrestling with this problem, see Sir George Greenwood, *Ben Jonson and Shakespeare* (1921) (Jonson's poem to Shakespeare celebrates not Shakespeare but the syndicate of unnamed learned men, including Bacon, who wrote his works); Gerald H. Rendall, *Ben Jonson and the First Folio Edition of Shakespeare's Plays* (Colchester, 1939) (the Earl of Oxford wrote Shakespeare's plays, as Jonson well knew, and the folio verses are lapwing); and Alden Brooks, *This Side of Shakespear* (New York, 1964) (Shakespeare merely polished the plays of others and got them performed; Jonson's verses are trying to tell us as much).

necessary he should be stop'd', etc. (655–9). 'Gentle' is a word which Jonson uses repeatedly of Shakespeare, as in his verses designed to accompany the frontispiece of Shakespeare's First Folio in 1623.

> This Figure, that thou here seest put,
> It was for gentle Shakespeare cut.
>
> (*Ungathered Verse*, 25. 1–2)

The word occurs again in Jonson's poem 'To the Memory of My Beloved, The Author, Mr William Shakespeare, and What he Hath Left Us' (*Ungathered Verse*, 26) which stands at the head of the commemorative poems in the same folio: 'Yet must I not give Nature all: Thy Art, / My gentle *Shakespeare*, must enjoy a part' (55–6). The word appears once more in the preliminary pages of the folio in the address 'To the Great Variety of Readers', signed by John Heminge and Henry Condell, but, as Steevens first suspected, possibly drafted in part by Jonson himself: Shakespeare, 'as he was a happie imitator of Nature, was a most gentle expresser of it. His mind and hand went together. . . .'[34] Thus launched into the critical vocabulary, the word 'gentle' recurs repeatedly in later tributes to Shakespeare, and forms an important ingredient in the eighteenth-century concoction of the dramatist's personality. It is perhaps worth pausing, however, to ask what Jonson may have meant when he called Shakespeare 'gentle', for I suspect that the reference may not be primarily or exclusively to Shakespeare's mildness of manner (as the eighteenth century believed) or to his station in life, but also to his fluency of composition. The word 'gentle' in the seventeenth century was commonly used of a river that was neither torpid nor in torrent, but which flowed steadily. Shakespeare himself uses the word in this way in *Lucrece*: 'Deep woes roll forward like a gentle flood' (1118). One of the commonest things that was said about Shakespeare in the seventeenth century was that his writings flowed with miraculous fluency; and it

---

[34] *The First Folio of Shakespeare*, The Norton Facsimile, prepared by Charlton Hinman (New York, 1968). Schoenbaum is dismissive of Steevens's theory: *Shakespeare's Lives*, 278. But there are several markedly Jonsonian turns of phrase in the address 'To the Great Variety of Readers': cf. in particular Jonson's *Epigrams*, 1, 3, 18; *Bartholomew Fair*, Induction, 85–112; 'Ode, to Himself' ('Come leave the lothed stage', Herford and Simpson, vi. 492–4), 1–6; *Ungathered Verse*, 8 ('To the Worthy Author, Mr John Fletcher'). The imagery of (textual) dismemberment and re-embodiment is paralleled in Jonson's dedication of *Sejanus* to Esmé Stuart, Lord Aubigny, in the 1616 folio. Jonson's famously dissenting views on Shakespeare's scarcely blotted papers are registered in *Discoveries*, 647 ff. For a fuller discussion, see W. W. Greg, *Shakespeare's First Folio* (Oxford, 1935), 17–21, 26–7, and (more sceptically) Herford and Simpson, xi. 140–4.

is this point that I believe Ben Jonson, like other seventeenth-century commentators, is often primarily intending when he uses the word 'gentle' in relation to his beloved friend.[35]

In eighteenth-century appropriations of the adjective by Shake-spere's admirers, the Jonsonian origins and inflexions of the word are quite ignored, as are the obvious warmth and affection with which Jonson customarily speaks of his great contemporary: 'for I lov'd the man, and doe honour his memory (on this side Idolatry) as much as any' (*Discoveries*, 654–5). That warmth is clearly apparent in Jonson's poem to the memory of Shakespeare that stands at the head of the 1623 folio: a poem that was widely read in the seven-teenth and eighteenth centuries, and was deeply influential in shaping opinion about the nature of Shakespeare's genius.[36]

It is a poem which employs the comparative and contrastive meth-ods of syncrisis on a grand and generous scale, ranking Shakespeare against a whole series of possible rivals, past and present, English and classical, allowing him to emerge triumphant as a writer second to none, a single star blazing in the literary firmament. The poem begins in deliberate hesitation, registering suspicion of both indiscriminate praise and comparative judgement. A minor Oxfordshire poet named William Basse had written a memorial elegy for Shakespeare

[35] See *OED*, 'gentle', 6b. Cf. Suckling, *Fragmenta Aurea, &c.* (1646): 'The sweat of learned *Johnson's* brain, / And gentle *Shakespear's* eas'er strain'; Sir John Denham, com-mendatory verses on John Fletcher (1647): 'Yet what from JOHNSONS oyle and sweat did flow, / Or what more easie nature did bestow / On SHAKESPEARS gentler Muse' (cf. Denham's wish that his own writing should emulate the passage of the Thames: 'Though deep, yet clear, though gentle, yet not dull', *Cooper's Hill*, 189 ff.); Margaret Cavendish, Duchess of Newcastle, 'General Prologue to All My Playes', *Playes* (1662): 'Yet Gentle *Shakespear* had a fluent Wit, / Although less Learning, yet full well he writ'; Richard Flecknoe, *A Short Discourse* (1664): 'Comparing [Jonson] with *Shakespear*, you shall see the difference betwixt Nature and Art; and with *Fletcher*, the difference betwixt Wit and Judgement: Wit being an exuberant thing, like *Nilus*, never more commendable than when it overflowes; but Judgement, a stayed and reposed thing, alwayes containing it self within its bounds and limits.' See C. M. Ingleby, L. Toulmin Smith, and P. J. Furnivall (comp.), and John Munro (ed.), *The Shakespeare Allusion-Book*, 2 vols. (1932), i. 407, 504, ii. 134, 85. Herbert Howarth takes the word 'gentle' in its social sense: 'Shakespeare's Gentleness', *Shakespeare Survey*, 14 (1961), 90–7; Honigmann demonstrates the inappropriateness of a behavioural interpretation of the word: *Shakespeare's Impact on his Contemporaries*, 14–21.

[36] The best accounts of the poem are those of T. J. B. Spencer, 'Ben Jonson on his Beloved, The Author, Mr William Shakespeare', in George Hibbard (ed.), *The Elizabethan Theatre*, vol. iv (1974), 22–40; Richard S. Peterson, *Imitation and Praise in the Poems of Ben Jonson* (New Haven, 1981), ch. 4; Lawrence Lipking, *The Life of the Poet: Beginning and Ending Poetic Careers* (Chicago, 1981), ch. 3; Sara van den Berg, *The Action of Ben Jonson's Poetry* (Newark, NJ, 1987), ch. 6.

in which he called upon learned Chaucer and rare Beaumont to 'lye /
A little neerer Spenser, to make roome, / ffor Shakespeare in your
threefold, fowerfold Tombe.' Jonson ridicules this bid to make the
English poets roll over in the great bed of fame to make room for
Shakespeare, whom he sees instead as a living author: 'My Shakespeare, rise.' Like Martial hailing Juvenal as 'meo Iuvenale', Jonson
subtly implies an intimacy with his fellow poet beyond the reach of
envy, beyond the need for comparison, the poem thus constantly
denying the comparisons that it seems to propose.

> That I not mixe thee so, my braine excuses;
> I meane with great, but disproportion'd *Muses*:
> For, if I thought my judgement were of yeeres,
> I should commit thee surely with thy peeres,
> And tell, how farre thou didst our *Lily* out-shine,
> Or sporting *Kid*, or *Marlowes* mighty line.
> And though thou hadst small *Latine*, and lesse *Greeke*,
> From thence to honour thee, I would not seeke
> For names; but call forth thund'ring *Æschilus*,
> *Euripides* and *Sophocles* to us,
> *Paccuvius*, *Accius*, him of Cordova dead,
> To life againe, to heare thy Buskin tread,
> And shake a Stage: Or, when thy Sockes were on,
> Leave thee alone, for the comparison
> Of all, that insolent *Greece*, or haughtie *Rome*
> Sent forth, or since did from their ashes come.

> (*Ungathered Verse*, 26. 25–40)

Modern readers may wonder why Jonson selected the not very well
known names of the Roman tragedians Pacuvius and Accius in this
passage. Jonson would have remembered that Pacuvius and Accius
are formally compared by Quintilian in a chapter in the *Institutes of
Oratory* in which Quintilian practises syncrisis extensively, bringing
several pairs of authors together for comparative assessment; and
that the comparison of Pacuvius and Accius had subsequently become a commonplace of classical criticism.[37] Syncrisis is the art that
Jonson recalls and, despite his apparent diffidence ('if I thought my
judgement were of yeeres, / I should commit thee surely with thy
peeres') practises throughout this passage, moving through a series
of witty and generous comparisons to his supreme tribute: 'He was

---

[37] Quintilian, *Institutio Oratoria*, x. i. 97; Horace, *Epistles*, II. i. 56.

not of an age, but for all time!' (43). No one in 1623 had ever praised Shakespeare in those terms, declaring him so firmly to be a writer equal or superior to any of the ancients, a writer 'for all time'.[38]

By the Restoration, however, Dryden could characterize this poem as 'an insolent, sparing, and invidious panegyric'.[39] Always ready to *commit* Shakespeare and Jonson against each other, Dryden helped, through this verdict, to perpetuate the notion of warfare between the two poets that existed even after Shakespeare's death. Those lines about Shakespeare's small Latin and less Greek were seen in the eighteenth century as clinching evidence of Jonson's malevolence in disparaging Shakespeare's gifts in order to brag about his own, and helped in turn to fashion a further contrast, between the formidably learned Jonson and the untutored genius, Shakespeare: a contrast we now know to have been greatly exaggerated.[40] In writing these lines Jonson may have remembered Quintilian's advice about how to praise another person: begin (says Quintilian) by mentioning the person's disadvantages, then go on to say how he overcame them: as for example, he was a small man, but very brave.[41] Jonson is saying: Shakespeare was not a classical scholar, did not aim to outgo the ancients: but, despite this, he exceeded them all. It is a serious and profound tribute. During Shakespeare's lifetime, as I have already suggested, Jonson was ready in some sense to vie with his rival, to test, sometimes humorously, his practice against that of Shakespeare. Jonson's memorial poem is deeply marked by Jonson's own ways of thinking about literature, and by his authorial presence. But it is not, as Dryden thought, a contestive poem. It is instead, ironically, the very cornerstone upon which the eighteenth-century construction of Shakespeare was to proceed.

The anxiety of influence is often thought to flow from the past, imposing a burden upon the present. The Bloomian model is patrilinear: sons fret about the great achievements of their fathers, which they can surely never hope to match. Feminists have looked quizzically at this model: Virginia Blain once suggested, only half-humorously, that women writers might find encouragement in the

---

[38] See Ch. 11 below.

[39] 'A Discourse Concerning the Original and Progress of Satire', *Of Dramatic Poesy*, ii. 75.

[40] T. W. Baldwin, *Shakespere's Small Latine and Lesse Greeke*, 2 vols. (Urbana, Ill., 1944); Emrys Jones, *The Origins of Shakespeare* (Oxford, 1977); and Ch. 12 below.

[41] *Institutio Oratoria*, III. vii. 10.

example of their aunts.[42] The sketch I have drawn of the evolving reputations of Jonson and Shakespeare raises another sort of question about the model which Bloom and Bate propose: for the present, as well as the past, imposes its burdens. Sons may struggle against the achievements of their fathers, but siblings also contest with one another. Martial and Juvenal, Jonson and Shakespeare, Dryden and Milton, Fielding and Richardson, Browning and Tennyson, Auden and Eliot, Murdoch and Lessing: such pairs of authors write in the knowledge that, whether they wish it or not, their work may be comparatively judged, and they themselves may be viewed as eager or hostile competitors. Sometimes these pressures lead to friendship, and sometimes not. In France, the relationships of Racine and Corneille, Rousseau and Voltaire, Sartre and Camus—writers whose work was routinely contrasted and compared—were marked by genuine tension and mutual dislike. In England, James Fenton, Professor of Poetry at Oxford, was formally challenged in 1994 by Adrian Mitchell to a Public Poetry Bout: a two-hour contest, beginning with a twenty-five-minute reading by each poet, followed by some 'shorter, wilder bouts . . . culminating in a flying exchange of insulting couplets and a farewell exchange by each fighter'. 'Shake hands and come out reciting', cried the challenger ringingly.[43] Such bardic postures may or may not be rooted in personal antagonism; they have their rhetorical precedents, and their own opportunities for self-advertisement and fun.

Jonson's relationship with Shakespeare was no doubt complex and at times uneasy. He was an independent and opinionated writer, and in his prologues and epilogues, inductions and choruses, he commented freely on the practice of his great contemporary. Some of Jonson's allusions to Shakespeare, 'the tother youth', are teasing; others seriously assert his own contrasting beliefs and principles, clearing a space for his own creative work. The notion of Jonson's warfare with Shakespeare and of his moroseness, malignity, and envy, was (however) an eighteenth-century invention, an intrinsic

[42] Harold Bloom, *The Anxiety of Influence: A Theory of Poetry* (New York, 1973); W. Jackson Bate, *The Burden of the Past and the English Poet* (1971); Virginia Blain, ' "Thinking Back Through our Aunts": Harriet Martineau and the Female Tradition', *Women: A Cultural Review*, 1 (1990), 223–39. See also Christopher Ricks, 'Allusion: The Poet as Heir', in R. F. Brissenden and J. C. Eade (eds.), *Studies in the Eighteenth Century*, vol. iii (Canberra, 1976), 209–40; see also Ch. 10 below.

[43] *Independent* (London), 20 Aug. 1994, 1.

part of the simultaneous construction of the modern idea of 'Shakespeare'.[44]

[44] Octavius Gilchrist's temperate and well-reasoned essay of 1808, *An Examination of the Charges Maintained by Messrs Malone, Chalmers, and Others, of Ben Jonson's Enmity, &c. Towards Shakespeare*, was followed by Gifford's acerbic essay ironically entitled 'Proofs of Ben Jonson's Malignity, From the Commentators on Shakespeare', prefixed to his edition of *The Works of Ben Jonson* in 1816. Gifford was an unfortunate champion of Jonson. He invented an absurd theory about Drummond's 'treachery' in luring Jonson to Hawthornden and then betraying his confidential remarks about Shakespeare. Critics such as Hazlitt appear to have disliked Jonson partly at least because they could not abide his editor: see 'Mr Gifford' in *The Spirit of the Age*, in William Hazlitt, *Complete Works*, ed. P. P. Howe after the edition of A. R. Waller and Arnold Glover (London, 1931), xi, 114, 115, 125; 'On Shakspeare and Ben Jonson', ibid. vi. 30–49. For modern reassessments of the relationship between the two dramatists see S. Musgrove, *Shakespeare and Jonson*, The Macmillan Brown Lectures (Auckland, 1957; repr. Folcroft, Pa., 1975); Jonas A. Barish (ed.), *Ben Jonson: A Collection of Critical Essays* (Englewood Cliffs, NJ, 1963), introduction; Ian Donaldson (ed.), *Jonson and Shakespeare* (1983); Anne Barton, *Ben Jonson: Dramatist* (Cambridge, 1984); Russ McDonald, *Shakespeare and Jonson: Jonson and Shakespeare* (Lincoln, Nebr. 1988); and Schoenbaum, *Shakespeare's Lives*.

3

Gathering and Losing the Self
Jonson and Biography

IN 1919 Gregory Smith began his study of Ben Jonson in the English Men of Letters series with these confident words:

We know more of Jonson than any of the great writers of his age. There are no mysteries, or at least great mysteries, in his literary career, and the biographer is not driven, with the Shakespearians, to conjectural reconstruction from the shards of record and anecdote. Even his personality stands forth fresh and convincing beside the blurred portrait of Marlowe, or Shakespeare, or Fletcher. For this fuller knowledge we are indebted to Jonson himself.[1]

Half a dozen years later, in the biographical essay that opens the first volume of the Oxford *Ben Jonson*, C. H. Herford expressed an even stronger belief in the immediate accessibility and legibility of Ben Jonson's character. 'The personality of Jonson', he wrote, 'detaches itself from the crowd of literary contemporaries with a distinctness by no means wholly due to the fact that our knowledge of it happens to be unusually full and clear.' For there was also, so Herford believed, 'something potent and distinctive in the *ethos* of the man.' 'Almost every sentence he wrote, however derivative in substance, carries an unmistakable relish of the man—is, in a greater or less degree, a document of the Jonsonian temperament and the Jonsonian will.'[2]

---

[1] *Ben Jonson*, English Men of Letters (1919), 1. Cf. Mark Eccles: 'Ben Jonson as a man stands out far more clearly than any other Elizabethan dramatist. He displayed his character in his plays and, still better, in his poems. He made a stronger impression on the educated men of his time than did either Shakespeare or Donne. No contemporary writer acquired more enemies, and few had more friends. Above all, his spoken words were set down by Drummond of Hawthornden—that forerunner of Boswell who put posterity more deeply in his debt by questioning Jonson and recording what he said than by all his writings. Jonson, in consequence, is the one dramatist of Shakespeare's time whose personality a biographer can hope to recapture . . .': 'Jonson's Marriage', *The Review of English Studies*, 12 (1936), 257.

[2] Herford and Simpson, i. 119. Herford was largely responsible for the biographical account of Jonson in the first volume of the Oxford edition, which was in turn based on the entry he had written for the *Dictionary of National Biography* in 1892.

Both scholars were writing in the far-off days before the advent of the new criticism and deconstructive theory, and before (even) the work of Freud had made a serious impact upon literary thinking in England. The personality of Ben Jonson which they invoke is coherent, stable, singular, and sharply defined. It is unproblematically evident in everything Jonson wrote. It resembles that of a minor character in a novel by Dickens, or, one might almost say, in an early comedy by Ben Jonson. It 'stands forth fresh and convincing', in Gregory Smith's words, spontaneously and explicitly declaring itself. There are 'no mysteries, or at least great mysteries' about the life of Ben Jonson, no need for the kind of 'conjectural reconstruction' that was evidently required in any attempted narrative of the life of Shakespeare, no scope for interpretation and guesswork. The 'fuller knowledge' that we enjoy of Jonson is apparently transmitted in a direct and unmediated way from the author, or subject, to the patient biographer, who acts seemingly as a kind of amanuensis or scholarly ghost.

The Oxford editors thought of Jonson as a writer who persisted in much the same ideas, convictions, and impulses from the beginning of his career to the end. The evidence for this view lay in a literary text that was assumed to be at once transparent and homogeneous. Jonson's work, Herford wrote,

is, in a rare degree, of a piece; we can distinguish its phases and its kinds; but the note of Jonsonian personality is singularly continuous; the apprentice challenging the veterans of Spain and the old poet indicting an Ode to Himself are the same; of the extraordinary power of inner growth, which astonishes us in a Dante, a Shakespeare, a Goethe, there is little trace in Jonson.[3]

It is hard to tell here whether a critical verdict has prompted a psychological conclusion, or the other way about, for the 'Jonsonian personality' that is invoked is in every sense a continuum, seamlessly encompassing apprenticeship and maturity, life and works, raw historical data and literary self-invention. No attempt is made to distinguish between Jonson's own tactical declarations of personal constancy and imperturbability, and the actual shifts, transformations, experiments, back-trackings, and inconsistencies which might be revealed by a closer scrutiny of his work as a whole, and the serpentine progress of his professional career. The claim to an easy recognition of 'something distinctive in the *ethos* of the man', though based on an unrivalled knowledge of Jonson's work, was in the final estimate little more than a subjective assertion, an editorial hunch of the kind that prompted similar judgements about the composition and dating of the canon. Those otherwise undatable works which deviated markedly from Herford and Simpson's 'potent and distinctive norm' were explained in terms of authorial senility, and dismissively assigned to the period of Jonson's so-called dotage. It is only in very recent years that scholars such as Anne Barton have begun to query the conventional Herford and Simpson view of Jonson's long, coherent, and consistent career that droops inexplicably into dotage some twenty years before the author's death, and to challenge many of the once firmly established Oxford datings. The revised Jonsonian chronology gives an altogether more irregular, various, and interesting view of the canon, and of the imaginative development of the author.[4]

If there was a measure of procedural circularity in the way in which the older biographical accounts of Ben Jonson were constructed, it may be remembered that circularity was a notion which greatly appealed to Jonson himself; so much, indeed, that on one occasion this large poet, tipping the scales at almost twenty stone, confessed that he exemplified circularity in his own person.[5] The figure of the circle, symbolizing integrity, perfection, impregnability, continuity, infinity, return, is to be found over and again throughout Jonson's writings.

> May windes as soft as breath of kissing friends
>   Attend thee hence; and there, may all thy ends,
> As the beginnings here, prove purely sweet,
>   And perfect in a circle alwayes meet.

> (*Epigrams*, 128. 5–8)

In bidding farewell to his friend William Roe, departing on his travels, Jonson wishes that Roe's return may be as peaceful as his setting out, his ends match his beginnings, his journeying—moral as well as geographical—take him circularly home to his starting-point, gently consolidating those qualities he already has. Change and disruption, like unfavourable winds, are excluded from this

---

4 Anne Barton, *Ben Jonson: Dramatist* (Cambridge, 1984).
5 *The Underwood*, 52, 'My Answer', 8.

magic circle; even in travel, stability is the thing. 'Stand forth my Object, then', Jonson writes to his friend the jurist John Selden,

> you that have beene
> Ever at home; yet, have all Countries seene:
> And like a Compasse keeping one foot still
> Upon your Center, do your Circle fill
> Of generall knowledge; watch'd men, manners too,
> Heard what times past have said, seen what ours doe.
>
> (*The Underwood*, 14. 29–34)

Home and abroad, times past and times present, are gathered and stabilized within the moral circle which Selden, in Jonson's figure, describes. 'How summ'd a circle didst thou leave man-kind / Of deepest lore, could we the Center find!', writes Jonson of the 'brave Infant of *Saguntum*', who returned at once to its mother's womb after glimpsing at its first emergence the horrors of the second Punic war (*The Underwood*, 70. 9–10). The infant's momentary life forms a perfect circle, ending where it began.

> Thou, looking then about,
> E're thou wert halfe got out,
> Wise child, did'st hastily returne,
> And mad'st thy Mothers wombe thine urne.   (5–8)

Writing of himself in 'An Epistle Answering to One That Asked to be Sealed of the Tribe of Ben', Jonson returns once more to the notion of centring and stability:

> Live to that point I will, for which I am man,
>   And dwell as in my Center, as I can,
> Still looking to, and ever loving, heaven;
>   With reverence using all the gifts thence given.
>
> (*The Underwood*, 47. 59–62)

How does a would-be biographer interpret this recurrent image? What, if anything, does it reveal about Jonson himself? How do we begin to read from *text* to *self*? It is tempting to assume that the circularity about which Jonson writes so constantly within his poems and court masques relates in some way to the movement of his own life and the shape of his career. 'Be alwayes to thy gather'd selfe the same', wrote Jonson to his friend Sir Thomas Roe,

> He that is round within himselfe, and streight,
> Need seeke no other strength, no other height;
> Fortune upon him breakes her selfe, if ill,
> And what would hurt his vertue makes it still.
>
> (*Epigrams*, 98. 9, 3–6)

Because Jonson asserts so often this notion of the round and gathered self, it seems almost as if his own integrated character is waiting there on the page, ready to be rolled or gathered into the biographer's briefcase. Yet the significance of the Jonsonian circle is perhaps less simple than at first appears.

In the induction to Jonson's last play, *The Magnetic Lady*, a boy admiringly describes the progress of the author's career in humours comedy from 'beginning his studies of this kind' in *Every Man In His Humour* to his most recent endeavour, *The New Inn*. Finding 'himselfe now neare the close, or shutting up of his Circle', Jonson (we are told) offers to the public this final comedy, *The Magnetic Lady* (Induction, 99, 104–5). This figure of the author's 'shutting up of his Circle' seems here to suggest a steady and deliberate progression in his career, which is now moving to a harmonious and perfect closure. Jonson's use of this figure, however, like the entire induction to *The Magnetic Lady*, may equally be seen as a brave attempt on Jonson's part to assert his undiminished power after the fiasco of *The New Inn*, which unfriendly critics had triumphantly cited as evidence of his creative deterioration and decline. The circular figure, in this view, can be seen as part of a rhetorical strategy which need not be accepted at face value, but seems rather to invite interpretation and a measure of resistance.[6]

The circle, like the gathered self, was of course an ideal notion, borrowed from the writings of classical and Renaissance authors: a statement of how, in a perfect world, one would like oneself and one's works to be viewed. It was not a description of how, in this necessarily imperfect world, things actually were, or of what one's character was actually like. Jonson significantly chose to adopt as his personal emblem the figure of a broken compass and an incomplete

---

[6] Thomas M. Greene's classic account, 'Jonson and the Centered Self', *Studies in English Literature 1500–1900*, 10 (1970), 325–48, while recognizing 'a strain of half-repressed envy for the homeless and centrifugal spirit' in Jonson's writing, tends generally to regard the circle as unproblematically descriptive of Jonson's character. John Enck entitles the final chapter of his *Jonson and the Comic Truth* (Madison, Wis., 1966) 'Shutting up of his Circle', accepting the terms in which Jonson chose to describe his own career.

circle. The motto accompanying this imprese was *deest quod ducere orbem*, 'that which might draw the circle' (or alternatively, 'that which might guide the world') 'is missing'.[7] The emblem and its motto serve as reminders of the unattainability of those qualities of closure, integrity, and perfection which Jonson simultaneously celebrates and asserts. The gap in the circumference of the circle is the gap between longing and fulfilment, between the ideal and the actuality. It is like the gap within our own boundaries of knowledge, the gap between text and life, the gap we attempt to bridge through interpretation, speculation, and guesswork. This chapter, which is itself quite speculative, is about those gaps, and how, if at all, they can be bridged.

❧

If the relationship between text and self is more problematical than an earlier generation of biographers believed, if there are gaps and contradictions within Jonson's apparent self-revelations, it seems worth asking what help the methods of psychoanalysis may bring. The first serious attempt to apply Freudian insights to an understanding of the character of Ben Jonson was made in 1948 by the American polymath Edmund Wilson in an essay entitled 'Morose Ben Jonson'.[8] Reacting against Herford and Simpson's edition of Jonson, which he found 'forbidding and fraught with asperities', and against T. S. Eliot's famous essay on Jonson which, he complained, 'minimises his glaring defects', Wilson set out to give a vivid account of those defects, which he chose to explain in psychoanalytical terms. Wilson thought Ben Jonson was what Freud had called an anal erotic, a person showing a strong disposition towards such qualities as orderliness, pedantry, parsimony, obstinacy, irascibility, vindictiveness. The chief evidence supporting this diagnosis lay, so Wilson thought, in Jonson's own writings. He quotes by way of example a few lines from the final act of *Cynthia's Revels*:

---

[7] *Conversations with Drummond*, 578–9 (Herford and Simpson, vol. i). The most complete account of this emblem is that of L. A. Beaurline in the epilogue to his *Jonson and Elizabethan Comedy* (San Marino, Ca., 1978).

[8] In Wilson, *The Triple Thinkers* (1952), 240–61. For another critique of this essay, see E. Pearlman, 'Ben Jonson: An Anatomy', *English Literary Renaissance*, 9 (1979), 364–93.

> When hath DIANA, like an envious wretch,
> That glitters onely to his soothed selfe,
> Denying to the world, the precious use
> Of hoorded wealth, with-held her friendly aide?
>
> (V. vi. 19–22)

'In these four lines', Wilson declares, 'you have the whole thing in the words that come to his pen: envy, denial, hoarding, withholding.' These are indeed words that come to Jonson's pen here, but only to be, as human qualities, quite specifically and explicitly repudiated. For the passage asserts the importance of values entirely contrary to those that Wilson finds in it and that he chooses to ascribe to the character of Ben Jonson himself; the four lines that he casually designates as representing 'the whole thing' being actually torn from a longer speech in which the character of Cynthia/Diana/Queen Elizabeth proclaims her liberality, generosity, and bounty. To read against the grain, to observe the positive force that lingers in apparent negations and denials, may indeed be an essential part of any attempted understanding of Jonson's character, as it is to the procedures of psychoanalysis, but Wilson seems scarcely to have noticed which way the grain is running in the first place, or what the speech more plainly declares.

It is Wilson's view that Jonson was morose in nature, like the character of that very name in *The Silent Woman*, who tries to shut himself away from the world in a house with double walls and treble ceilings and windows 'close shut, and calk'd', located in a lane too narrow for coaches to enter. This seems, to begin with, unlike the Ben Jonson who is known to have presided gregariously over sessions of wit and merry-making at the Apollo tavern. But it may further be asked why Jonson should be identified with a character such as Morose, who is so obviously subjected to comic ridicule within the play, rather than with a character such as (let us say) Truewit, the ingenious contriver of much of the comedy's action. And as drama is by its very nature dialogic, oppositional, multivocal, the identification of the playwright with just one of his own dramatic characters would seem in any case especially difficult to sustain. Wilson's apparent assumption is that, while Morose is indeed ridiculed and tormented throughout *The Silent Woman*, this form of dramatic attention reveals to the analytical eye the author's own deepest obsessions, attractions, and affinities. Jonson, he suggests, was in any case precisely the kind of author whom one can legitimately identify with his own dramatic characters, being—unlike Shakespeare—incapable of dispersing and disguising his imaginative sympathies, merely replicating within these characters his own grudges, fears, and sombre melancholy.

Though he attempts a variety of characters, they all boil down to a few motivations, recognizable as the motivations of Jonson himself and rarely transformed into artistic creations. Shakespeare expands himself, breeds his cells as organic beings, till he has so lost himself in the world he has made that we can hardly recompose his personality. Jonson merely splits himself up and sets the pieces—he is to this extent a dramatist—in conflict with one another; but we have merely to put these pieces together to get Jonson, with little left over.[9]

'Merely . . . merely': Wilson is here whistling his way through a complex hermeneutical problem with the same insouciance as the pre-Freudian biographers. He too assumes that the personality of the author is clearly and directly revealed within his writings, and that all you need do in order to discover him is pick up the textual pieces and put them together.

David Riggs's psychoanalytical reading of Ben Jonson in his recent biography rests on broadly similar assumptions. Like Edmund Wilson, whose essay he admires, Riggs seems to believe that certain scenes and characters within Jonson's plays offer a more or less transparent window on to Jonson's psychic condition. Riggs suggests, for example, that the scene in Jonson's early comedy *The Case is Altered* in which the miser Jacques buries his gold beneath a pile of horse dung shows the resentment that Jonson felt towards his stepfather. Jacques carries the dung onstage in a scuttle of a kind that Riggs fancies Jonson's stepfather, the bricklayer Robert Brett (no miser, so far as we know), might also have used in the course of his everyday labours when carrying mortar. According to Freud (in Riggs's account) the problems of anal erotics originate in the early difficulty they have in learning to control their bowels and thus progressing to the Oedipal stage, where they form a relationship with their fathers. Jonson's real father died before Jonson was born, and his stepfather seems to have been absent during Jonson's early infancy. Riggs writes:

[9] *The Triple Thinkers*, 242–3.

The scenes in which Jacques builds his cache of manure appear, then, to be the work of a man who suffers from the very malady that Freud describes: since Jonson never proceeded through the stage at which the child learns to cope with intergenerational conflict, when he fantasized about stepfathers, he instinctively regressed to the anal stage and soiled his foster parent with excrement.[10]

Perhaps the first and quite banal point to make about this analysis is that the association of money with excrement which the comedy here develops is thoroughly traditional, being found extensively in (for example) Renaissance popular art and proverbial lore. 'Money is like muck', noted Bacon, 'not good except it be spread.' Muck was (moreover) more generously spread, more generally visible, in earlier historical periods than it is today; not merely in the countryside, but in the city and the court. In seventeenth-century drawings of London, laystalls or dung-heaps are clearly visible on the street corners. In Jonson's time, the daily ceremony of the king easing his bowels, attended by the Groom of the Stool, was open to public view. Antony a'Wood reports that Charles II's nattily attired courtiers defecated freely in the fireplaces and other odd corners of the Oxford colleges in which they resided. As Alain Corbin's social history of smell in France reminds us, it is our society and our times that are exceptional in their methodical concealment of bodily processes. It is a modern fallacy to assume that references to excrement in the writings of Swift or Pope or Rabelais or Jonson necessarily signal some kind of authorial regression to an infantile state. In technologically advanced areas of the modern world, excrement may indeed be primarily associated with the experiences of infancy, but in early modern times these matters were less tidily confined.[11]

Even if we are convinced that this scene in Jonson's comedy must be read in autobiographical terms, however, the particular equation

---

[10] *Ben Jonson: A Life* (Cambridge, Mass., 1989), 31. For a more detailed critique, see my 'Life into Text', *Essays in Criticism*, 41 (July 1991), 253–61; on the general issues, see Stephen Greenblatt's 'Psychoanalysis and Renaissance Culture', in Patricia Parker and David Quint (eds.), *Literary Theory/Renaissance Texts* (Baltimore, 1986), 210–24.

[11] Bacon, 'Of Seditions and Troubles', in *The Works of Francis Bacon, Viscount St. Albans*, ed. J. Spedding, R. L. Ellis, and D. D. Heath, 14 vols. (1857–74), vi. 410; cf. Bacon's *Apophthegmes* (1625), 252; David Starkey, 'Representation Through Intimacy: A Study of the Symbolism of Monarchy and Court Office in Early Modern England', in Joan Lewis (ed.), *Symbols and Sentiments: Cross-Cultural Studies in Symbolism* (1977), 218; *The Life and Times of Antony a'Wood* (1961), 154; Alain Corbin, *The Foul and the Fragrant: Odor and the French Social Imagination* (Cambridge, Mass., 1986): trans. of *Le Miasme et la jonquille* (1982).

which Riggs proposes seems ultimately quite arbitrary. Why should the scene seriously provoke us to think about Jonson's stepfather? It would be as plausible to argue that he disliked misers, or theatre managers, who didn't pay him enough for his work. Here we are in a realm of utter guesswork, with no very plausible connection between play and playwright, and it seems best to admit this quite frankly.

The problem about the hypotheses I have just discussed is not that the very attempt to read from text to self is inherently ludicrous, but that the exercise demands a higher degree of sophistication and a greater readiness to consider the various interpretative hazards and options. It is not the ambition to cross the gap that is worrying, but the failure to realize that a gap is there. Recent theorists have cautioned against the wish to cross the gap at all, maintaining that the very notion of an authorial self discoverable within the text is a vulgar fallacy or humanistic illusion. Such theories obviously diminish the value of biography as an interpretative and intellectual enterprise. For reasons I want now to explain, I do not share this radical scepticism, or this low valuation of the practice of biography.

∿≋↝

Many of the logical inconsistencies and shortcomings of currently influential theories of literary authorship have been ably traced by (in particular) Sean Burke in his recent book on *The Death and Return of the Author*, and Lawrence Lipking in a skilful dissection of Roland Barthes's famous account of the author's death.[12] It is significant that biography itself should also have helped to explain why the death of the author has proved such an alluring doctrine to some of its major proponents over recent decades. David Lehman's 1991 biography of Paul de Man and David Macey's 1993 biography of Michel Foucault, for example, document some of the (sharply various) personal factors which seem to have strengthened the resolve of de Man, Barthes, and Foucault to reject conventional notions of authorial identity, visibility, and control in favour of

---

[12] *The Death and Return of the Author: Criticism and Subjectivity in Barthes, Foucault, and Derrida* (Edinburgh, 1992); Lawrence Lipking, 'Life, Death, and Other Theories', in Jerome J. McGann (ed.), *Historical Studies and Literary Criticism* (Madison, Wis., 1985), 180–98. See also Lipking's *The Life of the Poet: Beginning and Ending Poetic Careers* (Chicago, 1981).

alternative theories of readership and textuality.[13] Throughout a period in which formalist theory has attracted much support from within the academy, however, literary biography has never lost its powerful appeal to a wider scholarly and popular readership, whose collective interest cannot be dismissed as vulgar curiosity about the private lives of famous (or forgotten) authors. For literary biography is essentially an interpretative exercise of a twofold kind, illuminating works as well as lives, and the generally complex relationship that subsists between them. Biographers, like editors, necessarily move in the gap between self and text, testing biographical data against literary invention, measuring the fictionality of an author's work against its possible historicity, assessing the factors which may have helped to shape or sharpen a particular idea or a particular creative moment. That unusual tact and imagination are (equally) required for this kind of enquiry, that particular biographers may at times appear not to possess these qualities, are familiar facts that do not in themselves reduce or invalidate the significance of biography as a practice.

It is not easy to interpret the life of a writer such as Ben Jonson without attempting simultaneously to interpret his work. The self which Jonson projected within his writing is not identical with the Jonson who drank and argued at the Mermaid tavern, yet it is a legitimate and essential part of his total expressive life, of the self he fashioned through his doing and being, his thinking and saying and—not least—his writing. That writing becomes in turn, I believe, a legitimate and essential part of the total evidence which a biographer must confront and seek to explain.

Jonson's seeming presence within his writing is exceptionally vivid: he shows his rocky face and mountain belly; tells us, to the very pound, how much he weighs; speaks of his tendency to 'breake Chaires or cracke a Coach'; writes odes to himself; in the induction to one of his plays, lets it be known that he is watching from the wings; in the apologetical dialogue appended to another, permits the character of 'The Author' to walk onstage in order to remonstrate

---

[13] David Lehman's *Signs of the Times: Deconstruction and the Fall of Paul de Man* (New York, 1991) expands and documents earlier revelations about de Man's wartime articles for the Belgian collaborationist newspaper, *Le Soir*. David Macey's *The Lives of Michel Foucault* (1993) shows how Barthes and Foucault, practising homosexuals seeking professional advancement during an illiberal period in France, were attracted by the notion of textual impersonality: 'I am no doubt not the only one', declared Foucault, 'who writes in order to have no face' (*Lives*, p. xiii).

with the unappreciative audience.[14] In this respect Jonson is of course very different from an author such as Shakespeare. But what Jonson himself observed when praising the plays of Shakespeare, in which modern criticism tends to find its own reflection, was the indelible authorial stamp, the paternity of the text.

> Looke how the fathers face
> Lives in his issue, even so, the race
> Of *Shakespeares* mind and manners brightly shines
> In his well torned, and true-filed lines . . .
>
> (*Ungathered Verse*, 26. 65–8)

Jonson's work traces with giddying virtuosity the myriad intersections and overlappings of art and life. In his comedy *The Devil is an Ass* Fabian Fitzdottrell allows the young Wittipol to have fifteen minutes' conversation with his wife under strict conditions in return for the loan of a cloak that Fitzdottrell wishes to wear that day when visiting the playhouse. The play that Fitzdottrell is going to see is called *The Devil is an Ass*, by Ben Jonson. This intricate interleaving, this shimmering uncertainty about the nature of what Tom Stoppard delphically nominates 'the real thing', lies at the very centre of Jonson's thinking and of his art. Here are some lines on a Puritan preacher:

> I cannot think there's that antipathy
>   'Twixt *puritanes*, and *players*, as some cry;
> Though LIPPE, at PAULS, ranne from his text away,
>   To' inveigh 'gainst playes: what did he then but play?
>
> (*Epigrams*, 75)

Work and play, denial and indulgence, text and digression, text and self are all within Jonson's world inextricably involved and mutually reflected. In a highly suggestive passage in *Discoveries* Jonson writes as follows:

I have considered our whole life is like a *Play*: wherein every man, forgetfull of himselfe, is in travaile with the expression of another. Nay, wee so insist in imitating others, as wee cannot (when it is necessary) returne to our selves: like Children, that imitate the vices of *Stammerers* so long, till at last they become such; and make the habit to another nature, as it is never forgotten.   ('De vita humana', *Discoveries*, 1093–9)

---

[14] *The Underwood*, 9, 56, 23; *Bartholomew Fair*; *Poetaster*.

When life itself is likened to a literary artefact it is hard to keep the categories of 'self' and 'text' apart. The notion of selfhood which the passage proposes is itself characteristically complex, consisting, first, of the innate self which each of us originally possesses; then, of another, alien, self we may single out for emulation or imitation; next, of a process of 'travail' or becoming as we shift from the one character to the other; finally, of arrival and supersession, the accomplishment of the new self, the loss of the old.[15]

Since I am talking about the difficulties of interpretation I should add at this point that the passage I am wanting to adduce as central to Jonson's thinking was shown by Margaret Clayton just a few years ago to have been lifted more or less verbatim from the writings of the twelfth-century humanist John of Salisbury.[16] The problems posed by this revelation are characteristic of those presented by the *Discoveries* as a whole, which once were thought of as providing more or less direct and unimpeded access to Jonson's innermost thoughts and opinions. Swinburne regarded the *Discoveries* as a unique autobiographical document which revealed 'one of the noblest, manliest, most honest, and most helpful natures that ever dignified and glorified a powerful intelligence and an admirable genius', and lamented the fact that Shakespeare had not left behind a similar body of autobiographical writings for posterity. Subsequent scholarship began to show, however, that the *Discoveries* consisted largely of transcriptions from classical and Renaissance authors; such that by 1907 the French scholar Maurice Castelain, after many years of editorial labour, dejectedly ventured the opinion that *Discoveries* might without serious injustice be excluded from the Jonsonian canon.[17]

The problems here are multiple and perplexing. '*I have* considered our whole life is like a *Play* . . .': who is the speaker here, the 'I' who has considered the analogy between life and play? Is it John of Salisbury or is it Ben Jonson? What kind of *self* is actually revealed in

---

[15] For an acute analysis of the Jonsonian conception of the self, see Lawrence Danson, 'Jonsonian Comedy and the Discovery of the Social Self', *PMLA: Publications of the Modern Language Association*, 99 (1984), 179–93. Jonson's own professional progress is well described by Richard Helgerson, *Self-Crowned Laureates: Spenser, Jonson, Milton, and the Literary System* (Berkeley, 1983).

[16] Margaret [Tudeau] Clayton, 'Ben Jonson, "In Travaile with Expression of Another": His Use of John of Salisbury's *Policratus* in *Timber*', *The Review of English Studies*, NS 30 (1979), 397–408.

[17] A. C. Swinburne, *A Study of Ben Jonson* (1880), 130; Ben Jonson, *Discoveries*, ed. Maurice Castelain (Paris, n.d. [1907]), p. vii.

this text? What kind of appropriation or impersonation or hybridity or ventriloquism is occurring here? There are many similar moments in Jonson's classical verse imitations where the author is not speaking purely and unambiguously in his own unique voice, but is closely following the thought and language of particular works by Martial or Horace or Catullus: playing the part of an admired author, while seemingly 'forgetfull of himselfe'. Another section of the *Discoveries*, translated from yet another author, urges the necessity of the poet's perfecting the art of imitation, learning 'to convert the substance, or Riches of an other *Poet*, to his owne use. To make choise of one excellent man above the rest, and so to follow him, till he grow very *Hee*: or, so like him, as the Copie may be mistaken for the Principall' (2468–71). Faced with such cunning simulations and erasures of selfhood, the biographer may be tempted to abandon his search for a tangible subject, to assume with Maurice Castelain that the link between text and self is so tenuous as to be nearly invisible, and to conclude that such writings tell us nothing significant about the character and disposition of Ben Jonson himself. But Jonson's interest and attention must, to say the least, have been aroused by the passages he took pains to transcribe or translate in his commonplace book, and by the classical poets he imitated. He perceived in the writers of the past (as one might say) 'a part of himself', or of that self he sought assiduously to fashion: a stance, an attitude, that he strove to make his own; and this impulse is in itself an important psychological feature that a biographer needs to capture. Jonson's passion for emulation and imitation thus constitutes an essential and primary biographical fact. Literary personality, for Jonson, did not hinge upon notions of originality and individuality, did not consist in the achievement of a unique and unprecedented voice, in the finding of some essentialist *self*; it consisted rather of the gradual assumption of another self, in a process of deliberate play or travail through which one laboured to become the sort of person one most hoped to be. It was in this spirit and with these ends that Jonson sought diligently to become 'the English Horace'.

In his satirical comedy *Poetaster* Jonson presented the historical figure of Horace in such a manner that the correspondences with his English imitator would be evident. Not everyone was convinced. In *Satiromastix*, Thomas Dekker's scornful response to Jonson's play, the character Tucca accuses a young self-promoting poet of being a mere 'counterfeit Jugler, that steales the name of *Horace*'.

thou has no part of *Horace* in thee but's name, and his damnable vices: thou hast such a terrible mouth, that thy beard's afraide to peepe out: but looke heere you staring Leviathan, heere's the sweete visage of *Horace*; looke, perboylde-face, looke; *Horace* had a trim long-beard, and a reasonable good face for a Poet, (as faces goe now-a-dayes): *Horace* did not skrue and wriggle himselfe into great mens famyliarity, (impudentlie) as thou doost: nor weare the Badge of Gentlemens company, as thou doost thy Taffetie sleeves, tackt too onely with some pointes of profit: No, *Horace* had not his face puncht full of Oylet-holes, like the cover of a warming-pan: *Horace* lov'd poets well, and gave Coxcombes to none but fooles; but thou lov'st none, neither Wisemen nor fooles, but thy selfe: *Horace* was a goodly Corpulent Gentleman, and not so leane a hollow-cheekt Scrag as thou art . . . (v. ii. 244–5, 249–63)[18]

Dekker mercilessly exposes the gap in the circumference, the distance between the gathered, secure, authoritative, Roman self which Jonson aspired to attain, and the vulnerable, pushy, pimpled, self-absorbed, anxious self he still unhappily possessed. Jonson is brilliantly caught in that process of 'travail' between the one role and the other, screwing and wriggling his way from bricklayer to gentleman in a manner which his later pronouncements of sturdy social independence would seem to deny. Later, of course, he would fill the Horatian role more adequately, swelling both literally and metaphorically to classic proportions. The passage from *Satiromastix* is caricature, certainly, and therefore itself demands interpretation. Yet it brings us close enough to see that scraggy beard and pock-marked face, and guess what a sweat it must have been to play the English Horace.

❧

But what (to resume the search) can we gather about Jonson the man from his own text, as distinct from Dekker's? Let us return at this

---

[18]   *The Dramatic Works of Thomas Dekker*, ed. Fredson Bowers, 4 vols. (Cambridge, 1953), i. 380–1; i/j and u/v regularized. Cf. the attempt (early 1733) by Lady Mary Wortley Montagu and Lord Hervey to discredit Pope's similar claims to be 'the English Horace': '*Horace* can laugh, is delicate, is clear; / You, only coarsely rail, or darkly sneer: / His Style is elegant, his Diction pure, / Whilst none thy crabbed Numbers can endure; / Hard as thy Heart, and as thy Birth obscure.' (From *Verses Address'd to the Imitator of the First Satire of the Second Book of Horace*, in *Works of Lady Mary Wortley Montagu*, ed. Robert Halsband and Isobel Grundy (Oxford, 1977), 266.)

point to the character of Morose in *The Silent Woman*, and to a passage one might have expected Edmund Wilson to have quoted, though he does not. In the final act of the comedy, Morose, desperately seeking release from the noisy woman he has ill-advisedly married—who will ultimately turn out to be not a woman at all but a disguised boy—tells the two supposed lawyers, who have come to argue the case for and against his divorce, to speed through the formalities and come to the point.

I love not your disputations, or your court-tumults. And that it be not strange to you, I will tell you. My father, in my education, was wont to advise mee, that I should alwayes collect, and contayne my mind, not suffring it to flow loosely; that I should looke to what things were necessary to the carriage of my life, and what not: embracing the one, and eschewing the other. In short, that I should endeare my self to rest, and avoid turmoile: which is now growne to be another nature to me. So that I come not to your publike pleadings, or your places of noise; not that I neglect those things, that make for the dignitie of the common-wealth: but for the meere avoiding of clamors, & impertinencies of Orators, that know not how to be silent. And for the cause of noise, am I now a sutor to you. You doe not know in what a miserie I have been exercis'd this day, what a torrent of evill! My very house turnes round with the tumult! I dwell in a windmill! The perpetuall motion is here, and not at *Eltham*. (v. iii. 46–63)

Morose's wish 'that I should alwayes collect, and contayne my mind, not suffring it to flow loosely' interestingly resembles Jonson's own Horatian ideal, to 'Be always to thy gather'd selfe the same', 'round within himselfe, and streight', to 'dwell as in my Center as I can'. Morose's wish to resist the clamour and turmoil of public life, to retreat quietly into the private domain, can be paralleled in a number of Jonson's own poems, such as the epistle 'To Sir Robert Wroth' ('Let this man sweat, and wrangle at the barre, / For every price, in every jarre', etc.: *The Forest*, 3. 73–4). Morose's dislike of restless movement anticipates Jonson's own contempt for Inigo Jones's mobile scenic effects in the court masques; one scholar has noted that Jonson's attack on Jones, who is presented in the 'Expostulation' 'Whirling his Whymseys' (*Ungathered Verse*, 34. 73), is directed 'against scenes, lights and machines which *moved* before the spectators' eyes'.[19]

---

[19] W. A. Armstrong, 'Ben Jonson and Jacobean Stagecraft', in John Russell Brown and Bernard Harris (eds.), *Jacobean Theatre*, Stratford-upon-Avon Studies, 1 (1960), 51.

If it seems possible to glimpse in Morose's wish for stability and self-containment something of Jonson's own wishes and impulses, what follows from that? Does this mean, as Edmund Wilson believed, that Ben Jonson himself actually was temperamentally morose, anally erotic? Another, quite contrary, interpretation suggests itself: that in making fun of Morose's wish to shut himself away from the world, Jonson is humorously and critically exploring the limitations of an ideal to which, in its more considered form, he himself never-theless generally and substantially subscribed; that in the figure of the ludicrously misanthropic, misogynistic, curmudgeonly Morose Jonson is producing a picture not, in any simple sense, of himself but of what the admired Horatian ideal might lead to if obsessively, nar-rowly, myopically followed. Morose in this respect resembles that other well-intentioned, high-minded, civically responsible, equally ludicrous admirer of the writings of Horace, Justice Adam Overdo in *Bartholomew Fair*, who is in turn a kind of caricature of the morally upright figure of Cicero in Jonson's immediately previous, disastrously unsuccessful, play *Catiline*.[20] An interpretation roughly along these lines might suggest in turn another and quite different picture of the kind of person Jonson may have been: more humor-ous, more flexible, more self-critical, less monolithic, and (in a word) less morose.

Central to Jonson's thinking about the nature of personal identity is a contrast that is developed extensively throughout his drama and his non-dramatic verse between *the gathered self*—collected, con-sistent, contained, morally stalwart, but tending towards stodginess and solipsism—and what might be called *the loose self*, a personal-ity more labile and mercurial, ready to shift opportunistically from one role, one voice, one stance to another, and another; a self that in its very instability is at once deeply attractive and deeply untrust-worthy. This latter type engaged Jonson's dramatic energies and imaginative sympathies to a surprising degree. It is represented within his dramatic work by such characters as Brainworm, Mosca, Volpone, Face, Subtle, who move with such virtuosity from part to part, changing a visor swifter than a thought, that it is difficult finally to say who they are, what their basic character may be. Volpone moves from playing the part of a dying magnifico to that of Scoto of

---

[20] See Jonas Barish, *Ben Jonson and the Language of Prose Comedy* (Cambridge, Mass., 1960), 204–13, 319.

Mantua, himself a dazzling charlatan, mimicking him with such fidelity that, as Mosca admiringly says, 'SCOTO himselfe could hardly have distinguish'd!' (II. iv. 36). Later he disguises himself as a Commendatore, demanding of Mosca, 'Am I then like him?'. 'Oh, sir, you are he', Mosca responds, 'No man can sever you' (V. v. 1–2). When Volpone finally comes face to face with Celia he cannot tell her who he is, merely describe excitedly his own talents in mimicking the identity of others, proposing to her a seemingly unending round of erotic games in which they might assume a series of feigned and ever-changing identities. Sir Epicure Mammon in *The Alchemist* is a slow-witted variant on this basic model, wishing to multiply infinitely his pleasures and his own unlovely character:

> For I doe meane
> To have a list of wives, and concubines,
> Equal with SALOMON, who had the *stone*
> Alike, with me: and I will make me, a back
> With the *elixir*, that shall be as tough
> As HERCULES, to encounter fiftie a night. . . .
>
> I will have all my beds, blowne up, not stuft:
> Downe is too hard. And then, mine oval roome,
> Fill'd with such pictures, as TIBERIUS tooke
> From ELEPHANTIS: and dull ARETINE
> But coldly imitated. Then, my glasses
> Cut in more subtill angles, to disperse,
> And multiply the figures, as I walk
> Naked between my *succubae*. My mists
> I'le have of perfume, vapor'd 'bout the roome
> To loose our selves in; and my baths, like pits
> To fall into . . .
>
> (II. ii. 34–51)

There is some irony in the fact that Mammon's erotic tastes should resemble those of Jonson's beloved Horace, who, as Suetonius reveals, 'was immoderately lustful; for it is reported that in a room lined with mirrors he had harlots so arranged that whichever way he looked, he saw a reflection of venery'.[21] 'Loose our selves in', in the folio spelling, or 'lose ourselves in', as Mammon is no doubt also suggesting, the two words being at this time interchangeable both in spelling and significance: the loose self threatens always to be the lost

[21] *The Lives of Illustrious Men*, in *Suetonius*, trans. J. C. Rolfe, Loeb Classical Library, 2 vols. (1914).

self. What Morose in *The Silent Woman* most fears is that through inadvertence he 'flow loosely', thereby losing his carefully garnered self.[22]

Jonson's own life, as I have already indicated, was itself more loose and mobile than his sturdy self-declarations cared to admit. He zig-zagged his way up through the social registers from labourer to soldier to actor to playwright to court poet, became sufficiently intimate with James I to risk, in work written for him, both jokes and stern advice, clung anxiously and precariously to royal favour under Charles I while simultaneously professing to disdain the court. He repeatedly scorned and threatened to leave the public theatre for which he nevertheless continued to write. He changed his religion, and changed it again. He wrote repeatedly of the virtues of a settled life, of dwelling contentedly at home, but left his wife and his home, and during the years of his maturity shifted from house to house, living under the protection of patrons. '*I have* considered our whole life is like a *Play*': much of Jonson's life was lived with and through plays, alongside fellow actors, who shifted constantly from role to role, perpetually changing voice and face and place and costume. The court itself, as Jonson saw it, was a kind of theatre, a centre of disguise and play-acting and social manipulation. Living as he did in and between such unstable worlds, it is not surprising that Jonson aspired so firmly to the ideal of the gathered self, nor that his imagination was simultaneously drawn to the idea of a self that was not fast but loose, duplicitous, mercurial.

In one of his brilliant and compassionate essays in *The Man Who Mistook his Wife for a Hat*, the New York clinical neurologist Oliver Sacks describes the case of a Mr Thompson, who simply could not remember from moment to moment who he actually was, and who consequently invented, even within the course of the briefest conversation, a whole series of quite different personalities for himself, a string of wonderful and diverse self-fictions, between which he slipped with spell-binding confidence and dexterity. So far as he himself was concerned, all of these roles and all of these stories were

---

[22] Similar fears and polarities are found elsewhere in Jonson's writing. Cf. e.g. the advice given by the elder Knowell to Stephen in *Every Man In His Humour* (folio), I. i. 76–82: 'Nor would I, you should melt away your selfe / In flashing braverie, least while you affect / To make a blaze of gentrie to the world, / A litle puffe of scorne extinguish it, / And you be left, like an unsavourie snuffe, / Whose propertie is onely to offend. / I'Id ha' you sober, and containe your selfe . . .'.

perfectly true, for by the time he came to the next story he had forgotten the one he had just told. Sacks comments:

Such a frenzy may call forth quite brilliant powers of invention and fancy—
a veritable confabulatory genius—for such a patient must *literally make
himself (and his world) up every moment*. We have, each of us, a life-story,
an inner narrative—whose continuity, whose sense, *is* our lives. It might be
said that each of us constructs and lives a 'narrative', and that this narrative
is us, our identities.

If we wish to know about a man, we ask 'What is his story—his real,
inmost story?'—for each of us *is* a biography, a story. Each of us *is* a singular narrative, which is constructed, continually, unconsciously, by, through,
and in us—through our perceptions, our feelings, our thoughts, our actions; and, not least, our discourse, our spoken narrations. Biologically,
physiologically, we are not so different from each other; historically, as
narratives—we are each of us unique.[23]

Ben Jonson certainly did not appear to suffer from Korsakov's disease: he maintained well into old age a powerful memory and a
powerful sense of who he was and who he wanted to be, that is constantly reinforced in many of the narrations that he told about himself. But as I have suggested, that sense of who he was and who he
wanted to be contained an element of duality, even of multiplicity:

> Let me be what I am: as *Virgil* cold;
>   As *Horace* fat; or as *Anacreon* old . . .
>
>   (*The Underwood*, 42. 1–2)

'What I am' is compounded in part of what the great figures of the
past once were. In his talks with the Scottish poet William
Drummond at Hawthornden over the winter of 1618/19, Jonson revealed a personality that is in other ways less secure, less singular
than that presented robustly within his poetry. 'He hath consumed a
whole night', reported Drummond, 'in lying looking to his great toe,
about the which he hath seen tartars and turks Romans and
Carthaginions feight in his imagination' (*Conversations with
Drummond*, 322–4). And Jonson throughout his lifetime told other
dramatic narratives, too, which, though not ostensibly about himself, are deeply concerned with the puzzles of selfhood, with the
nature of duplicity, with metamorphosis and the loss of stable identity, with figures who seem to behave like Mr Thompson, shifting

---

[23] *The Man Who Mistook his Wife for a Hat* (1985), 105.

giddily from moment to moment, from character to character, loosing and losing themselves. If we want in turn to tell our narrative about the kind of person we reckon Ben Jonson to have been, we need, I think, to listen carefully to all these stories, all of which need interpreting and weighing against each other and against external evidence, none of which explains itself, none of which can be wholly set aside. After such listening, our own story may perhaps begin.

4

Jonson's Duplicity: The Catholic Years

'I, OFT, have heard him say, how he admir'd / Men of your large profession', says Mosca ingratiatingly to the lawyer Voltore in the first act of *Volpone*,

> that could speake
> To every cause, and things mere contraries,
> Till they were hoarse againe, yet all be law;
> That, with most quick agilitie, could turne,
> And re-turne; make knots, and undoe them;
> Give forked counsell; take provoking gold
> On either hand, and put it up: these men,
> He knew, would thrive, with their humilitie. . . .
>
> (I. iii. 52–60)

Jonson here imagines a juridical system that is as pliable as the criminal energies it seemingly attempts to contain, turning and returning as occasion and advantage offer. The lawyer's readiness to take bribes from any source is benignly regarded as another proof of the legendary even-handedness of the law, and his ability to argue for opposing causes is admired as a form of rhetorical virtuosity and personal abasement: 'these men, / He knew, would thrive, with their humilitie'. Two of Jonson's epigrams darkly celebrate similar skills in a lawyer named Cheverel. The skin of the cheverel or kid makes the softest and most malleable of gloves, that can be turned inside out in a moment: as can the lawyer.

> No cause, nor client fat, will Chev'rill leese,
> But as they come, on both sides he takes fees,
> And pleaseth both. For while he melts his greace
> For this: that winnes, for whom he holds his peace.
>
> (*Epigrams*, 37)

Jonson was later to present in *The Devil is an Ass* another representative of the law appropriately named Sir Paul Eitherside.

'Either hand', 'both sides', 'Eitherside': duplicity of this sort lies at the very heart of Jonson's drama and of his social vision: it is the basis (one might almost say) of the Jonsonian social contract, the premiss from which his narrative energies spring. Double-dealing seems to have held a deep fascination for Jonson, though he was at pains to repudiate any suggestion that his own life might have been in any way duplicitous. In his poetry, Jonson characteristically presents himself as a man of simple, devout, and single aspirations, 'Still looking to, and ever loving, heaven', possessed of a 'Character' that can at once be 'read' (*The Underwood*, 47. 61, 73). There is nothing lurking around the corner, no other or either side to be examined, no hint of those multiple, variable aspects of selfhood that are delightedly explored in the writings of Montaigne, or of Sir Thomas Browne. The only changes to which Jonson elsewhere in his poetry concedes he may be subject are those inflicted by increasing age and girth, in a process of progressive self-reification by which, as he grows older and fatter, he becomes—not different, but ever and more intensively *himself*.[1]

Jonson was similarly insistent about the single, unchanging qualities of those whom he admired and sought to praise: Pembroke, for example, 'whose noblesse keeps one stature still, / And one true posture, though beseig'd with ill' (*Epigrams*, 102. 13–14). There was of course a second side to William Herbert, Earl of Pembroke, as Clarendon's later account of the man makes clear.[2] Jonson must have known this other side, but one stature, one posture, is all he here seemingly wishes to declare.[3] This tactical suppression of complicating evidence might, in a strict moral accounting, itself be reckoned a form of mild duplicity. Yet what is remarkable about Jonson's epigram to Pembroke is its larger vision of a society that is itself—not duplicitous exactly, but morally divided, separated into opposing sides.

> I Doe but name thee, PEMBROKE, and I find,
>   It is an *Epigramme*, on all man-kind;
> Against the bad, but of, and to the good:
>   Both which are ask'd, to have thee understood.
> Nor could the age have mist thee, in this strife

---

[1] E.g. *The Underwood*, 52, 71.
[2] Edward Hyde, Earl of Clarendon, *The History of the Rebellion*, ed. W. Dunn Macreay, 6 vols. (Oxford, 1888), ii. 71–4.
[3] See Ch. 11 and n. 33, below.

> Of vice, and vertue; wherein all great life,
> Almost, is exercis'd: and scarse one knowes,
> To which, yet, of the sides himselfe he owes.
>
> (*Epigrams*, 102. 1–8)

The problem in dealing with a Voltore or a Cheverel or a Sir Paul Eitherside, as with a Mosca or Volpone, is that one never quite knows if they are allies or adversaries: for they will be, as interest dictates, now this, now that, opportunistically on either side. The problem touched on in the poem to Pembroke is of a deeper kind, involving metaphysical as well as empirical knowledge, knowledge of the self as well as of society. In the great strife of vice and virtue, the poem suggests, most humans *do not themselves know* quite where they belong: 'scarse one knowes / To which, yet, of the sides himselfe he owes'. 'Scarse one': it would be possible to argue that the poem here registers a passing, tactful doubt about the precise moral status even of Pembroke himself, briefly subverting the confident declarations with which it begins. Jonson's dualistic vision and his insistence on the limitations of human knowledge are strongly reminiscent of Calvin, whose influence has been traced elsewhere in his writing; but the reference, as I want in a moment to suggest, may carry a wider signification as well.[4]

Jonson's strenuous attempts to dissociate himself and those he admires from the world of double-dealing which so evidently continues to fascinate him, to stabilize and simplify his own moral position, often paradoxically suggest an actual complexity and dividedness of character quite at odds with his own protestations, and with the biographical portrait of the morally integrated author which C. H. Herford presented seventy years ago in the first volume of the Oxford *Ben Jonson*. More recent accounts by Anne Barton, David Riggs, and others have revealed a very different Ben Jonson, more fractured in temperament and conduct, more experimental, various,

---

[4] See W. Kerrigan, 'Ben Jonson Full of Scorn and Shame', *Studies in the Literary Imagination*, 6 (1973), 199–217. Calvin berates 'those who, only covered with a mask, claim for themselves before the world the chief place among the pious', and finds in the writings of Paul evidence for the existence of 'two kinds of people: one, from the whole race of Abraham; the other, separated from it, and being withdrawn under the eyes of God, hidden from human sight': *Institutes of the Christian Religion*, ed. John T. McNeill, trans. Ford Lewis Battles, 2 vols., The Library of Christian Classics (Philadelphia, 1960), bk. III, ch. xxii, sect. 6. The political implications of Jonson's epigram to Pembroke are analysed by Robert C. Evans, *Ben Jonson and the Poetics of Patronage* (Lewisburg, Pa., 1989), 107–18.

and digressive in his creative processes.[5] Riggs's 1989 biography posits a deeply divided personality, oscillating between 'reckless self-assertion and rationalistic self-limitation', between 'defiant risk taking and sober retrenchment': 'two protagonists' (as Riggs puts it) battling for supremacy within 'a single life'.[6] Using the insights of Freudian analysis, Riggs locates the origins of this divided self in the traumas of Jonson's childhood: the prenatal death of his father, the remarriage of his mother, the uneasy relationship with his stepfather who had usurped his mother's affection and was later to push him towards a detested trade.

Even in the case of a living subject, a hypothesis of this kind must, in the nature of things, remain quite speculative. With a 400 year-old subject about whom only fragmentary evidence relating to the formative years is available, the hypothesis is inevitably even more attenuated. Is there another kind of evidence which might be invoked in relation to the theory of Jonson's divided life, and are there other, more obvious, questions that might be asked about it?

Take for example, this familiar passage from the *Conversations with Drummond* (631–2): 'Of all stiles', noted Drummond of Jonson, 'he loved most to be named honest, and hath of that ane hundreth letters so naming him.' What interpretation does this comment invite? Jonson's emphasis, to begin with, naturally stirs suspicion. 'A man who has a hundred letters vouching for his honesty', as David Riggs nicely puts it, 'clearly anticipates that people are going to call him a liar or a hypocrite.'[7] The sense of potential reversibility here is curiously similar to that in Jonson's creative work: in *Epigrams*, 115, for example, where 'the town's honest man' is satirically exposed as an entirely contrary creature, the town's 'arrant'st knave'. Those hundred letters seem to serve for Jonson as a hundred nails, pinning the word 'honest' the right way about. There may well be a psychological explanation for Jonson's interest in this form of categorical instability, in the ease with which apparent moral absolutes might be 'preposterously transchangd',[8] and perhaps, who knows, it might be found, if we could ever recover and

---

[5] Anne Barton, *Ben Jonson: Dramatist* (Cambridge, 1984); David Riggs, *Ben Jonson: A Life* (Cambridge, Mass., 1989); E. Pearlman, 'Ben Jonson: An Anatomy', *English Literary Renaissance*, 9 (1979), 364–93.

[6] *Ben Jonson*, 2.   [7] Ibid. 257.

[8] Lorenzo in *Every Man In His Humour* (quarto), V. iii. 307. Cf. *Measure for Measure*, II. iv. 16: 'Let's write "good angel" on the devil's horn', etc.

truly understand them, in the formative, familial experiences of his early childhood. But concentration on that line of enquiry may divert attention from other more immediate social pressures operating upon Jonson in the course of his adult life.

What *are* those hundred letters, for example, and what exactly can Jonson have been talking about? It is not easy to say, but here is a guess. Letters testifying to a person's honesty were commonly required in this period in cases of litigation, particularly but not only in the Star Chamber.[9] Shakespeare himself produced similar letters in his negotiations with Henry Chettle over the 'upstart crow' passage in Greene's *A Groatsworth of Wit*. Chettle's formal apology to Shakespeare noted that 'divers of worship have reported his uprightnes of dealing, which argues his honesty, and his facetious grace in writting, that aprooves his Art'.[10] Jonson, being in and out of the courts at frequent intervals throughout his career on charges ranging from murder to seditious utterance, would in all likelihood have required many such testimonies to his own character—a hundred letters, as he might exasperatedly have said in the course of an evening's conversation at Hawthornden. One kind of documentary evidence that was required of him on several occasions in 1605–6 by the Consistory Court related to his and his wife's churchgoing and to the nature of his own religious convictions. 'They are both to Certify of their diligent & ordinarie going to Churche', reads one of several court entries during this period, of Jonson and his wife; 'he is to Certify how he is satisfied in the scruple he made of his receyving the Co[mmun]ion by them he was referred unto to conferr w[i]th.'[11] This may or may not be the kind of certification to which Jonson was referring in his talks with Drummond. But the repeated legal necessity to produce documentary evidence concerning his character, beliefs, and disposition may go some way towards explaining the general manner—pre-emptively, emphatically self-justifying—in which Jonson was often prompted to write about himself.

Six hundred miles from London, in the romantic isolation of Hawthornden, Jonson in his late forties showed Drummond a more varied, more versatile face, admitting to contradictions and

[9] C. J. Sisson, *Lost Plays of Shakespeare's Age* (Cambridge, 1936), 8.

[10] From H[enry] C[hettle], *Epistle to Kind-Harts Dreame* (London, n.d., S.R. Dec. 1592), sigs. A3^v–4, repr. in E. K. Chambers, *William Shakespeare: A Study of Facts and Problems*, 2 vols. (Oxford, 1930), ii. 189, u/v spellings regularized.

[11] Herford and Simpson, i. 222.

flexibilities of character that his more public pronouncements had often denied. Towards the end of the *Conversations*, Drummond notes some of the paradoxes of belief and temperament to which Jonson had confessed during his time in Scotland.

> for any religion, as being versed in both.
> interpreteth best sayings and deeds often to the worst:
> oppressed with fantasie, which hath ever mastered his
> reason, a generall disease in many poets.   (690–3)

The word 'any' ('for any religion') is used here in the now obsolete sense, still current in northern dialects, of 'either': 'one of *two* things indifferently', as the *OED* puts it. Ignoring the Reformed Church of Scotland and nonconformist sects south of the border, Jonson speaks of the two major religions of which he has had intimate and continuing experience, 'as being versed in both', the Church of England and the Church of Rome. Versed initially in the ways of the Roman Church while in prison in 1598, perhaps by the Yorkshire Jesuit, Father Thomas Wright, Jonson was (so to speak) re-versed back into the ways of the established church in 1606 on the instructions of the Consistory Court, which required him to engage in formal and regular theological disputation with no lesser personages than the Dean of St Paul's and the Chaplain of the Archbishop of Canterbury.[12] Though Jonson did not officially return to the Church of England until 1610, he was obliged in the mean while, as we have just seen, to report regularly to the Consistory Court on the progress of his beliefs.

What Jonson did believe precisely during those years is open, however, to speculation; as is, notoriously, the precise nature of his involvement with Guy Fawkes and his fellow conspirators in 1605, the year preceding the Consistory Court's order that he take theological instruction. Can Jonson, who denounced spies and spying with such vigour, himself have acted (as Barbara De Luna suggests) as a

---

[12] Theodore A. Stroud, 'Ben Jonson and Father Thomas Wright', *ELH: A Journal of English Literary History*, 14 (1947), 274–82, and 'Father Thomas Wright: A Test Case for Toleration', *Biographical Studies, 1534–1829*, 1 (1951–2), 189–219, with an 'addition' by B. Fitzgibbon, SJ, 261–80; Ian Donaldson, 'Jonson's Italy: *Volpone* and Fr. Thomas Wright', *Notes and Queries*, 19 (1972), 450–2; Thomas Wright, *The Passions of the Mind in Generall*, ed. Thomas O. Sloan (Urbana, Ill., 1971), introduction, and the introductions to the Garland repr. of same work, ed. William Webster Newbold, The Renaissance Imagination, vol. xv (New York, 1986), 3–16, 61–2; Arnold Pritchard, *Catholic Loyalism in Elizabethan England* (Chapel Hill, 1979), 61–7; Herford and Simpson, i. 221.

government counter-agent? Which side was he actually on at the time of the conspiracy? Was he, as De Luna believes, *pretending* to be a Catholic, or was he indeed a 'seducer of youthe to the popishe Religion', as the court presentment of 1606 alleged?[13] These questions can probably never be conclusively answered. And while Jonson celebrated his return to the Church of England in 1610 in characteristic style, quaffing the entire contents of the cup at his first attendance at Communion, that determined gesture did not quite disguise his lingering interest in the religion which he had now formally renounced. In 1612–13 he listened attentively to theological disputations in Paris between Protestant and Catholic champions. At Hawthornden in 1618–19 he talked with Drummond about the Catholic poet and martyr Robert Southwell, tortured by Topcliffe in the Tower in 1592 and ultimately dispatched by Sir Edward Coke with the calm instruction 'that he should be carried to Newgate from whence he came, and from thence to be drawn to Tyburn upon an hurdle, and then to be hanged and cut down alive, his bowels to be burned before his face, his head to be striken off, his body to be quartered and disposed at Her Majesty's pleasure'. Jonson would almost certainly have been familiar with these details, though Drummond perhaps was not. His note of Jonson's account reads laconically: 'That Southwell was hanged yett so he had written that piece of his the burning babe he would have been content to destroy many of his' (180–2). During his later life Jonson maintained a close friendship with Catholics such as Kenelm Digby, with whom he is likely to have discussed the decision to exclude from the second folio (as from the first) a number of poems addressed to other Catholics—even the highly accomplished 'Ode Allegorike', written for his schoolfriend and fellow convert to Catholicism, the poet Hugh Holland.[14]

'. . . and scarse one knows, / To which, yet, of the sides himselfe he owes': Jonson's religious allegiances from the late 1590s to his death

---

[13] B. N. De Luna, *Jonson's Romish Plot: A Study of 'Catiline' and its Historical Context* (Oxford, 1967); Herford and Simpson, i. 222. For Jonson on spies, see *Conversations with Drummond*, 256–60; *Epigrams*, 59, 101. 36; *Sejanus*, II. 442 ff., etc.

[14] Christopher Devlin, *The Life of Robert Southwell, Poet and Martyr* (New York, 1956), 283; *Conversations with Drummond*, 180–2. Jonson's 'Ode Allegorike' prefixed to Holland's *Pancharis* (1603) is printed by Herford and Simpson as *Ungathered Verse*, 6. On Southwell and Holland, see also L. I. Guiney, *Recusant Poets* (New York, 1939); for Digby, see R. T. Peterson, *Sir Kenelm Digby* (London, 1956), and Robert C. Evans, *Jonson and the Contexts of his Time* (Lewisburg, Pa., 1994), ch. 8.

in 1637 are not easy—may not always have been easy for Jonson himself—precisely to determine. The 'sides' to which he refers in his epigram to Pembroke may not simply be those imagined in the great Calvinistic divide of the damned and the elect, the vicious and the virtuous, but also, by extension, the two major churches of post-Reformation England. Amongst the manuscripts which perished in the fire of 1623 which Jonson ruefully mentions in 'An Execration upon Vulcan' are his writings on philosophical and religious matters dating back to the time of his conversion to Catholicism in the late 1590s:

> And twice-twelve-yeares stor'd up humanitie,
>   With humble Gleanings in Divinitie,
> After the Fathers, and those wiser Guides,
>   Whom Faction had not drawne to studie sides.
>
>   (*The Underwood*, 43. 101–4)

Those 'wiser Guides' are pre-Reformation theologians, writing before the great European spiritual and political crisis that had brought into being the sharply polarized and embattled world of 'faction', of *sides*, the modern spiritual state which Jonson and his contemporaries had inherited.

'Duplicity' may seem an unduly severe word for the quality in Jonson's personality and creative life that I am seeking to define. If, despite protestations of constancy, Jonson changed his religion, then changed it again; if the precise nature of his allegiances is often unclear, and he seemed 'For any religion, as being versed in both', he was still emphatically different from those flexible lawyers whom he derisively attacked. Writing in *The Lives of the English Poets* of Dryden's adoption of Catholicism, Dr Johnson drily remarks, 'That conversion will always be suspected that apparently concurs with interest'.[15] Ben Jonson's conversion to Catholicism spectacularly failed to concur with interest: the last years of Elizabeth's reign and the early years of James's were certainly not, in terms of social advancement, a good time to become a Catholic in England. New legislation following the execution of the gunpowder plotters in 1606 added to the number of penalties and prohibitions already imposed

---

[15] Samuel Johnson, *The Lives of the English Poets*, ed. George Birkbeck Hill, 3 vols. (Oxford, 1905), i. 377.

upon Catholics during Elizabeth's reign.[16] A further and even more severe increase in penalties in 1610 following the assassination in Paris of Henri IV—himself a celebrated commuter between the Protestant and Catholic faiths—was perhaps the precipitating event returning Jonson finally in that year to the side of orthodoxy.[17] Jonson was certainly not a trimmer nor an opportunist, not a Cheverel nor an Eitherside, and his protestations of honesty were no doubt in large measure justified. But it is remarkable that his imagination was so strongly taken, especially in these Catholic years, by the notion of duplicity, a word which does accurately denote the kind of divided life, part hidden, part public, that he would have been obliged to lead throughout this period, and the behavioural and rhetorical strategies that he would at times have been forced to adopt.

In this regard, Jonson's life was not unique or even especially un-usual. Many individuals, of course, and many entire families in this period shifted their religious allegiances or disguised them with such skill that it is not easy even today to say with confidence to which side they belonged. What is nevertheless remarkable about Jonson's time as a Catholic is that it coincided almost exactly with what is com-monly accepted as being, even by those who argue for the revaluation of his late work, the most brilliant and fertile period of his entire career; a career to which, as David Kay suggested many years ago, he was at this time attempting quite deliberately to give a particular shape.[18] It was a period in which Jonson was determinedly establish-ing, under James VI and I, a central and significant position as poet at court. How exactly did Jonson balance and reconcile his private spiritual life and public career ambitions throughout this period? How, to put the question more bluntly, did the Catholic poet survive and flourish at the (largely) Protestant court? 'His faith', as Robert Evans has accurately remarked of Jonson, 'however much it may have made for some uncertainty and insecurity, does not seem to have much retarded his career.'[19] Why should it not have done so?

---

[16] David Matthew, *Catholicism in England* (1955); Edward Norman, *Roman Catholicism in England from the Elizabethan Settlement to the Second Vatican Council* (Oxford, 1985); John Bossy, *The English Catholic Community, 1570–1850* (1975).

[17] Riggs, *Ben Jonson*, 175–6. No trace remains of a work by Jonson entitled *Motives*, printed in Oct. 1622, mentioned by Antony a'Wood and thought by Herford and Simpson (xi. 586) to have been an account of 'the "motives" for his conversion from Catholicism in 1612'.

[18] See W. David Kay, 'The Shaping of Ben Jonson's Career', *Modern Philology*, 67 (1970), 224–37; and the same author's *Ben Jonson: A Literary Life* (1995).

To a degree, it is true that talented artists flourished at the court in this period whatever and despite their beliefs. William Byrd, a Catholic, directed the music of the Chapel Royal under Elizabeth, and attended the coronation of James I although he and his family were under investigation at the time for so-called Popish practices, and he himself had actually been excommunicated since 1598.[20] Anne of Denmark was herself a convert to Catholicism, and there were powerful ambivalences and contradictions within James's own religious position, that were especially evident during the negotiations for the Spanish match from 1613, and more generally in his controversial choice of advisers during the later years of his reign.[21] A central element in James's strategy of government, as Kenneth Fincham and Peter Lake have argued, was indeed his toleration of loyal Catholics and crypto-Catholics, such as Jonson's 'mortal enimie', Henry Howard, Earl of Northampton, who brought Jonson before the Privy Council to answer charges 'both of popperie and treason' in relation to *Sejanus*.[22]

It is worth recalling, furthermore, that at a much earlier stage of his life the young James had been placed at the very centre of an ambitious Catholic plot, orchestrated from the Continent, aimed at restoring by force the Catholic religion in both England and Scotland. The prime agent in this conspiracy was the father of one of Jonson's most important future patrons during his Catholic period, Esmé Stuart, the seventh Seigneur d'Aubigny. I want now to look more closely at Jonson's connection with this family, and speculate on its significance to the questions I have just asked.

෴

[20] *DNB*, entry for Byrd, William.

[21] On Anne of Denmark's conversion, see William Forbes-Leith SJ, *Narratives of Scottish Catholics under Mary Stuart and James VI* (Edinburgh, 1885), 263–7, 272–3, and Albert J. Loomie, 'King James I's Catholic Consort', *Huntington Library Quarterly*, 34 (1971), 303–16. Unlike Henrietta Maria after her, Anne agreed not to proselytize, and her religion was tolerated on this understanding. It is possible that Anne was persuaded to Catholicism by Lady Henrietta Stuart, the sister of Jonson's patron, whom James had married to the Catholic Earl of Huntley: see Caroline Bingham, *James I of England* (1981), 55–6.

[22] 'The Ecclesiastical Policies of James I and Charles I', in Kenneth Fincham (ed.) *The Early Stuart Church, 1603–1642* (Basingstoke, 1993), 23–49; *Conversations with Drummond*, 325–7; Linda Levy Peck, *Northampton: Patronage and Policy at the Court of James I* (1982). Erica Veevers examines the relationship of Catholicism and Caroline court culture in her *Images of Love and Religion: Queen Henrietta Maria and Court Entertainments* (Cambridge, 1989).

The Stuarts of Aubigny were a Catholic branch of the Scottish royal family, who resided in France from 1422 to 1672, commanded two military companies, the Scots Men-at-Arms and the Scots Guards, and were vigorously involved in all of the major French wars of the period.[23] The two companies grew out of a small élite band of Scottish men-at-arms appointed to serve with the personal guard of the king of France under the direction of Sir John Stuart of Darnley, who in 1423 was granted the Seigneurie of Aubigny in Berry as a reward for his help against the English.

Esmé Stuart senior, sixth Seigneur d'Aubigny, and father of Jonson's future patron, was an impoverished, adventurous, charming, untrustworthy, and strikingly handsome man, 'of comelie proportioun', wrote a contemporary, 'civile behaviour, readbeardit, and honest in conversation'.[24] He had loyally participated in the Guisian slaughter of Protestants in Paris on St Bartholomew's Day, 1572, and after Morton's deposition from the regency of Scotland in 1578, was regarded by Catholic authorities as the ideal agent to send as adviser to the 12-year-old James VI, in order, as one Jesuit privately wrote, to 'settle the affairs of Scotland'.[25] The following year James was accordingly encouraged to invite his cousin Esmé, whom he had never seen, to visit Scotland and witness his state entry into Edinburgh. Aubigny, then in his mid-twenties and struggling with inherited debts, arrived in Scotland bedecked in jewellery and attired in the latest French fashions. Too long cooped up at Stirling Castle with the unamiable George Buchanan, the young James was entirely bedazzled, plunging with characteristic abandon into the first of his famous political romances.

[23] The principal sources for this account of the Stuarts of Aubigny are: Eileen Cassavetti, *The Lion and the Lilies: The Stuarts and France* (London, 1977); Lady Elizabeth Cust, *Some Account of the Stuarts of Aubigny in France [1422–1672]*, privately printed (1891); Sir William Fraser, *The Lennox*, 2 vols. (Edinburgh, 1874); Sir Robert Gordon of Gordonstoun, *A Genealogical History of the Earldom of Sutherland From its Origins to the Year 1630* (Edinburgh, 1813); David Moysie, *Memoirs of the Affairs of Scotland 1577–1603* [ed. J. Dennistoun], privately printed at the Bannatyne Club, 39 (Edinburgh, 1830); Andrew Stuart, *Genealogical History of the Stewarts From the Earliest Period of their Authentic History to the Present Times* (1798). Forbes-Leith's *Narratives of Scottish Catholics* is an especially valuable source, containing letters from the Vatican's secret archives which more fully disclose the nature of Aubigny's mission to Scotland in 1579.

[24] Moysie, *Memoirs*, 25.

[25] Letter of 15 May 1579 from the Bishop of Ross in Paris to Cardinal de Como in Rome: Forbes-Leith, *Narratives of Scottish Catholics*, 134–6.

The story of James's disastrous liaison with his irresistible French cousin is a familiar chapter in the annals of Scottish history, but the ultimate impact of this affair on the next generation of Stuarts and hence on the life of Ben Jonson has not to my knowledge been examined. As James's infatuation grew, he began rapidly to devolve titles, honours, assets, and political responsibilities upon Esmé Stuart. From his great-uncle Robert, on whom the title had been conferred only three years earlier, James wrenched the earldom and estates of Lennox, and bestowed them upon Esmé. By October 1581 James had converted this earldom to a dukedom, given his cousin precedence over all other Scottish peers, and appointed him regent of Scotland. To calm the growing and understandable suspicion of the ministers of the kirk, James persuaded Esmé Stuart to undergo instruction in the Presbyterian religion. On 17 March 1579, in the presence of the provost, baillies, council, and ministers of Edinburgh, Esmé Stuart formally renounced his Catholicism and declared himself a convert to the religion of Scotland, promising 'not only to ratefie the same befoir the King, bot to die thairfoir gif neid beis, desyring thame to esteime it ane vpricht and sinceire zeale without hypocretie'.[26] Despite these loyal protestations, Esmé Stuart remained in close and constant touch with the Guises in France and the Spanish ambassador in Paris, who in 1582 sent two Jesuits secretly to Scotland with letters of credence from Philip II of Spain and from the Pope, instructing him to raise an army, invade England, secure the release of Queen Mary, and thus help to restore the Catholic religion in both England and Scotland. This bold conspiracy was thwarted through the sudden capture of James himself by the Earl of Gowrie. Held prisoner at Ruthven Castle, James was forced by Gowrie to order Esmé Stuart's immediate departure from Scotland. By the time of his arrival in Paris in May 1583, however, Esmé was gravely ill, and within a few days was dead; Jesuit observers were convinced that he had been poisoned in London on the journey home. On his deathbed, Esmé asked that his body be buried at Aubigny, and that his heart be sent to James in Scotland, to whom he also professed his devoted affection, and recommended the care of his children.[27]

Devastated by these events, James issued a proclamation declaring that Esmé Stuart had died in the Presbyterian faith, and threatening

[26] Moysie, *Memoirs*, 26.
[27] Forbes-Leith, *Narratives of Scottish Catholics*, 183 n. 2; Cust, *Some Account of the Stuarts of Aubigny*, 94.

the death penalty to any who were so foolhardy as to deny the assertion.[28] He ordered that Esmé's eldest son Ludovic be fetched at once
from France to Scotland, to assume the title Duke of Lennox, and
composed an allegorical poem figuring the young boy as a new
phoenix, happily found in the ashes of the fire that had destroyed its
splendid parent.[29] Not long after, James also sent for two of
Ludovic's sisters, whom he married to the earls of Huntley and of
Mar. The second son—also named Esmé and the central figure in
this story, imperfectly known to modern scholarship—stayed behind
in France to inherit the title of seventh Seigneur d'Aubigny, administer the estate, and serve the cause of Henri IV.[30] In 1601 Esmé was
visited by his brother Ludovic, now Scottish ambassador to Paris,
who appears to have persuaded him to visit Scotland and meet with
James. Esmé Stuart was certainly in Scotland on 1 April 1603, when
he signed a deed agreeing to surrender Aubigny to his brother should
Ludovic ever wish to return permanently to France.[31] He must have
met James at this moment, and have accompanied the royal progress
south, which departed from Edinburgh on 5 April with Lennox and
the French ambassador in the retinue.[32] On arrival in London, Esmé
appears to have taken up more or less permanent residence in
England. He was naturalized as an Englishman on 24 May 1603, and
is mentioned in the state papers almost every year thereafter until his
death in 1624. He would, however, have returned at intervals to

[28] Moysie, Memoirs, 46.

[29] 'Ane Metaphoricall Invention of a Tragedie Called Phoenix', The Poems of James VI
of Scotland, ed. James Craigie, 2 vols., The Scottish Text Society (Edinburgh, 1955), i,
39–59. James figures the phoenix as feminine. Many years later Jonson was to recall this
poem in an epithalamion written to celebrate the marriage of Esmé Stuart's granddaugh-
ter Frances with Jerome Weston: 'Force from the Phoenix, then, no raritie / Of Sex, to rob
the Creature, but from Man, / The king of Creatures, take his paritie . . .' (The
Underwood, 75. 81–3). (The phoenix was traditionally regarded as sexless, but ever since
Petrarch had compared Laura to a phoenix, poets had commonly treated it as feminine:
see W. H. Matchett, The Phoenix and Turtle (The Hague, 1965), introduction.)

[30] He was formally received as proprietor of the lands of Aubigny and performed foy
and hommage for the Seigneurie in Paris on 8 Apr. 1600: see Stuart, Genealogical History
of the Stewarts, 266.

[31] This document, along with Esmé Stuart's signature, is reproduced in Fraser, The
Lennox, ii. 343. Andrew Stuart believes that Esmé was in Scotland in 1601, but cites no evidence: Genealogical History, 266.

[32] Not to mention the ambassador's wife, who was 'carried betwixt Edinburgh and
London by eight pioneers or porters; one four to relieve the other four by turns, carrying
her in a chair with slings': The True Narration of the Entertainment of His Royal Majesty,
from the time of his departure from Edinburgh till his receiving at London . . . (1603), in
C. H. Firth (ed.), An English Garner (1903), 20.

Aubigny to see to his affairs, and visit his formidable mother, Katherine de Balsac, who lived on into the 1630s to a great age.[33]

James treated the young Esmé with particular affection. He created him a Gentleman of the Bedchamber, thus placing him in the powerful innermost group of royal advisers, within a structure established by Esmé senior on the French model in 1580, and now controlled by Aubigny's brother Ludovic, Duke of Lennox.[34] In February 1609 James arranged for Aubigny's marriage to the wealthy Katherine Clifton, daughter and heir to Sir Gervase Clifton, sealing the match with a substantial gift of £18,000.[35] Esmé appears to have lacked the tougher political skills of Ludovic, who watched over him as 'a loveing brother' and 'a carefull father'.[36] Ludovic died unexpectedly in February 1624, and Esmé inherited the dukedom, along with his brother's other Scottish titles and offices. He might also have succeeded Ludovic as controller of the Bedchamber, but was outmanœuvred by James, Marquis of Hamilton, who swiftly married his eldest son to the Duke of Buckingham's niece in order to manipulate his way into this office.[37] Esmé survived his brother by a mere five months, dying of spotted fever on 31 July 1624 while still in his mid-forties. James was deeply affected by his death. 'It is scarce credible', wrote one observer, 'what greiff the king conceaved for the sudden and unexpected death of his deir and neir cusin, haveing so latelie lost his eldest brother.'[38] The king took upon himself the care

---

33 DNB, entry for Stuart, Ludovick, second Duke of Lennox and Duke of Richmond, 1574–1624; Calendar of State Papers (Domestic), James I, 1603–1610 (1857); 1611–1618 (1858); 1619–1623 (1858); Cust, Some Account of the Stuarts of Aubigny, 95.

34 Neil Cuddy, 'The Revival of the Entourage: The Bedchamber of James I, 1603–1625', in David Starkey et al. (eds.), The English Court: From the Wars of the Roses to the Civil War, (1987), 173–225. The restructuring of the royal household was a central purpose of Esmé Stuart's visit: Forbes-Leith, Narratives of Scottish Catholics, 134–6.

35 The irascible Sir Gervase (later Lord Clifton of Leighton Bromswold) complained bitterly about the terms of the marriage settlement, quarrelled in 1612 with Aubigny and his wife, and threatened to remarry in order to bilk her expectations. In 1617 he vowed to kill the Lord Keeper and was as a consequence fined and committed to the Tower. In 1618 (in the words of John Chamberlain) Clifton 'killed himself for ennui, though the suits with his daughter were ended'. Aubigny inherited his goods and chattels. Calendar of State Papers (Domestic), James I, 1611–1618 (1858), 42, 127, 505, 511, 584, 596. In 1619 Aubigny was created Lord Stuart of Leighton Bromswold and Earl of March. It was rumoured that during his residence in France Aubigny had been contracted, possibly married, to Gabrielle de Bueil, daughter of Louis, Count de Sancerre: see Cust, Some Account of the Stewarts of Aubigny, 96–7.

36 Gordon, A Genealogical History, 385.   37 Ibid. 386.

38 Ibid. 389. Aubigny is buried in Westminster Abbey, near the tomb of Mary, Queen of Scots.

and education of Esmé's 12-year-old son James, now fourth Duke of Lennox, dispatching him to Cambridge, admitting him to the Bedchamber, conferring upon him, his brother, and his mother a handsome annual pension, and granting him a table in the king's house 'as a speciall grace and favour to that familie, which no other subject in Britane had'.[39]

Jonson's relationship with Aubigny appears to have developed quite early in James's reign, and to have flourished throughout the central and most difficult period of Jonson's time as a Catholic. Though Drummond's notes on the matter are characteristically ambiguous and have as a consequence been variously interpreted, it is clear that Jonson was lodging with Aubigny in 1604, when he translated Horace's *Ars Poetica*, and that he stayed with him then, or returned to him later, for a period of five years: 'He maried a wyfe who was a shrew yet honest', writes Drummond; '5 yeers he had not bedded w[i]t[h] her, but remained w[i]t[h] my Lord Aulbanie.'[40] This passage is often regarded as reflecting, a little humorously, on the quality of Jonson's marital life, as perhaps indeed it does. It certainly hints at the existence an unusually close relationship between the two men.[41] But the passage may also tell us something about Jonson's religious life, and the manner in which he sought to sustain simultaneously his private spiritual beliefs and his seemingly contradictory ambitions for professional advancement at court. To lodge in the house of a noble Catholic family was a familiar stratagem for recusants who wished regularly to hear a private Mass and to escape the interrogations of the Consistory Court. Robert Southwell had found sanctuary in this fashion with Lord Vaux and later at the

---

[39] Ibid. 390.

[40] *Conversations with Drummond*, 85–6, 254–5. Mark Eccles, 'Jonson's Marriage', *The Review of English Studies*, 12 (1936), 257–72, argued that Jonson's main period of residence with Aubigny was 1613–18. His views have recently been accepted by David Riggs, in *Ben Jonson*, 191, 192, 204, 369–70 n. The Oxford editors were less convinced, but finally wondered if Jonson could have paid two visits to Aubigny, 'a shorter one about 1604 and a longer in 1613–18': Herford and Simpson, xi. 576–7. None of these accounts considers the possibility that Jonson's period of residence with Aubigny and his Catholic period were significantly connected.

[41] Jonson's sexual preferences were the subject of contemporary innuendo. In *Satiromastix* Dekker portrayed Horace/Jonson in dubious liaison with Asinius Bubo, who addresses him constantly as 'ningle' (e.g. v. ii. 310–11); Tucca refers to Horace as a 'thin bearded hermaphrodite' (I. ii. 344–5). Both terms mean 'homosexual'. These gibes are perhaps in part conventional. For rumours of a possible homosexual relationship between Jonson and Weaver, see E. A. J. Honigmann, *John Weaver: A Biography of a Literary Associate of Shakespeare and Jonson* (Manchester, 1987), 48–9.

Countess of Arundel and Surrey's house in the Strand.[42] To lodge with a noble Catholic who was also a close, dearly regarded, and well-placed relative of the king was a move that is wholly intelligible without our needing to develop too elaborate a theory of the Jonsons' domestic unhappiness. The separation of the Jonsons may have been in part at least strategic; Ben's answers to recusancy charges in April 1606 could well have been an attempt to protect his wife by stressing the separateness of their lives, the difference between his beliefs and hers, and his honest inability to report precisely on her behaviour. He himself, he insisted to the court, could not receive communion until he resolved certain scruples of conscience; 'but his wife he sayethe for a[n]y thing he knowethe hathe gone to Churche & used alwayes to receyve the Co[mmun]ion and is appoynted to receyve the Co[mmun]ion to morow'.[43]

It is likely in any case that the Jonsons' five-year separation was not absolute. Their house was located in Blackfriars, presumably within easy reach of the Blackfriars Theatre, where the King's Men frequently played, and The Alchemist (for example) is now thought to have been performed.[44] Aubigny also lived in Blackfriars. On Lord Cobham's conviction in 1603, his great house near Playhouse Yard next to the Blackfriars Theatre, now Apothecaries' Hall, had been forfeited to the Crown, and had passed to Aubigny's brother Lennox. It is thought Aubigny himself lived here during this period.[45] Movement between the two residences would not have been difficult. The Epistle Dedicatory to Volpone in 1607 is significantly signed 'from my house in the Blackfriars', and (as David Kay has recently observed) the recorded christening of an infant Benjamin Jonson, 'son to Benjamin', in February 1608, suggests that some kind of bedding must have occurred between the Jonsons in the middle of the preceding year.[46] Aubigny's house would have been an interesting

---

42   Devlin, The Life of Robert Southwell, 131 ff.

43   Herford and Simpson, i. 221.

44   R. L. Smallwood, ' "Here, in the Friars": Immediacy and Theatricality in The Alchemist', The Review of English Studies, 32 (1980), 142–60.

45   P. M. Handover, Arbella Stuart: Royal Lady of Hardwick and Cousin to King James (1957), 239.

46   Kay, Ben Jonson 94–5. In 1607 James granted to Aubigny the large building in Clerkenwell, once the priory of St John's, where Edmond Tilney, Master of the Revels, had hitherto maintained his spacious offices and lodgings. See Richard Dutton, Mastering the Revels: The Regulation and Censorship of English Renaissance Drama (Basingstoke, 1991), 34.

location for the dramatist who was soon to write a comedy about a quick-witted man leading a double life in a large and partly neglected house 'here, in the Friars', whose indulgent master was sometimes out of town. (Is it pure coincidence that Aubigny, like Lovewit, appears to have had estates in Kent, and an interest in the cultivation of hops?)[47]

Jonson's epistle to 'that rare wife / Other great wives may blush at', Lady Katherine Aubigny (*The Forest*, 13. 110–11) testifies to the affection and intimacy that existed between Jonson and the Aubigny family. His shorter poem to her husband—'To whom I am so bound, loved Aubigny'—also published in the 1616 folio, suggests that without Aubigny's protection both Jonson and his work might literally have perished.

> How full of want, how swallow'd up, how dead
> I, and this *Muse* had beene, if thou hadst not
> Lent timely succours, and new life begot . . .

> (*Epigrams*, 127. 6–8)

The poem itself is designed 'To thank thy benefits', paying a debt to Aubigny which is not merely personal, but shared also by posterity. Jonson's folio dedication of *Sejanus* speaks again of an indebtedness to Aubigny, who had witnessed that play's unhappy theatrical initiation, and warmly acknowledges 'the bond your benefits have, and ever shall hold upon me'. Jonson's letter of thanks on release from prison in 1605 after the troubles of *Eastward Ho!*, figures himself and his fellow authors as 'double bound' to the 'Noble favours' of the unnamed patron, almost certainly (again) Lord Aubigny.[48]

Perhaps there were other bonds of gratitude which held Jonson to Aubigny. Why did the Consistory Court charges against the Jonsons apparently come to nothing? De Luna thought that they were trumped-up charges which were quietly forgotten when the political moment passed. But Herford, more plausibly, believed that the charges were genuine, and wondered whether 'some powerful influence . . . may have intervened' on the Jonsons' behalf.[49] It is tempting to ask whether Aubigny was not this 'powerful influence',

---

[47] Aubigny was an exporter of beer. *Calendar of State Papers (Domestic), James I, 1603–1610* (1857), 33, 141, 644; *1611–1618* (1858), 196.

[48] Herford and Simpson, i. 198. See also *A Seventeenth-Century Letter-Book: A Facsimile Edition of Folger MS.V.a.321*, transcribed and annotated by A. R. Braunmuller (Newark, NJ, 1983), 374–5 (fo. 89ʳ), 415.

[49] Herford and Simpson, i. 43.

and whether this was not one of the many 'benefits' and 'timely suc-
cours' which Jonson owed to his skilfully protective patron. Like
much else about Jonson's Catholic period, this possibility must remain at the level of conjecture, but it is the closest I can get to answering the question with which I began.

The story of Esmé Stuart senior is a reminder, if reminder be
needed, of the scale upon which religious and political duplicity
could be practised in early modern Europe, of the stakes for which
the game might be played, the status of those who contrived and endeavoured to control the game from afar, and the tragic consequences in this case for the double-dealer who sat at the table,
holding his cards very close to the chest. The story of Esmé Stuart the
younger, in so far as it can be read, seems a happier one, of a man
who moved with relative ease between France, Scotland, and
England, maintaining the Catholicism of his upbringing in the
Protestant country of his adoption, protecting a writer of exceptional talent during an exceptionally dangerous and professionally critical period of his career. The story is a reminder also of that
other kind of duplicity—honestly motivated, no doubt, but no less
complex in its behavioural and creative effects and consequences—
that Jonson himself was sometimes obliged to practise. His letters
and dedications protesting the innocence of his writings, like his reported testimonies to the Consistory Court, sound at moments like
the utterances of a man not unfamiliar with the jesuitical practices of
equivocation.

And Jonson was, after all, trained as an actor. In the view of one
Catholic commentator, however, he was not trained quite well
enough. Amongst the great chorus of eulogistic verses mourning the
death of Jonson in 1637 are to be found these less harmonious lines
by Thomas Willford, for whom Ben Jonson, having failed to play the
great drama of his Catholic beliefs decisively through to the fifth act,
was not a man whose life could be whole-heartedly applauded.

> Here *Johnson* lies, who spent his days,
> In making sport, and Comicke plays:
> His life a Play, perform'd the worst,
> The last Act did disgrace the first,
> His part he plaid, exceeding well,
> A *Catholike*; untill he fell
> To Sects and Schismes, which he did chuse,
> Like to a fiction of his Muse.

He staid there 'till the *Scene* was past,
Without a *Plaudit* given at last:
So ill he plaid, the later part,
The *Epilogue*, did brake his heart.
When Death his bodie did surprise,
The Fatall *Sisters* clos'd his eyes,
And took him to his tyring roome,
Where I will leave him to his doome;
But wish that I could justly raise
Memorialls of eternall praise.
But Ben, from whence thy mischiefe grew,
I mourne, but must not say, A due:[50]

[50] 'An Epitaph upon the most learned Comedian and moderne Poet, *Benjamin Johnson*, who left the *Church* and died Anno Dom[in]i, MDCXXX[VII]': Herford and Simpson, xi. 493–4.

5

Jonson's Magic Houses

JONSON more than once compared the art of writing with that of building. A writer, he declared, arranges words within a sentence in much the same way that a builder brings stones together to form a wall. 'The congruent, and harmonious fitting of parts in a sentence, hath almost the fastning, and force of knitting, and connexion', Jonson wrote in *Discoveries* (1976–80), 'As in stones well squar'd, which will rise strong a great way without mortar.' What a writer finally created was an object like a house. Its various parts should be

so joyn'd, and knitt together, as nothing in the structure can be chang'd, or taken away, without impairing, or troubling the whole; of which there is a proportionate magnitude in the members. As for example; if a man would build a house, he would first appoint a place to build it in, which he would define within certaine bounds: So in the Constitution of a *Poeme*, the Action is aym'd at by the *Poet*, which answers Place in a building; and that Action hath his largenesse, compasse, and proportion. (*Discoveries*, 2683–91)

Literary works vary in scale and magnitude, as do different kinds of building: 'a Court, or King's Palace, requires other dimensions then a private house'. The parts come together to form a whole 'as a house, consisting of diverse materialls, becomes one structure, and one dwelling'. Episodes and digressions 'are the same that household stuffe, and other furniture are in a house' (*Discoveries*, 2691–2, 2791–2, 2748–9). The analogies are traditional, yet at the same time congenial to Jonson's creative imagination.[1] It is characteristic of Jonson to perceive literary works in spatial terms: as objects laid out and built up like courts or palaces or private houses, to be walked around, observed, inhabited, their details and proportions and the relationship of their parts appreciatively assessed. And it is equally characteristic of Jonson to speak of literary works as objects which

[1] Jonson is following Vives, *De Ratione Dicendi*, bk. i (1555), and Heinsius, *De Tragoediae Constitutione* (1611); Heinsius is in turn following Aristotle, *Poetics*, chs. vii and viii (where these analogies are not, however, to be found).

are consciously, solidly, monumentally constructed: built to last. To the Lord Treasurer, Richard Weston, Earl of Portland, Jonson writes:

> . . . though I cannot as an Architect
> In glorious Piles, or Pyramids erect
> Unto your honour: I can tune in song
> Aloud; and (happ'ly) it may last as long.
>
> (*The Underwood*, 77. 25–8)

'Architect' (the profession of Inigo Jones) is a word which Jonson elsewhere utters with hostility or contempt, but 'glorious' here concedes a counter-truth.[2] Architect and poet, it is tacitly admitted, may have certain aims and functions in common: each is concerned with construction and commemoration, and, up to a point, the terminology of the one art may be equably appropriated for the other.

However suggestive the analogy may have been for Jonson, it also had its limits. It was not altogether a happy coincidence that Jonson himself had actually worked as a builder in the early 1590s. From time to time his enemies drew unkind comparisons between his past and present occupations. Jonson is 'the wittiest fellow of a Bricklayer in England', declares one of the characters drily in the second part of *The Return from Parnassus*, and his companion at once takes up the cue: he is 'so slow an Inventor, that he were better betake himself to his old trade of Bricklaying: a bould whorson, as confident now in making of a booke, as he was in times past in laying of a brick'.[3] Making a book, laying a brick: put the two activities so humorously together, and the analogy itself at once becomes absurd; Jonson is seen as an intellectual navvy, a thoughtless wielder of flat, heavy objects. Modern readers, nurtured on Romantic images of organic form, are likely to be especially sensitive to the limitations of the analogy between writing and building. Leavis's famous comment about Milton comes to mind: 'a good deal of *Paradise Lost* strikes one as being almost as mechanical as bricklaying'.[4]

---

[2] 'Architect': *Epigrams*, 115. 30; cf. *Ungathered Verse*, 34. 37.

[3] *The Return from Parnassus*, pt. II, 1. ii. 293–9, in *The Three Parnassus Plays (1598–1601)*, ed. J. B. Leishman (1949), 244.

[4] 'Milton's Verse', in Leavis, *Revaluation* (1962), 60. For the background to this remark, and a more detailed account of the metaphors used in Jonsonian criticism, see Ian Donaldson, 'Damned by Analogies: Or, How to Get Rid of Ben Jonson', *Gambit: International Theatre Review*, 6 (1972), 38–46. On the organic metaphor, see G. S. Rousseau (ed.), *Organic Form: The Life of an Idea* (1972).

Nineteenth-century critics were wont to allude with routine distaste to Jonson's early career as a manual labourer. For Carlyle, Jonson was 'the rugged Stonemason, the harsh, learned Hodman'; for Macaulay, 'Ben's heroic couplets resemble blocks rudely hewn out by an unpractised hand, with a blunt hatchet'.[5] Felix Schelling put the matter succinctly: 'We cannot expect the laws which govern organic growth to coincide with those controlling constructive ingenuity; a house is built, a tree grows, and the conscious and self-controlled development of such a man as Jonson is alien to the subtle and harmonious unfolding of a genius like Shakespeare's.'[6]

'A house is built, a tree grows': the distinction is a telling one, but it is a distinction which Jonson himself might be said to have anticipated. His own collections of verse and prose are significantly entitled *The Forest*, *The Underwood*, *Timber*, and the promise which these titles offer—of spontaneous organic growth, of multiform things 'promiscuously growing'—is as important to an understanding of Jonson's aesthetic as is the imagery of artisanship, labour, and rational planning.[7] Building was in any case an art which Jonson regarded with wariness and suspicion. In 'An Expostulation with Inigo Jones' (*Ungathered Verse*, 34) building is represented as the product and symbol of 'the money-gett, Mechanick Age' (52); it trades merely in externals—in painting and carpentry, cloth and deal-board for the court masque, in 'Purbeck stone' for the new Banqueting House at Whitehall—lacking the life and 'soul' which poetry can impart.[8]

Jonson's animus against building is also apparent in 'To Penshurst' (*The Forest*, 2). It is Penshurst's praise that it has not been 'built to

---

[5] Thomas Carlyle, *Historical Sketches of Notable Persons and Events in the Reigns of James I and Charles I* (n.d. [1898]), 74; Lord Macaulay, *Critical and Historical Essays Contributed to the Edinburgh Review* (1878), 705.

[6] *Ben Jonson and the Classical School* (Baltimore, 1898), 24.

[7] On the arboreal metaphor, see in particular Alastair Fowler, 'The Silva Tradition in Jonson's *The Forest*', in Maynard Mack and George deForest Lord (eds.), *Poetic Traditions of the English Renaissance* (New Haven, 1982), 163–80. 'Promiscuously growing': see 'To the Reader', prefixed to *The Underwood*.

[8] On the Jonson–Jones quarrel and collaboration, see D. J. Gordon, 'Poet and Architect: The Intellectual Setting of the Quarrel between Ben Jonson and Inigo Jones', in *The Renaissance Imagination: Essays and Lectures by D. J. Gordon*, collected and edited by Stephen Orgel (Berkeley, 1975), 77–101, and Stephen Orgel's introductions to his edition of *The Complete Masques of Ben Jonson*, and to Stephen Orgel and Roy Strong, *Inigo Jones: The Theatre of the Stuart Court*, 2 vols. (1973). A. W. Johnson discusses the influence of architectural thinking on Jonson's literary work in *Ben Jonson: Poetry and Architecture* (Oxford, 1994).

envious show' in the manner of other ostentatious houses of the day, but stands, 'an ancient pile', as though rooted in the grounds from time immemorial.[9] The point is made in another way in the poem's concluding lines:

> Now, PENSHURST, they that will proportion thee
>   With other edifices, when they see
> Those proud, ambitious heaps, and nothing else,
>   May say, their lords have built, but thy lord dwells.   (99–102)

Building in itself is nothing: what matters is the life that animates a building. Though remarkably precise in its physical and topographical detail, Jonson's poem is not essentially concerned with the bricks and stones and mortar of Penshurst, but with the kind of life that the *house*, in its fullest sense—a dynasty and a household, an edifice and an estate—is capable of fostering and sustaining. 'Thy lord dwells': but, as J. C. A. Rathmell has shown, it was an awkward fact that Lord Lisle, who was undergoing personal difficulties at the time when Jonson wrote the poem, did not in fact dwell at Penshurst as regularly and faithfully as he should have done.[10] The master of Penshurst plays a marginal role throughout Jonson's poem, despite the final tribute that is paid to him. One might contrast the way in which Jonson locates Lord Bacon centrally within York House, and centrally within his own birthday poem to him:

> Haile, happie *Genius* of this antient pile!
> How comes it all things so about thee smile?
> The fire, the wine, the men! and in the midst,
> Thou stand'st as if some Mysterie thou did'st!
>
> (*The Underwood*, 51. 1–4)

The central character within 'To Penshurst' is instead Penshurst itself, which is at once the subject and recipient of the poem. Penshurst is imbued with a life and consciousness of its own. Jonson speaks to the house with tenderness:

---

[9] Penshurst was built *c.* 1340, over 200 years before the Sidney family came to live there. Jonson may be contrasting the antiquity of Penshurst with the brash modernity of such buildings as Knole and Theobalds. See G. R. Hibbard, 'The Country House Poem of the Seventeenth Century', *Journal of the Warburg and Courtauld Institutes*, 19 (1956), 159–74; Alastair Fowler, *Conceitful Thought* (Edinburgh, 1975), 114–34, and *The Country House Poem* (Edinburgh, 1994); and Don E. Wayne, *Penshurst: The Semiotics of Place and the Poetics of History* (1984).

[10] 'Jonson, Lord Lisle, and Penshurst', *English Literary Renaissance*, 1 (1971), 250–60.

> Nor, when I take my lodging, need I pray,
> For fire, or lights, or livorie: all is there;
>   As if thou, then, wert mine, or I raign'd here . . .   (72–4)

'As if thou, then, wert mine': the words might almost be uttered to a lover. In such a house, the guest feels like a king ('or I raign'd here'): and thus by a natural transition Jonson shifts to an account of the unexpected visit to Penshurst one night of King James and his son Prince Henry, who glimpsed the glow of fires from the windows of the house while hunting in the nearby woods.

> What (great, I will not say, but) sodayne cheare
> Didst thou, then, make 'hem! and what praise was heap'd
>   On thy good lady, then! who, therein, reap'd
> The just reward of her high huswifery;
>   To have her linnen, plate, and all things nigh,
> When she was farre: and not a roome, but drest,
>   As if it had expected such a guest!   (82–8)

Who looked after the royal party? Though Jonson tactfully praises the forethought of Lady Lisle, he also makes it clear that she and her husband were actually not at home when the king and his son chanced by. The king and his entourage, the poem wittily suggests, were cared for *by the house itself*, which made them 'sodayne cheare'. 'Not a roome, but drest, / As if it had expected such a guest!': 'drest' (the word is aptly and humorously chosen for its double reference) as a person might be dressed; each room thoughtfully 'expected such a guest'. By these and other similar touches throughout the poem, Jonson creates a sense of Penshurst as a kind of magic house, animated and sentient, with a mind and will and influence all its own: expectant, beneficent, welcoming, enabling.

Jonson elsewhere writes of other buildings which are magically animated. As King James entered the city of London in 1603, Jonson declared in the *Panegyre* he had written to welcome him, 'every windore griev'd it could not move / Along with him' (45–6).

> All the aire was rent,
> As with the murmure of a moving wood;
> The ground beneath did seeme a moving floud:
> Walls, windores, roofes, towers, steeples, all were set
> With severall eyes, that in this object met.   (60–4)

The eyes seem to belong not to the city's inhabitants, but to the city itself, straining to glimpse its new monarch. Another house with a will of its own is that which expects the new bride Frances Howard after her marriage to the Earl of Essex in the masque *Hymenaei*:

> Haste, tender *lady*, and adventer;
> The covetous *house* would have you enter,
>   That it might wealthy bee,
>   And you, her mistris see:
> Haste your owne good to meet;
> And lift your golden feet
> Above the *threshold*, high,
> With prosperous *augury*.   (477–84)

Jonson was to develop the trope of the animated house most fully not in the court masque (despite the opportunities for scenic metamorphosis which the form offered), nor in his non-dramatic poetry, but in his plays written for the public stage. It is to these that I want now to turn.

ᐷᕇᐸ

Part of Jonson's great power as a dramatist lies in his understanding of the pressures and excitements associated with confined spaces. No dramatist before him (and none after, until recent times) so fully explores the psychology of urban indoor living, so instinctively perceives the correspondence between the fixed space of a house and the fixed space of the stage on which the actors must work. To think of a play by Jonson is to think at once of the house in which its action occurs. There is Morose's house in *The Silent Woman*, strategically situated in a lane too narrow to admit carts and coaches, its door quilted, its windows shut and caulked, its walls and ceilings doubly and trebly reinforced, its master living fearfully within by candlelight. There is Agrippina's house in *Sejanus* where the spies Opsius and Rufus stow themselves in their holes between the roof and the ceiling in the hope of hearing seditious talk below. There is Corvino's house in *Volpone*, where the hapless Celia is confined, a chalk line drawn on the floor beyond which she must not stray, the window giving on to the piazza—the 'publike windore' from which she has dropped her handkerchief to the supposed mountebank Scoto of Mantua—closed off: 'I will have this bawdy light dam'd up' (II. v. 3, 50). And there is that mysterious, enticing house where the

Magnifico himself apparently lies dying: a house to which each of the legacy-hunters in turn is irresistibly drawn and which each dearly wishes to possess; a house from which Volpone himself is in the end excluded by the skilful manœuvrings of his own servant and seeming ally, Mosca. The idea of a man and his wealth confined to a house is imaginatively central to the play. (John Aubrey thought the character of Volpone was modelled on that of Captain Thomas Sutton, the financier, who ended his days 'in Fleetstreet at a Wollen draper's shop, opposite to Fetter-lane; where he had so many great Chests full of money, that his chamber was ready to groane under it, and Mr. Tyndale, who knew him . . . was afrayde the roome would fall'.) The houses in Jonson's plays are by turns comforting, protective, sinister, attractive. They are not merely 'settings': they are also in a deep symbolic sense what the plays are about.[11]

The confined locations of Jonson's dramas can generate a high degree of stage excitement; they can also generate a range of psychological and metaphorical meaning. In *The Silent Woman*, Morose's obsessive concern with living alone and undisturbed in his own house ('Is the dore shut?', II. v. 3) suggests a way of life entirely contrary to that which Jonson depicts at Penshurst, where 'all come in, the farmer and the clowne' to enjoy the 'open table' that the master of the house provides (48, 27). Morose's house offers no such hospitality: even his wedding breakfast must be forcibly brought into the house from outside, against his wishes. The revellers and tormentors violate his solitary and solipsistic way of life in a kind of parody of the sexual act that should rightfully consummate his wedding ('this horne got me entrance, kisse it', says Truewit, II. iv. 10). The house in which Morose has shut himself remains a thing of bricks and mortar and quilted doors, lacking in life and vitality. Though Morose has chosen to marry, he will never establish (in a further, generational sense of the word) a house of his own: his wife, as the final busy moments of the play reveal, is no woman and therefore no wife. Morose's own desperate confession of physical impotence, wrung from him in the seconds before this final revelation,

[11] On Sutton, see *Aubrey's Brief Lives*, ed. O. L. Dick (Harmondsworth, 1962), 347. Robert C. Evans tests the credibility of this story in *Jonson and the Contexts of his Time* (Lewisburg, Pa., 1994), ch. 3, 'Thomas Sutton: Jonson's Volpone?'. Jonson may also have remembered Barabas's 'Infinite riches in a little room', *The Jew of Malta*, I. i. 37. In 'The First West End Comedy', *Proceedings of the British Academy*, 68 (1982), 215–58, Emrys Jones suggestively considers Jonson's settings in relation to urban growth and development in early seventeenth-century London.

is a fiction devised to secure his divorce, but it retains its symbolic appropriateness as a characterization of his total way of life, shut up within his own house. This way of life is contrasted with that of the absurdly 'open' man, Sir Amorous La Foole, whose house spills its progeny with disconcerting fecundity to all points of the compass: 'They all come out of our house, the LA-FOOLES o' the north, the LA-FOOLES of the west, the LA-FOOLES of the east, and south—we are as ancient a family, as any is in *Europe*' (I. iv. 37–40). Literal and metaphorical meanings of the word 'house' play off against each other here, as so often elsewhere in Jonson's writing. The reckless disclosures of La Foole, who invites guests to plays and suppers 'aloud, out of his windore, as they ride by in coaches' (I. iii. 34–5), is contrasted with the determined isolationism of Morose, who ensures that all his windows are closed up.

Corvino, another stopper-up of windows and social pleasures, forbids his wife a view over the piazza yet grants her access to the house's rearward prospects, and himself, by a process of Freudian association, one avenue of sexual gratification.

> Then, here's a locke, which I will hang upon thee;
> And, now I thinke on't, I will keepe thee backe-wards;
> Thy lodging shall be backe-wards; thy walkes back-wards;
> Thy prospect—all be backe-wards; and no pleasure,
> That thou shalt know, but backe-wards . . .
>
> (II. v. 57–61)

To close off the windows at the front of the house and leave the back ones open is entirely in character for Corvino, whose apparent absolutism is never what it seems. His mind, like his house, is not quite closed: through one loophole he will rashly argue his escape from the mental fortress he has established, dragging his wife to the very bedside of the man who most wishes to possess her. In *Sejanus* (to offer one more instance of Jonson's suggestive trafficking between the literal and the metaphorical) what those spies in Agrippina's ceiling overhang is an entire dynasty and its fortunes, not simply a physical structure. 'It is a noble constancie you shew / To this afflicted house', says Latiaris to Sabinus as the spies crawl to their crannies (IV. 115–16), and the timing of his remark deftly enlarges its symbolic sense. The simple stage action of the spies' concealing themselves in the rafters of the house gives menacing particularity to the larger affliction of which Latiaris speaks.[12] The house already contains the elements of its own destruction.

Nowhere in his work, however, does Jonson more subtly explore the tensions of domestic living, nowhere does he more skilfully elaborate the manifold meanings of that seemingly simple concept, a 'house', than in his comic masterpiece, *The Alchemist*. No other house which Jonson created more fully deserves the epithet 'magic' than that house in Blackfriars where three confidence tricksters ply their trade.

❧

The action of *The Alchemist* is played out within strict limits both of time and space. Though modern editions of the play sometimes obscure this fact, the entire action, apart from the scenes in Act V in the lane outside, takes place within a single room of Lovewit's house. There are rooms opening off this area—most notably, Subtle's laboratory, which (significantly and suggestively) is never fully revealed—and there are rooms to which Mammon and the Spanish Count are permitted to retire for their amorous engagements. Somewhere 'within', too, is the privy where the luckless Dapper is hurriedly stowed at a critical moment of the play, there to be forgotten. The acting area itself, however, is confined: no use is made of the inner rooms or upper stage for acting purposes, allowing for a concentration of effect which, as E. K. Chambers observed many years ago, is quite unprecedented in the English theatre.[13]

This sense of enclosure is important to the total effect of the play, stimulating for audience and characters alike various sensations of curiosity, nervousness, and claustrophobia. Lovewit's house in Blackfriars, like Volpone's house in Venice, serves as a 'honeypot', a 'center attractive', a powerful magnet to draw the curious and unwary; what goes on within the house is a constant source of speculation and fascination.[14] The house itself serves as a trap: a trap that

---

[12]   See Francis Berry, 'Stage Perspective and Elevation in *Coriolanus* and *Sejanus*', in Ian Donaldson (ed.), *Jonson and Shakespeare* (1983), 163–78.

[13]   *The Elizabethan Stage*, 4 vols. (Oxford, 1923), iii. 123. Cf. W. A. Armstrong, 'Ben Jonson and Jacobean Stagecraft', in John Russell Brown and Bernard Harris (eds.), *Jacobean Theatre*, Stratford-upon-Avon Studies, 1 (1960), 43–61: 47.

[14]   *The Honeypot* was the apt first title of the Joseph Manciwiecz–Rex Harrison film version of *Volpone* (later called *It Comes Up Murder*). 'Center attractive': *The Magnetic Lady*, Induction, 108–9.

may also be sprung on the tricksters themselves, who (unlike Volpone and Mosca) have no legitimate claim to occupy the house and use it in the way they do. The house is set in a neighbourhood, and there is the constant risk that the activities of Dol, Subtle, and Face and their victims will be overheard or overlooked. The conspirators are nervous on this matter right from the start of the play, and in their more reckless and rebellious moments choose to provoke each other by raising their voices.

DOL   Will you have
  The neighbours heare you? Will you betray all? . . .
FACE   Will you be so lowd? . . .
SUBTLE I wish, you could advance your voice, a little. . . .
FACE   You might talke softlier, raskall.
SUBTLE   No, you *scarabe*,
  I'll thunder you, in peeces.
                    (I. i. 7–8, 18, 32, 59–60)

Within the house, there is a similar fear of being overheard; it is as though the walls were paper-thin. When Sir Epicure Mammon is given his opportunity to court Dol Common, Face tells him that his wooing is all too audible in the next room.

FACE Sir, you are too loud. I heare you, every word,
  Into the laboratory. Some fitter place,
  The garden, or great chamber above.
                    (IV. i. 170–2)

During a later quarrel with Subtle, Face threatens to call out 'And loose the hinges' (IV. iii. 82) so Dol can know that Subtle, contrary to the terms of the alliance, has designs upon Dame Pliant. A single cry might suffice to destroy the conspiracy. At the beginning of Act V, a confused neighbour is to tell Lovewit that three weeks earlier he heard 'a dolefull cry' emanating from the house while he sat up mending his wife's stockings: 'like unto a man / That had beene strangled an houre, and could not speake' (v. i. 33, 36–7). Not long afterwards, *Dapper cryes out within* (v. iii. 63, s.d.), shattering the fiction which Face has hastily devised to explain for Lovewit's benefit what has been occurring in the house while he has been away.

  The constant knocking at the door of the house heightens the sense of nervous apprehension; it is not always at first clear whether a new caller is friend or foe. 'Is he the Constable?' asks Kastril suspiciously after the entrance of Ananias at IV. vii. 44. In Act V, the master himself is seen knocking repeatedly at the door of his own house. After his admission the knocking continues, for later in the act Mammon, Tribulation, Ananias, Surly, and Kastril return to the house with Officers, noisily demanding entry. 'Harke you, thunder', says Face to Subtle, coolly offering to him and to Dol a means of escape from the trap that has now closed upon them:

> All I can doe
> Is to helpe you over the wall, o' the back-side;
> Or lend you a sheet, to save your velvet gowne, DOL.

(V. iv. 132–4)

By a variety of small touches, Jonson thus makes us acutely aware of Lovewit's house as a potentially confining place: as a box or prison within which the action of the comedy is played out. Dol spies from the windows of the house, as from a loop-hole, into the lane outside, and communicates with unwanted callers by means of a speaking tube: 'Thorough the trunke, like one of your *familiars*' (I. iv. 5). At moments of high excitement, Face and Subtle rebound within the house like balls within an enclosed court:

FACE   Let us be light, though.
SUBTLE   I, as balls, and bound
> And hit our heads against the roofe for joy:
> There's so much of our care now cast away.

(IV. v. 98–100)

The supposed Spanish don is lured, as though to a prison: fettered by Dol's fair looks, he is to be 'throwne / In a downe-bed, as darke as any dungeon' (III. iii. 41–3).

The fixed setting of *The Alchemist* also creates an air of mystery. What cannot be seen from outside the house or from the single room to which most of the visitors gain access is darkly guessed at. The house is constantly spoken of as something more than a house. Mammon fancifully pictures it as '*novo orbe*', 'the rich *Peru*', 'a meere *Chancell*' for Subtle's high art (II. i. 2, V. iii. 2). His companion, Surly, sceptically convinced that the place is nothing but a bawdy house, nevertheless aggrandizes it in his sterner denunciations, speaking gravely of 'The subtilties of this darke *labyrinth*' and of 'the knaveries of this *Citadell*' (II. iii. 308, IV. vi. 9).[15] For other

---

[15] *Epigrams*, 7, 'On the New Hot-House', turns on a similar ambiguity concerning a building's actual use and function.

visitors, the house is the residence of a 'cunning man' (I. ii. 8) who can advise them on many matters, a centre of social, religious, and alchemical mysteries. Abel Drugger, an ardent believer in the mystical significance of the art of building, visits the house in Blackfriars in order to consult with Subtle on the construction and disposition of the tobacconist's shop which he is about to erect for himself. Subtle solemnly advises him of the most auspicious orientation for the shop, and urges him to bury a lodestone beneath its threshold, 'To draw in gallants, that weare spurres: The rest, / They'll seeme to follow' (I. iii. 70–1)—advice that humorously reminds us of the magnetic effect that the house in which Subtle himself operates appears to exercise on those who visit it (Drugger himself has been drawn in, as if by the heels).[16] The neighbours with whom Lovewit talks in the lane at the beginning of the fifth act cannot confidently say what has been going on within the house: whether and how it has been used, whether and by whom it has been visited, whether 'open house' has been maintained, or (as Face asserts) the doors have been securely locked for the past three weeks. 'We were deceiv'd, he sayes', admits one neighbour, lamely (V. i. 42). The house in Blackfriars is capable of being whatever people most want it to be: it is a shell within which their fantasies may be projected, a sounding-board for the imagination. When Lovewit finally enters the house, he finds it strangely desolate and abandoned:

> Here, I find
> The emptie walls, worse then I left 'hem, smok'd,
> A few crack'd pots, and glasses, and a fornace,
> The seeling fill'd with *poesies* of the candle:
> And MADAME, with a *Dildo*, writ o' the walls.
>
> (V. v. 38–42)

For Ananias, on the other hand, this is not just an empty house: it is 'a cage of uncleane birds', 'this den of theeves' (V. iii. 47, V. v. 93). Even as he denounces the place, Ananias, like Surly, makes it sound

---

[16] Cf. the discussion in *The Magnetic Lady*, Induction, 74–85, of the magnetic effect of dramatic titles, which draw audiences into the playhouse: as Damplay believes, through the Vitruvian 'portall, or entry to the worke'. Derek Walters has pointed out to me that Drugger's conviction that his shop must be appropriately arranged in order to ensure harmony and good fortune is precisely congruent with Feng Shui, the traditional Chinese art of geomancy. Was Feng Shui or a similar art practised in Jonson's London? For an account of Feng Shui, see Derek Walters, *Chinese Geomancy* (Longmead, Shaftesbury, Dorset, 1989), and id., *The Feng Shui Handbook* (1991).

grander, more mysterious, more compelling, than Lovewit's sober account has suggested. Ananias will go to Amsterdam:

> I will pray there,
> Against thy house: may dogs defile thy walls,
> And waspes, and hornets breed beneath thy roofe,
> This seat of false-hood, and this cave of cos'nage.

(V. v. 112–15)

'Cage', 'den', 'seat', 'cave': this is no ordinary house, but a magical place, a centre of spiritual enchantment.

The 'house' against which Ananias determines to direct his vengeful prayers is the physical edifice in Blackfriars whose inner rooms he and his companions have now at last penetrated; it is also the entire dynasty and household of Lovewit, which Ananias believes to be responsible for the downfall and humiliation of the Brethren. The 'house' of Lovewit at present comprises exactly three people, Lovewit himself, his new wife Dame Pliant, and his servant Jeremy, alias Face; Ananias's terrible curse aggrandizes the strength of this house even as it threatens its destruction. The imagination that can convert a common London dwelling-house into a Spenserian 'cave of cos'nage' can equally convert three people into an Old Testament dynasty.

The comedy is much concerned with the creation of such imaginary dynastic 'houses'. Sir Epicure Mammon, after catching a subliminal glimpse of Dol Common, is easily persuaded that she is 'A lords sister' (II. iii. 221) and scholar of divinity, now crazed in her wits. When Surly expresses some scepticism about the circumstances of this supposed lady, Sir Epicure at once protests that he knows her family well: her brother is 'one I honour, and my noble friend, / And I respect his house' (II. iii. 277–8). Having so swiftly persuaded himself of his familiarity with this house, Mammon has no difficulty in complying with Face's stipulation before his eventual meeting with the lady.

FACE And you must praise her house, remember that,
    And her nobilitie.
MAMMON   Let me, alone:
    No *Herald*, no nor *Antiquarie*, Lungs,
    Shall doe it better.

(IV. i. 19–22)

Left alone with Dol, Mammon praises the 'strange nobilitie' of her eye, her lip, her chin:

> Me thinkes you doe resemble
> One of the *Austriack* princes.
> FACE   Very like,
> Her father was an *Irish* costar-monger.
> MAMMON The house of *Valois*, just, had such a nose.
> And such a fore-head, yet, the *Medici*
> Of *Florence* boast.
>
> (IV. i. 54–60)

Such a lady, he believes, ought rightfully to live not in 'This nooke, here, of the *Friers*', but rather should 'come forth, / And tast the aire of palaces' (IV. i. 131, 134–5): her aristocratic house deserves a grander physical house to set off its dignities and beauties.

In preparing Mammon for this encounter, Face has warned him that he must make no mention of divinity to the lady, 'For feare of putting her in rage'.

> MAMMON   I warrant thee.
> FACE   Sixe men will not hold her downe. And then,
> If the old man should heare, or see you—
> MAMMON   Feare not.
> FACE The very house, sir, would runne mad.
>
> (IV. i. 10–13)

'The very house': Face is conjuring up another household to rival that of the supposedly aristocratic lady whom Mammon is about to meet; this 'house' consists of Subtle, its apparent master, and his mysterious retinue (none other than Face and Dol, in their many guises). But Face's words also contain the further humorous suggestion that the building which they now inhabit would itself be affected by so grave a transgression as the mention of scriptural controversy. In his meeting with Dol, Mammon contrives to break not only Face's prohibition but also that of Subtle, who has told him that if the elixir is to come to perfection, he must practise perfect chastity, paying no regard to the opposite sex. Face has warned Mammon that once the lady falls into her fit, she

> will discourse
> So learnedly of *genealogies*,
> As you would runne mad, too, to heare her, sir.
>
> (II. iii. 240–2)

And it is of genealogies—of the rise and fall of ancient families—
that Dol indeed discourses in her '*fit of talking*', prompted by
Mammon's indiscreet mention of his wish to establish a fifth monarchy.

> DOL And so we may arrive by *Talmud* skill,
>   And profane *greeke*, to raise the building up
>   Of HELENS house, against the Ismaelite,
>   King of *Thogarma*, and his *Habergions*
>   Brimstony, blew, and fiery; and the force
>   Of King ABADDON, and the Beast of *Cittim*:
>   Which *Rabbi* DAVID KIMCHI, ONKELOS,
>   And ABEN-EZRA doe interpret *Rome*.
>
> (IV. v. 25–32)[17]

The pandemonium climaxes with the entrance of Subtle and '*A great
crack and noise within*'. It is indeed as though the very house has now
run mad, the edifice itself responding to Mammon's folly.

> SUBTLE   Hangs my roofe
>   Over us still, and will not fall, o justice,
>   Upon us, for this wicked man!
>
> (IV. v. 78–80)

Meanwhile, in another part of the house, Surly is at large, disguised as a Spanish Count. Almost the first words which Surly utters
in this role concern the nature of the house:

> SURLY   *Por dios, Sennores, muy linda casa*!
> SUBTLE   What sayes he?
> FACE   Praises the house, I thinke,
>   I know no more but's action.
> SUBTLE   Yes, the *Casa*,
>   My precious DIEGO, will prove faire inough,
>   To cossen you in. Doe you marke? you shall
>   Be cossened, DIEGO.
> FACE   Cossened, doe you see?
>   My worthy *Donzel*, cossened.
> SURLY   *Entiendo*.
>
> (IV. iii. 34–40)

---

[17] Dol's ravings are neatly lifted from the Puritan writer Hugh Broughton's *A Concept
of Scripture* (1590); Dol quotes chiefly from Broughton's commentary on Daniel's interpretation of Nebuchadnezzar's dream (Dan. 2), concerning the progressive degeneration
of kingdoms.

'*Entiendo*', 'I understand'—as Surly indeed does understand, more thoroughly than either Face or Subtle realizes. Surly professes to praise the house as a *brothel*, which is indeed what he privately believes it to be; it is an assignation that he is seemingly after, and he pretends to a certain connoisseurship in the necessary arrangements surrounding these matters. When Surly arrives, however, the only available lady of the house, Dol Common, is busy with Sir Epicure, and Face proposes to Subtle that they must persuade Dame Pliant to stand in for Dol:

FACE What dost thou thinke on't, SUBTLE?
SUBTLE   Who, I? Why—
FACE The credit of our house too is engag'd.

(IV. iii. 69–70)

Face makes their enterprise sound like that of a firm of international bankers, and it is especially revealing that the two of them should adopt such language in private conversation. 'The credit of our house': 'credit' means both credibility, the primary meaning of the word, and financial solvency. For Face and Subtle, the two things are closely connected, for people put their money where their beliefs are, and it is thus upon belief that they constantly endeavour to play. But how are Dame Pliant and her brother Kastril to be persuaded to accept this substitution? The argument which convinces them both is that of social advancement: the Spanish Count (they are told) is keen to marry the widow, and, as Kastril contentedly remarks, 'This match will advance the house of the KASTRILS' (IV. iv. 88).

Kastril's phrase confers upon an obscure country family the pomp and status of a noble European dynasty. The advancement of the house of the Kastrils is to proceed more modestly than Kastril himself anticipates. The aristocratic claims of the supposed Spanish Count, like those of the supposed lady whom Mammon ardently pursues, are to prove wholly fraudulent. The 'houses' to which these characters seemingly belong exist merely in the imagination. So too does the commercial house which Subtle and Face profess to operate, and the house of retainers which Face pretends Subtle has in his employ. Both in the literal and the metaphorical senses of the phrase, the three confidence workers have *no house* to support their enterprises. In the opening scene of the play Face cuttingly reminds Subtle that he is in fact a houseless person, a vagabond, and that it is he, Face, who has provided him with the house in which he now operates—a house, as Subtle is quick to respond, which does not belong to Face, either.

FACE I ga' you countenance, credit for your coales,
   Your stills, your glasses, your *materialls*,
   Built you a fornace, drew you customers,
   Advanc'd all your black arts; lent you, beside,
   A house to practise in—
SUBTLE   Your masters house?
FACE Where you have studied the more thriving skill
   Of bawdrie, since.
SUBTLE   Yes, in your masters house.

(I. i. 43–9)

The alliance between Subtle, Face, and Dol is as temporary and uncertain as their period of occupancy of Lovewit's premises; theirs is a *house* in which little credit can be placed.

The various houses thus far described in *The Alchemist* are 'magic' in the sense that they lack a basis in reality, existing principally in the hopes and fantasies and perceptions of the characters themselves. The almost empty house in Blackfriars is capable of becoming whatever its occupants and visitors most wish it to become: closely inspected after the event, it proves to be an almost empty house in Blackfriars. Lovewit's house (in short) is irresistibly like that other house—situated, in all probability, in Blackfriars too—where this very play was first presented in 1610 by the King's Men.[18] These two houses of illusion are in fact *the same house*, and the charlatans who arouse and exploit the fantasies of their victims are (when all is said and done) members of the company of the King's Men, who use similar arts to somewhat similar ends. For the playhouse is, *par excellence*, a magic house, a wooden frame animated and transformed by the skills of the actors, men who pretend to be what they are not, playing in a house that seems to be what it is not: closely inspected after the event, it is merely a wooden frame, an almost empty house in Blackfriars. 'Good faith, sir, I beleve, / There's no such thing' says Face to his master Lovewit in the last act of the play, coolly dismissing the confused gossip of the neighbours: ''Tis all *deceptio*

---

[18] I follow F. H. Mares, editor of the Revels edition of *The Alchemist* (1967), p. lxv, in believing it more likely that the play was first presented at Blackfriars than at the Globe, as Herford and Simpson assert. For a fuller argument on this matter, see R. L. Smallwood's ' "Here, in the Friars": Immediacy and Theatricality in *The Alchemist*', *The Review of English Studies*, NS 2 (1980), 142–60; and Ch. 3 above.

visus' (v. iii. 61–2). What has been glimpsed in and around Lovewit's house is simply an optical illusion, *deceptio visus*, lacking any basis in reality. And, in a double sense, this might be regarded as true: for the confidence tricksters have indeed traded in deception, not substance, and (moreover) they themselves have been impersonated by a group of actors, whose business is likewise to deceive. Lovewit's house is thus a powerful analogue and symbol of the playhouse itself, with which it is in a sense coterminous. The charlatan's art is not unlike that of the dramatist and his actors, and there is thus a further uncomfortable resemblance between the audience who are currently enjoying this comedy and the gulls whom the charlatans are currently exploiting. Both groups of people have wandered expectantly into a house in Blackfriars where their fantasies are entertained; both groups have been gently relieved of their cash. *Caveat spectator.*

Though the warning note is there, it would be a mistake (I believe) to regard *The Alchemist* merely as a parable on the perils of theatre-going, or as a costive diatribe against 'the loathed stage'. Jonson certainly exhibits from time to time what Jonas Barish has called the 'anti-theatrical prejudice',[19] but it is impossible to ignore the zest and high spirits with which the illusory arts are planned and executed. For the theatre, as the play reminds us, is a magic house in a pleasurable as well as a delusive sense, and the playwright's and actors' aim is not to drive their customers from the doors, but instead 'To feast you often, and invite new ghests' (V. v. 165). The play is (so to speak) its own lodestone, placed beneath the threshold to draw in visitors to the theatre. The London theatres were in fact closed for substantial periods around the time of the first performance of *The Alchemist*, on account of the plague; if there was a risk of contagion in such public congregations as the play now attracted, there must also now have been a particular pleasure for actors and audience alike in seeing the playhouse open and full of life.[20] The plague is an important background to the play itself: it is on account of the plague that Lovewit has shut up his London house and gone off to tend his hopfields in the healthier air of Kent. Like the authorities responsible for the closure of the playhouses, Lovewit is watching the weekly mortality figures in London in order to decide when to reopen his house.[21]

---

[19] 'Jonson and the Loathed Stage', in id., *The Antitheatrical Prejudice* (Berkeley, 1981).
[20] F. P. Wilson, *The Plague in Shakespeare's London* (Oxford, 1927), 123–7.
[21] *The Alchemist*, I. i. 182–3, IV. vii. 115–18. On the effect of mortality rates on the theatre closures, see Wilson, *The Plague in Shakespeare's London*, 51–5.

When he returns earlier than Face, Subtle, and Dol have calculated, Face hastily concocts a story that the house has been infected by plague during Lovewit's absence: the cat that kept the buttery had the disease a week before Face noticed it, and so (Face continues) he locked the house up prudently for a month,

> Purposing then, sir,
> T'have burnt rose-vinegar, triackle, and tarre,
> And, ha' made it sweet, that you should ne'er ha' knowne it.
>
> (v. ii. 11–13)

Though the story is a fabrication, there is another, deeper, sense in which Face—as Lovewit himself is soon to recognize—has sweetened and revived his master's house. For this house has never been, in the fullest sense, a *house* since the death of Lovewit's first wife, as Subtle's contemptuous attack upon Face in the opening scene of the play indirectly reveals.

> You, and the rats, here, kept possession.
> Make it not strange. I know, yo'were one, could keepe
> The buttry-hatch still lock'd, and save the chippings,
> Sell the dole-beere to *aqua-vitae-men*,
> The which, together with your *christ-masse* vailes,
> At *post and paire*, your letting out of counters,
> Made you a pretty stock, some twentie markes,
> And gave you credit, to converse with cob-webs,
> Here, since your mistris death hath broke up house.
>
> (I. i. 50–8)

Into this cobwebby house, 'broke up' and run down since the death of his late mistress, Face brings new life and energy—and, for his master, a new wife, Dame Pliant, who 'Will make you seven yeeres yonger, and a rich one' (v. iii. 86). This is not illusion: it is flesh and blood, solid cash and solid 'happinesse' (v. v. 147). A real magic has been worked within the near-dead house, and a new and living one established.

⤜❧⤐

The title-page of Jonson's *Discoveries* carries a tag from Persius (*Satires*, iv. 52): *tecum habita, ut noris quam sit tibi curta supellex*— 'live in your own house, and recognize how poorly it is furnished'.

Time and again throughout his writing, Jonson praises those who live soberly and stoically 'at home' within their own houses, recognizing how poorly (or how sufficiently) they are furnished. Sir Robert Wroth is praised as one who can avoid the temptations of the court and city, and can 'at home, in thy securer rest, / Live, with unbought provision blest' (*The Forest*, 3. 13–14). The speaker of 'To the World' vows to 'make my strengths, such as they are, / Here in my bosome, and at home' (*The Forest*, 4. 67–8). John Selden has 'all Countries seene' yet remained 'Ever at home' (*The Underwood*, 14. 30). Sir Kenelm Digby is celebrated as an embodiment of virtue: 'And he is built like some imperiall roome / For that to dwell in, and be still at home' (*The Underwood*, 78. 7–8). To dwell 'at home' is to recognize—undeceived, undeceivingly—one's own peculiar strengths and limitations. Errant characters within Jonson's comedies are often, as a final, chastening punishment, *sent home*. In Act V, Scene iii of *Volpone*, for example, each of the legacy hunters is curtly advised by Mosca to 'go home'. 'Goe home, and use the poore sir POL, your knight, well', he says to Lady Would-be, 'For feare I tell some riddles' (44–5). To Corvino: 'Go home, be melancholique too, or mad' (60). To Corbaccio: 'Goe home, and die, stinke' (74). And to Voltore: 'Good faith, you looke / As you were costive; best go home, and purge, sir' (100–1). In the following scene, the great traveller Sir Politic Would-be, tormented by the disguised Peregrine, clambers laboriously beneath a tortoise shell, vowing 'to shunne, this place, and clime for ever; / Creeping, with house, on backe' (V. iv. 87–8). The tortoise, which carries its own house for ever on its back, was a familiar emblem of integrity, policy, and self-containment: it remained for ever at home.[22] At the end of *Volpone* the Avocatori send the innocent Celia 'Home, to her father, with her dowrie trebled' (V. xii. 144): Celia, who has been so obsessively shut away by her husband Corvino in that other house in '*an obscure nooke of the piazza*' (II. ii. 38) until the one catastrophic enforced venture to an apparently safe, apparently private house elsewhere, which has led to public exposure and humiliation.

The private house is thus for Jonson an important symbol of what has been called 'the centered self', that modest, gathered, stable, singular make of personality to which Jonson seemingly

---

[22] Ian Donaldson, 'Jonson's Tortoise', *The Review of English Studies*, NS 19 (1968), 162–6; John W. Creaser, 'The Popularity of Jonson's Tortoise', *The Review of English Studies*, NS 27 (1976), 38–46.

aspired.[23] As one ponders this symbol in relation to Jonson's own art and life, however, certain ironies are evident. 'Live in your own house, and recognize how poorly it is furnished' is (to begin with) a curious motto to affix to a commonplace book so densely furnished with transcriptions of the writings of other authors. 'Live in your own house'? The arts of imitation, appropriation, and impersonation were clearly of absorbing interest to Jonson, both in literature and in life: imaginatively speaking, he lived in many other 'houses', just as—in the most literal sense—he chose for many years to leave his own house and live contentedly in the homes of various friends and patrons.[24] Though Jonson vowed on more than one occasion to leave 'the loathed stage', it was in that magical house—delusive and unstable in its presentations and its rewards—that he was, paradoxically, most at home.

Within the world of his comedies, a part at least of Jonson's complex sympathies is reserved for the shifty and the shiftless, the men and women who live by their wits, not their estates, who have neither a fixed identity nor a fixed home. To hide oneself away from the world in a fortified and soundproofed house, as Morose in *The Silent Woman* attempts forlornly to do, is—as that comedy shows—to prize that 'centered self' more highly than the freedom and openness which make a person truly human. It may be a fit punishment for Sir Politic Would-be that he is forced finally to creep within the shell of a tortoise, but that creature is scarcely a satisfactory model for human emulation. The fox, that devious and lively sallier-out from home, seems altogether more engaging in its ways.

It is one of the ironies of Jonson's own life that during his final years, crippled by strokes and palsy, he was confined to a single room of his house in Westminster; now at last constantly 'at home', as house-bound and bed-bound as his own dramatic character Volpone had once feigned to be. Grossly overweight, he lay (his muse, he complained, as restricted as he)

---

[23] Thomas M. Greene, 'Ben Jonson and the Centered Self', *SEL: Studies in English Literature 1500–1900*, 10 (1970), 325–48.

[24] On Jonson's residency with Esmé Stuart, Lord Aubigny, see Ch. 4 above. In 1602 Jonson was living with Sir Robert Townshend (*The Diary of John Manningham*, ed. R. B. Sorlien (Hanover, NH, 1976), 187, 380–1); in 1603 he was staying, probably briefly, with Sir Robert Cotton in Conington in Huntingdonshire (*Conversations with Drummond*, 262). The journey to Scotland took Jonson away from London for the best part of a year in 1618/19; during this period he lodged with many friends and acquaintances.

> . . . block'd up, and straightned, narrow'd in,
> Fix'd to the bed, and boords, unlike to win
> Health, or scarce breath . . .
>
> (*The Underwood*, 71. 10–12)

The single room that had been so favourite a theme and setting in his plays was now his own daily and unvarying experience. In 1631 a friend possessed of a touching thoughtfulness and humour presented the invalid with a pet fox: 'w[hi]ch Creature', wrote Jonson, 'by handling, I endeavoured to make tame, aswell for the abateing of my disease, as the delight I tooke in speculation of his Nature'.[25] And what did the fox think about his own enforced confinement to an urban house? As it happens, an answer of sorts is to hand. Writing to the Earl of Newcastle shortly before Christmas 1631, Jonson reports a dream he has recently had. A servant arrives at his bedside and announces, 'Master, Master the Foxe speakes'.

Whereat, (mee thought) I started, and troubled, went downe into the Yard, to witnes the wonder; There I found my Reynard, in his Tenement the Tubb, I had hyr'd for him, cynically expressing his owne lott, to be condemn'd to the house of a Poett, where nothing was to bee seene but the bare walls, and not any thing heard but the noise of a Sawe, dividing billatts all the weeke long, more to keepe the family in exercise, then to comfort any person there with fire, save the Paralytick master; and went on in this way as the Foxe seem'd the better Fabler, of the two.

The fox informs his master that the cellar is infested with moles. The royal molecatcher is fetched, but announces that there is nothing he can do; only the king or some nobleman can remedy the situation: 'This kind of Mole is called a *Want*, w[hi]ch will distroy you, and your family, if you prevent not the workeing of it in tyme, And therefore, god keepe you and send you health.' A 'want' is a species of mole, and Jonson's house—as he wittily and beseechingly reports to Newcastle—is undermined by a *want*: is there nothing that his lordship can do at this Christmas time to relieve it?[26] The imagination that had once been stirred (if Aubrey is to be credited) by the thought of Thomas Sutton's confinement to a house which threatened to

---

[25] Jonson to the Earl of Newcastle, 20 Dec. 1631: Herford and Simpson, i. 213–14.
[26] The same wordplay is found in Jonson's 'Epistle Mendicant' to Lord Weston, the Lord High Treasurer, written in the same year: '*Disease*, the Enemie, and his Ingineeres, / *Want*, with the rest of his conceal'd compeeres, / Have cast a trench about mee, now, five yeeres': *The Underwood*, 71. 4–6.

collapse through the weight of chests of money is now exercised by a meditation on his own confinement, and by the fantasy of the collapse of his own house through 'want'. In his greatest comedy, a man behaves like a fox; in this dream of his old age, a fox behaves like a man, frankly discussing with its master the miseries of confined living, and the perils that threaten their house. The constrained and the free, the centred and the eccentric, the housed and the houseless, the fast and the loose, remained to the end of Ben Jonson's life the great polarities between which his creative imagination moved.

6

Clockwork Comedy
Time and The Alchemist

THE ALCHEMIST, as Coleridge recognized long ago, is one of the world's most brilliantly plotted plays.[1] Its design is cleverer, more intricate, more elegant, more surprising than that of any comedy of Shakespeare; it as cunning as clockwork. *The Alchemist* may be compared with clockwork in another, more literal, sense too, for the time-scheme of the play is organized with extraordinary precision, plotted to the very moment. For most of the characters in the comedy, moreover, time itself is a matter of the deepest consequence, always at the forefront of their consciousness, sharpening their particular ambitions and visions of the world. Time impinges in *The Alchemist*, as characteristically in Jonson's comedies, with an urgency and precision rarely encountered in the world of Shakespearian comedy or romance. Even in those plays of Shakespeare in which time is felt to be a matter of great practical or psychological consequence, the formal organization of dramatic time may seem, by Jonsonian standards, to be curiously lax or wayward. Jonson himself was notoriously unimpressed by Shakespeare's seemingly more casual artistry, as his passing gibes at Shakespeare's late plays in the Induction to *Bartholomew Fair* and the *Conversations with William Drummond* testify. These comments are sometimes taken as evidence of Jonson's pedantry or of his personal enmity towards Shakespeare. Yet it is worth reflecting on the deeper dramatic logic that may have prompted Jonson's responses, which ultimately reveal more about his own theatrical practices than about those of his great contemporary.

⁓⁂⁓

[1] *Table Talk* (1835), in James Thornton (ed.), *Table Talk from Ben Jonson to Leigh Hunt* (1934), recording his comment, made *c*.1823, on the 'perfect' plot of *The Alchemist*.

At the end of the first act of *The Magnetic Lady* the wretched critic Damplay, asked for his opinion on the play thus far, magisterially observes that its action appears to be inconclusive. The Boy who serves as the author's spokesman in these little symposia between the acts asks Damplay in some surprise whether he normally looks for conclusions in the first act of a play, rather than in the fifth: 'But you would have all come together, it seemes: The Clock should strike five, at once, with the Acts.' The well-made play (this analogy implies) runs like a well-regulated clock, moving with dependable exactitude to its patiently awaited climax. Some writers, it is true—the Boy goes on, warming to the task of derision—seem to have abandoned the clock entirely as a measure of dramatic time, their plays representing the passage not of minutes and hours but of years and generations, grandly extending the accustomed boundaries of dramatic time and space:

So, if a Child could be borne, in a *Play*, and grow up to a man, i' the first Scene, before hee went off the Stage: and then after to come forth a Squire, and bee made a Knight: and that Knight to travell betweene the Acts, and doe wonders i' the holy land, or else where; kill Paynims, wild Boores, dun Cowes, and other Monsters; beget him a reputation, and marry an Emperours Daughter for his Mistris; convert her Fathers Countrey; and at last come home, lame, and all to be laden with miracles. (Chorus after Act I, 11–24)

The kind of narrative which Jonson ridicules here contrasts sharply with his own dramatic invention, which was always precisely contained within what Jonson called 'fit bounds' of time and space. 'Now, in every Action it behooves the *Poet* to know which is his utmost bound', Jonson wrote in the *Discoveries* (2735-7), 'how farre with fitnesse, and a necessary proportion, he may produce, and determine it.' The writer first marks the dramatic territory, calculating the precise limits of the intended action before *producing* the narrative—drawing it out—and ultimately *determining* it, bringing about its conclusion.

For, as a body without proportion cannot be goodly, no more can the Action, either in *Comedy*, or *Tragedy*, without his fit bounds. And every bound, for the nature of the Subject, is esteem'd the best that is largest, till it can increase no more: so it behooves the Action in *Tragedy*, or *Comedy*, to be let grow, till the necessity ask a Conclusion: wherein two things are to be considered; First, that it exceed not the compasse of one Day: Next, that there be place left for digression, and Art. (2739-47)

The contrasts are worth noticing within this passage, which speaks of amplitude as well as compactness, of digression as well as linearity, of natural growth as well as artful control. Though Jonson is following Aristotle here (through the mediation of a Renaissance commentator) the passage perfectly describes the controlled narrative excitements and surprises of his own theatrical practice.

In Jonson's dramatic world, time, like territory, is strictly limited, fiercely competed for, precisely calibrated: the dramatic 'bounds' are always carefully set. In *The Devil is an Ass*, for example, Fabian Fitzdottrel allows the young gallant Wittipol to pay court to his wife, Frances Fitzdottrel, for a period of fifteen minutes in exchange for the gift of a new cloak. As the interview begins, the two men carefully synchronize their watches, Fitzdottrel reminding Wittipol that he stay within

> Your quarter of an houre, alwaies keeping
> The measur'd distance of your yard, or more,
> From my said Spouse: and in my sight and hearing.

(I. vi. 67–9)

Within these imposed limitations, Wittipol chooses to speak to Frances Fitzdottrel about the limitations that are also imposed upon human beauty and human life. Obedient to her husband, Frances makes no reply.

> WITTIPOL . . . ere your spring be gone, injoy it. Flowers,
>   Though faire, are oft but of one morning. Thinke,
>   All beauty doth not last untill the *autumne*.
>   You grow old, while I tell you this. And such,
>   As cannot use the present, are not wise . . .
>
>   What doe you answer, Lady?
> FITZDOTTREL   Now the sport comes
>   Let him still waite, waite, waite: while the watch goes,
>   And the time runs.

(I. vi. 128–32, 135–7)

For Fitzdottrel, time is a marketable commodity: every moment has its value. While Fitzdottrel narrowly contemplates the movements of the dial-plate, Wittipol urges Mrs Fitzdottrel to contemplate the larger movements, losses, and possibilities of their individual lives, prefigured within this segment of time: 'You grow old, while I tell you this.' The time-scheme of the entire play is marked and bounded with equal care: within it, Jonson creates a complex and ironic pattern of conflicting hopes, expectations, and regrets concerning the passage of time.

Such exact control and 'bounding' of the drama, such heightened awareness of the ticking of the clock, are characteristic of Jonson's methods. At the outset of *The Staple of News* the young heir Pennyboy Junior delightedly regards his chiming watch, waiting eagerly for the striking of the hour that signals the arrival of his majority. In *The New Inn* the chambermaid Prue is allowed to play for a single day the role of sovereign of sports at the inn, and in turn permits her mistress's lover, Lovel, two hours to prosecute his courtship. As this period of licensed wooing draws towards its close, Lady Frampul wishes it would never stop: 'O, for an engine to keepe backe all clocks!' (IV. iv. 230). These clearly bounded periods of time within Jonson's drama resemble and are in turn contained by those clearly bounded periods for which his playgoers have consented to stay in the theatre: the 'two short houres' mentioned in the prologue to *The Alchemist*, or the 'two houres and an halfe, and somewhat more' set down in the Scrivener's Articles of Agreement with the audience in the Induction to *Bartholomew Fair*, during which they covenant to remain 'with patience' 'in the places, their money or friends have put them in' (77–80). For Jonson's theatre-goers as for the characters within his dramas, the clock is often seen as an ultimate arbiter, setting the limits within which the action is to be played out, and signalling the manner in which success or failure is to be decided.

In 1652 Thomas Berney was aptly (if lavishly) to liken Jonson's dramatic powers to those of 'th'hour telling Sun, the Rectifier / Of Clocks and Watches'.[2] Other dramatists, Berney implied, might set their watches by Jonson's models of dramatic practice. If there is one play above all that might warrant such hyperbolic praise, it is surely that masterpiece of comic timing and mistiming, Jonson's clockwork comedy, *The Alchemist*.

⤬

The action of *The Alchemist* is precisely delimited, and may be precisely dated. The play was first performed in 1610, and the action is

---

[2] Quoted in G. E. Bentley, *Shakespeare and Jonson: Their Reputations in the Seventeenth Century Compared*, 2 vols. (Chicago, 1945), ii. 83.

supposed to occur in the same year. A mass of topical references gives a general sense of contemporaneity, and several further references invite us to make an even more exact dating. Dame Pliant, who is said to be 19 years of age, admits that she could never endure a Spaniard since the Armada year of 1588, and that (she says) was three years before she was born in 1591: plus nineteen equals 1610. In the fifth act the indignant Ananias, robbed (as he believes) of his expected riches, tells Lovewit of the exact date upon which Subtle undertook to deliver the elixir to the Puritan brethren:

> Were not the shillings numbred,
> That made the pounds? Were not the pounds told out,
> Upon the second day of the fourth weeke,
> In the eight month, upon the table dormant,
> The yeere, of the last patience of the *Saints*,
> Sixe hundred and ten?

(V. v. 100–5)

—that is to say, upon 23 October 1610. This is a strange way of computing time, in relation to the ending of the world that the millenarians anticipated would arrive in AD 2000. The 'last patience of the *Saints*' of which Ananias now impatiently speaks is the patience that should enable them to endure the final millennium until the expected doomsday—or possibly the patience the Brethren must show until Subtle at last delivers the promised elixir. The same ambiguity flickers through the original transaction between Subtle, Ananias, and Tribulation Wholesome earlier in the play:

TRIBULATION   But how long time,
    Sir, must the *Saints* expect, yet?
SUBTLE   Let me see,
    How's the moone, now? Eight, nine, ten dayes hence
    He will be *silver potate*; then, three dayes,
    Before he *citronise*: some fifteene dayes,
    The *Magisterium* will be perfected.
ANANIAS About the second day, of the third weeke,
    In the ninth month?
SUBTLE   Yes, my good Ananias.

(III. ii. 125–32)

Subtle's promise is for delivery on 16 November, which is 'some fifteene dayes' hence: thus the action of the play must be supposed to occur on 1 November, a week after Tribulation Wholesome first 'told out' the pounds in expectation of an imminent fortune.[3] The Puritans' businesslike insistence upon the exact dates of contractual promise, payment, and delivery contrasts and blends bizarrely with their larger computation of the time remaining until the arrival of the Last Judgement (which, it was traditionally rumoured, would be preceded by a period of *tribulation*).[4] Their lives are governed entirely by expectation, both commercial and apocalyptic.

To its earliest audiences, the action of *The Alchemist* would therefore have appeared to have been occurring in the immediate present: *right now*. The very immediacy of the play, its precise contemporary dating, carries, perhaps, its own gently satirical implications, like Swift's ironical reference to 'the taste of wit calculated for this present month of August, 1697' in the Preface to his *Tale of a Tub*, or the mock-topical titles of Fielding's play *The Historical Register for the Year 1736* and of Pope's poem 'One Thousand Seven Hundred and Forty'. In each of these works a writer with a powerful sense of the historical past and some confidence in a future readership gravely imitates the manner of those who are locked within the consciousness of their own times, unable to look before or after, victims of fashion and hence of the relentless and exposing movement of time.

1610 was a plague year in London. At its height that year, the plague brought thirty to forty deaths per week.[5] At the opening of the second act of *The Alchemist*, Mammon promises Surly that, armed with the elixir, he will 'undertake, withall, to fright the plague / Out o' the kingdome, in three months' (II. i. 69–70), and Surly replies that the actors will be grateful to him, for during 1610 the theatres had been closed for five months in order to curb the spread of infection. This sharp reminder of the risks attendant upon theatre-going cannot have been altogether comforting to the London audiences of 1610.

---

[3] Herford and Simpson, followed by later editors of the play, see a discrepancy between the dates indicated in v. v and in III. ii, failing to observe that 23 October is the date on which the Brethren's money was 'told out', and that on the present date of 1 November the Brethren are impatient, and 'will not venter any more' (II. v. 65). Jonson's own calculations are in fact perfect.

[4] Frank Kermode, 'Waiting for the End', in Malcolm Bull (ed.), *Apocalypse Theory and the Ends of the World* (Oxford, 1995), ch. 11.

[5] See F. P. Wilson, *The Plague in Shakespeare's London* (Oxford, 1927); Paul Slack, *The Impact of the Plague in Tudor and Stuart England* (1985); Cheryl Lynn Ross, 'The Plague of *The Alchemist*', *Renaissance Quarterly*, 41 (1988), 439–58.

When the play opens, both Face and Subtle know that there is a
limit to the period of time for which they can occupy Lovewit's
house, but do not know precisely when that limit will be reached.
Face seems not to be anxious about Lovewit's return.

> O, feare him not. While there dyes one, a weeke,
> O' the plague, hee's safe, from thinking toward *London*.
> Beside he's busie at his hop-yards, now:
> I had a letter from him. If he doe,
> Hee'll send such word, for ayring o' the house
> As you shall have sufficient time, to quit it:
> Though we breake up a fortnight, 'tis no matter.

(I. i. 183–8)

On this false reckoning about the amount of time available to them,
the entire operation of Face, Subtle, and Dol is based. When Lovewit
unexpectedly returns, they anxiously squabble over the cause of
their mistake.

SUBTLE   You said he would not come,
> While there dyed one a weeke, within the liberties.
FACE No: 'twas within the walls.
SUBTLE   Was't so? Cry' you mercy:
> I thought the liberties. What shall we doe now, Face?

(IV. vii. 115–18)

Neither the 'liberties' (the wider, suburban area of London) nor the
'walls' (the stricter city limits) have in fact been mentioned by Face in
the original exchange, yet it is characteristic of Jonson's dramaturgy
that time and territory—chronological and geographical *bounds*—
should here be so intimately and critically linked.

At the outset of the play, Face, Subtle, and Dol know they must
move fast, but don't know *how* fast: their tenure of the house is temporary, the period of their 'festivall dayes' or 'holy-day' (III. iii. 53, V.
iii. 9) unknown. Their deceptions and counter-deceptions are dependent entirely upon speed. In the fourth act of the play Subtle, unable
to win Dame Pliant for himself, decides to let the importunate
Spanish Count have a private assignation with her before Face
sweeps her off.

> I will the heartilier goe about it now,
> And make the widdow a punke, so much the sooner,
> To be reveng'd on this impetuous FACE:
> The quickly doing of it is the grace.

(IV. iii. 101–4)

'The quickly doing of it is the grace': this sentiment underlies much of the action of the three tricksters. Speed is the secret of their survival, as it is of their deceptions; a speed which paradoxically converts the most low-minded of actions—prostituting your closest colleague's intended bride—into a 'grace', an act worthy almost of admiration. Those who suffer defeat in this play do so not because they are less virtuous or even necessarily because they are less intelligent—Surly has his own moral values, and is shrewd enough after his own manner—but rather because they are ultimately too slow. Lovewit, who shares his servant Face's quickness of mind and action, is finally to turn mischievously upon Surly and tell him that Dame Pliant could not bring herself to care for someone who moves as slowly as Surly does. True, Surly darkened his face, dyed his beard, dressed as a Spaniard, protested his love for Dame Pliant,

> And then did nothing. What an over-sight,
> And want of putting forward, sir, was this!
> Well fare an old Hargubuzier, yet,
> Could prime his poulder, and give fire, and hit,
> All in a twinckling.
>
> (V. v. 54–8)

Abel Drugger, equally hopeful of gaining Dame Pliant's hand, is even slower: 'He stay'd too long a washing of his face' (V. v. 120).

This delight in celerity, in 'the quickly doing of it', is a central impulse in the play: for the tricksters, it becomes almost an end in itself, a game, a competition. The quarrel between Face and Subtle that opens the play eventually reaches a truce, and is shifted into another mode, when they agree to compete against each other to see 'who shall sharke best' that day (I. i. 160). Within the already limited period of time that is at their disposal, they set themselves this narrower limit, deliberately creating another reason to race the clock. The day thus takes on a special significance for Face and Subtle, as it will for certain of their victims; in the course of the play, they will come to characterize it as 'lucky', 'good', or 'ill', gambling with fortune in a manner not unlike that of those whom they set out to deceive (III. iii. 27, IV. vii. 113).

Thus the comedy's time-scale begins to acquire its gradations: a particular year, a particular month, a particular (but cavalierly and approximately reckoned) period of occupancy for the house, a particular day upon which Face and Subtle decide to compete against each other. And within that day, as the comedy proceeds, finer gradations of time begin to be established. The events of the play are organized with extraordinary precision: 'organized' by Jonson, and organized, too, up to a point, by Subtle, Face, and Dol, who watch the clock sharply throughout. Yet these three are capable of making mistakes; their concentration sometimes lapses; and unforeseen events erupt, throwing their careful plans awry, and demanding of them ever quicker and more ingenious thought and action. The comedy presents a wonderful counterpoint of control and random-ness, of planned action and spontaneous improvisation, of discip-line and anarchy. From the mistimings that occur within the highly regulated programme of the day, the fun begins.

The Alchemist opens in the morning (Jonson's Oxford editors, who draw up an hour-by-hour timetable of events, guess at 9 a.m.[6]) and runs through until the early afternoon; ' 'tis not yet deepe i'the after-noone', says Face towards the end of the play (V. ii. 30). The organization of time within the first two acts of the play gives some indication of the careful construction of the whole. Scarely is the quarrel between Face and Subtle patched up when the first customer of the day arrives, Dapper the lawyer's clerk. Dapper made his appointment to visit 'the cunning-man' this morning while drinking with Face at the Dagger in Holborn the night before. A normally punctual and fastidious man, Dapper is now unsure whether he is late or early for the appointment, as he has lent his watch to an acquaintance with an even more pressing engagement, 'and so was rob'd / Of my passe-time' (I. ii. 7–8). ('Passe-time' suggests the harm-less pleasure that Dapper habitually derives from this toy. 'Watches, at this time, were scarce and dear, and seem to have conferred some kind of distinction upon their possessors', Jonson's nineteenth-century editor William Gifford explains.[7]) It suits Face to pretend that Dapper is late, and that he himself was therefore just leaving the house, having tired of waiting. Face bustles like a brisk receptionist with a patient whose late arrival has thrown the doctor's morning's time table awry; he can insist that Dapper will just have to wait his turn. Dapper will do so eventually in the privy, his mouth stuffed with a gag of gingerbread, until he can endure no longer. Face intro-duces Dapper now to Subtle, who promises in turn to introduce him to the Queen of Fairy, but not yet; for the Queen herself does not rise

---

[6] Herford and Simpson, x. 49–50.
[7] The Works of Ben Jonson, ed. William Gifford and Francis Cunningham, 3 vols. (1904), ii. 10–11. Cf. the fussing of Asotus over his watch in Cynthia's Revels, IV. iii.

until noon. Dapper must go away, apply some drops of vinegar at suitable orifices, fast, and perform other solemn rites of preparation. At one o'clock he may come again. 'Can you remember this?'—'I warrant you.' (I. ii. 171). Exit Dapper. Already at the door is the next client, the tobacconist Abel Drugger, but contending with Drugger for entry are several 'good wives', equally anxious for a consultation with Subtle; they are fobbed off by Face 'till after-noone' (I. iii. 2).

Drugger is seeking specialist advice from Subtle concerning the layout of his shop, and the interpretation of his almanack. He asks that Subtle look over the almanac, 'And crosse out my ill-dayes, that I may neither / Bargaine, nor trust upon them' (I. iii. 95–6). This very day is actually to prove an ill one for Drugger, if only he knew it, but then it is also to prove an ill day for the sage whom he now so trustingly consults. Drugger is told to leave the almanac for Subtle to study, is sent away, and bidden to return in the afternoon. As Drugger leaves, the women are still clamouring for admission, along with another client, 'your giantesse, / The bawd of *Lambeth*'. 'Not, afore night', Dol tells them through the speaking tube (I. iv. 2–4), casting forward to a period that actually lies beyond the time-span of the play. By nightfall—though Dol does not yet know it—the master of the house will have returned, the conspiracy will have collapsed, and Dol and Subtle will have vanished over the back fence; and the women, no doubt, will call again, pleading ever more loudly for admittance.

At the end of Act I, Sir Epicure Mammon is seen

> Comming along, at far end of the lane,
> Slow of his feet, but earnest of his tongue,
> To one, that's with him.
>
> (I. iv. 7–9)

Subtle has looked for him 'With the sunnes rising: Marvaile, he could sleepe!' (I. iv. 12). For this is a special day for Mammon, too: the day upon which, after ten months' apparent labour, Subtle has promised that the elixir will at last be ready. In Jonson's day an epicure was commonly thought of as a person who made pleasure his chief good, and who disbelieved in a future life; the here and now was all that mattered.[8] And it is about the here and now that Sir Epicure at first

---

[8] See George A. Panichas, *Epicurus* (New York, 1967); N. W. De Witt, *Epicurus and his Philosophy* (Minneapolis, 1954). Cf. Carlo Buffone, the 'incomprehensible epicure' of *Every Man Out of His Humour* (Grex, 338). Sir Epicure Mammon's vision of solitary feasting (II. ii. 72 ff.) is contrary to the spirit of Epicurus, who maintained that 'To eat and

appears to be talking, his thoughts being seemingly focused entirely
upon the present: 'Now', 'This is the day', 'This Day', 'This night'
are his characteristic phrases (II. i. 1, 6, 8, 29). On closer scrutiny,
however, it will be seen that it is not the present moment about which
Mammon speaks, but the moment that is about to arrive: he lives in
a state of perpetual excited anticipation; 'shall' and 'will' are the
commonest and most eloquent words upon his lips. Mammon is like
a comic version of Macbeth, so haunted by a vision of the future that
the present ceases to have any validity or significance: 'nothing is but
what is not' (*Macbeth*, I. iii. 141). He inhabits a world of prophecy
and dream; 'If his dreame last', says Subtle, 'hee'll turne the age, to
gold' (I. iv. 29).

Mammon's imagination fastens upon the nature of time, and the
way it can be manipulated once he is possessed of the elixir. He believes that he will have the power to defy and to collapse time, moving with unimaginable speed to reverse its normal destructive
processes:

> In eight, and twentie dayes,
> I'll make an old man, of fourscore, a childe. . . .
>
>   'Tis the secret
> Of nature, naturiz'd 'gainst all infections,
> Cures all diseases, comming of all causes,
> A month's griefe, in a day; a yeeres, in twelve:
> And, of what age soever, in a month.
> Past all the doses, of your drugging Doctors.
> I'll undertake, withall, to fright the plague
> Out o' the kingdome, in three months.

(II. i. 52–3, 63–70)

Mammon believes that with the elixir one may live for ever, liber-
ated from common fears and apprehensions. 'I see no end of his
labours', says Subtle of Mammon (I. iv. 25), and Mammon himself
sees no ends of any kind: no end to his sexual and gastronomic delights, no end to his powers, no end to his life. Mammon is in this respect quite unlike his philosophical namesake Epicurus, who was
acutely interested in the necessary limits of human pleasure and of
human life. True pleasure, Epicurus argued, depends upon a calm
recognition of these limits: 'Infinite time contains no greater

drink without a friend is to devour like the lion and the wolf': quoted in Carlo Diano,
'Epicureanism', *Encyclopedia Britannica*, 15th edn. (Chicago, 1983) vi. 911–14.

pleasure than limited time, if one measures by reason the limits of pleasure.'[9] Unthinking pleasure, on the other hand, cannot succeed in dispelling the fears and pains which a consciousness of these limits will impose:

If the things that produce the pleasures of profligates could dispel the fears of the mind about the phenomena of the sky and death and its pains, and also teach the limits of desire and of pains, we should never have cause to blame them: for they would be filling themselves full with pleasures from every source and never have pain of body or mind, which is the evil of life.[10]

With more irony than he knows, Mammon speaks to Subtle of the task of Sisyphus, 'dam'd / To roule the ceaselesse stone' (II. iii. 208–9). Mammon himself seeks the hedonist's counterpart to this instrument of torment: a stone that will bring ceaseless pleasure. Yet the task of finding that stone will itself be ceaseless, for Subtle's strategy is perpetually to promise, and perpetually to delay.

Jonson allows us to glimpse a curious affinity between Mammon's attitude to time and that of the Puritan brethren. With one part of his mind, Mammon believes in a world of unending pleasure. With another part, however, he believes—as do Ananias and Tribulation—in a coming apocalypse. In conversation with Dol Common, Mammon reveals himself to be a Fifth Monarchy man, awaiting the millennium.[11] At the end of the play, frustrated of all his hopes, he dramatically revises the probable date of the ending of the world:[12]

> I will goe mount a turnep-cart, and preach
> The end o'the world, within these two months.
>
> (V. v. 81–2)

When Subtle meets Mammon in the second act he rebukes him for his excessive eagerness to view the results of Subtle's still unconcluded labours:

---

[9] *Principal Doctrines*, xix, in Whitney J. Oates (ed.), *The Stoic and Epicurean Philosophers* (New York, 1940), 36.

[10] *Principal Doctrines*, x, ibid. 35–6.

[11] See P. G. Rogers, *The Fifth Monarchy Men* (1966); B. S. Capp, *The Fifth Monarchy Men: A Study in Seventeenth-Century English Millenarianism* (1972); Theodore Olson, *Millennialism, Utopianism, and Progress* (Toronto, 1982); E. L. Tuveson, *Millenium and Utopia: A Study of the Background of the Idea of Progress* (Berkeley, 1949).

[12] Millenarians, like other apocalyptic sects, have always been ready to revise the likely date of the ending of the world if disappointed in their first prediction, as Frank Kermode points out in *The Sense of an Ending* (1967).

> Sonne, I doubt
> Yo'are covetous, that thus you meet your time
> I'the just point: prevent your day, at morning.

(II. iii. 4–6)

Through his 'ungovern'd hast', Mammon may ruin the entire experi-
ment; more 'patience' is required: so Mammon, too, is sent away, and
bidden to return in two hours' time. Mammon is anxious to see not
only the elixir but also Dol Common, whom he believes to be the in-
sane and sexually available sister of a lord; spurred by this double incentive, he will arrive once more at the opening of the fourth act with
characteristic punctuality, 'i'the onely, finest time' (IV. i. 1).

The day's timetable is now growing more crowded. Mammon's
suspicious companion Surly is informed—by Face himself, in the
guise of Subtle's laboratory assistant, Lungs—that Captain Face
wishes to see him 'i'the *Temple*-church, / Some half houre hence, and
upon earnest businesse' (II. iii. 289–90). As these various appoint-
ments accumulate, Face, Subtle, and Dol begin to lose perfect control over the order of events. Before Face can get away to keep his
appointment in the Temple Church, other visitors arrive. Ananias
comes first, and is sent away at once to fetch his elders and return
within 'threescore minutes' (II. v. 84). (He and the elders are to arrive
with supreme punctuality in the third act. 'O, Are you come?', Subtle
is to ask; ''Twas time. Your threescore minutes / Were at the last
thred, you see . . .', III. ii. 1–2[13].) Drugger comes next, bringing news
of Kastril and his sister, the delectable Dame Pliant. Kastril is a man
whose deepest wish is to keep up with contemporary fashion, to live
for the present moment:

> a gentleman, newly warme in'his land, sir,
> Scarse cold in'his one and twentie; that do's governe
> His sister, here: and is a man himselfe
> Of some three thousand a yeere, and is come up
> To learne to quarrell, and to live by his wits,
> And will goe downe againe, and dye i'the countrey.

(II. vi. 57–62)

Kastril has journeyed from the safety of the country to plague-
infested London at a time when sensible Londoners like Lovewit have

---

[13] F. H. Mares, in his Revels edition of *The Alchemist* (1967), plausibly suggests that
Subtle may produce an hour-glass at this moment.

been prudently heading in the opposite direction. Nothing is more important to him than to catch the fashion of the moment; after that he can return to the country, and, like a mayfly, die.

Always at the back of these busy comings and goings is our consciousness of Face's impending appointment with Surly in the Temple Church. At last Face makes his escape, but in Act III he is to return to the house and confess that he has missed Surly. Face and Subtle have been temporarily outwitted: for the suspicious Surly is soon to return to the house in his Spanish disguise in an attempt to discover what is really going on. Like every other visitor, Surly will be sent away, having been given a new time at which to return. His next visit is to cause a different kind of disruption to the carefully managed timetable of the day, for it has been forgotten that Mammon has been told to return at exactly the same hour, and that both men are determined to enjoy an assignation with the same woman, Dol Common.

The temporal organization of the remaining acts of *The Alchemist* might be examined with equal minuteness, but the superlative technical precision with which the events of the play are plotted, timed, and set in motion will by now be fully apparent. Jonson's dramaturgy is, at the lowest level, a rich source of humour. So complex does the programming of events become in *The Alchemist* that the audience, like the characters themselves, are capable of forgetting that certain arrangements have been agreed upon. It is a wonderful moment in the theatre when Face at last believes that he has explained everything satisfactorily to Lovewit and has brought events once again under his control, and a stifled cry is suddenly heard: Dapper, desperately thrust into the privy long ago in a moment of crisis, has now eaten through his gag of gingerbread and can hold out no longer: 'For gods sake, when wil her *Grace* be at leisure?' (V. iii. 65).

But if this were all that could be said of Jonson's 'clockwork' skills, then his achievement might seem more nearly comparable to that of Feydeau than to that of Shakespeare. An examination of the organization of time in *The Alchemist* does more, however, than reveal Jonson's great cleverness in dramatic engineering, for it will also be evident that time, and the attitudes which people display towards it, are a central preoccupation of the play. The comedy's formal structure elegantly bears and enacts a central theme: as in *Volpone*, Jonson explores the nature of human expectation, and the various ways in which people hope, 'Each greedy minute' (I. i. 80), to have their most covetous dreams fulfilled. In Shakespearian comedy time often operates as a benign and clarifying force, dispelling error, rewarding devotion, and restoring that which is lost. It is to this property in time that the characters, at their most bewildered, often make appeal:

> O Time, thou must untangle this, not I;
> It is too hard a knot for me t'untie.
>
> (*Twelfth Night*, II. ii. 38–9)

Well, Time is the old justice that examines all such offenders, and let Time try. (*As You Like It*, IV. i. 178–80)

In *The Alchemist* time is viewed in other ways. For many of the characters, time is a commodity in which it is profitable to invest. Expectation may be governed by self-interest, while couched in the language of devotion: 'But how long time, / Sir, must the *Saints* expect, yet?' (III. ii. 125–6). The comedy reveals bizarre correspondences between the views of time taken by characters of apparently contrary temperament and disposition: between the Puritans' apocalyptic habits of mind, and the sensuous expectations of Sir Epicure Mammon; between the gambling instincts of Dapper, and those of Face and Subtle; between Kastril's manner of living for the moment, and that of the rogues with whom he finds himself allied. To examine the time-scheme of *The Alchemist* is to discover more fully what the play is centrally about.

⁓✻⁓

The scorn which Jonson expressed for those loosely constructed dramas about knights wandering in the holy land, like Sir Philip Sidney's earlier strictures against similar contemporary breaches of the classical unities, may look like a rearguard action mounted in defence of a hopeless cause.[14] The logic of common experience, the ultimate verdict of theatrical history, seem to stand against him. 'Time is, of all modes of existence, most obsequious to the imagination', Samuel Johnson persuasively reasoned a century later in defence of Shakespeare's more elastic dramaturgy; 'a lapse of years is as easily conceived as a passage of hours. In contemplation we easily contract

---

[14] *An Apology for Poetry*, ed. Geoffrey Shepherd (1965), 134–5.

the time of real actions, and therefore willingly permit it to be contracted when we only see their imitation.'[15] By Victorian times, these
arguments would seem self-evidently true, and the very principles of
Jonson's classical dramaturgy, as admiringly anatomized by Dryden
(for example) in *The Essay of Dramatic Poesy*, were to look profoundly dated and questionable. 'Dryden's praise is based on grounds
which to me are naught', wrote Trollope dismissively in the margins
of his copy of Cunningham and Gifford's *Ben Jonson* after rereading
The Silent Woman in 1876.

I never think of asking how many days are taken in 'As You Like It', or even
quarrel with 'A Winter's Tale' because of the lapse of time. Who really now
loves a play the better because the scenes are laid in two contiguous
houses,—except the proprietor who has to furnish the properties? That
feeling is over.[16]

To Victorian readers nurtured on the three-decker novel and the long
poem, the formal constraints of the classical theatre as represented
by a dramatist such as Jonson were to seem intolerable. 'Five acts to
make a play?' wrote Elizabeth Barrett Browning questioningly in
Aurora Leigh,

> And why not fifteen? why not ten? or seven?
> What matters for the number of the leaves,
> Supposing the tree lives and grows? . . .
>
> I will write no plays.[17]

An organic image, the tree, replaces the mechanical image of the
clock, a time-bound art being reconceived in terms of vegetable
growth whose movement is imperceptible to the human eye.

    The distant reverberations of such questions are still to be felt in
the modern theatre, where the humorously eccentric clocks of
Samuel Beckett sound, in a different register, a similar protest against
the tyranny of classical assumptions concerning the proper regulation of theatrical time. In an early piece by Beckett entitled *Le Kid*, a
parody of Corneille's *Le Cid*, an elderly gentleman with a long, white
beard named Don Diegue (originally played in performance by

[15] 'Preface to Shakespeare' (1765), in *Johnson on Shakespeare*, ed. Arthur Sherbo, vol.
vii. of the Yale Edition of the Works of Samuel Johnson (New Haven, 1968), 78.
    [16] Trollope's annotated copy of the Gifford–Cunningham *Ben Jonson* is now in the
possession of the Folger Shakespeare Library, Washington, DC.
    [17] *Aurora Leigh*, ed. Margaret Reynolds (Athens, Oh. 1992), bk. V, pt. 2, 229–332, 267.

Beckett himself) enters anxiously clutching a small alarm clock; as he embarks upon a lengthy soliloquy, the hands of another huge alarm clock painted on the backdrop are seen—first by the audience, then by Don Diegue himself, to turn at ever-accelerating speed, while the small clock in his hands begins agitatedly to sound its alarm, gradually drowning the increasingly nonsensical words of the soliloquy.[18] The energetic alarm clock of *Endgame*, to whose clamorous peal Hamm and Clov listen so intently, randomly punctuates their general consciousness of a formless time which enfolds them, stretching ever onward, always promising the end which seemingly never comes.

Beckett's dramatic world is one from which the notion of 'fit bounds' has vanished, and the divine watchmaker mysteriously taken his leave. While Jonson's *The Alchemist* may seem to present an entirely secular and even cynical view of human behaviour—the very Puritans in this play are greedy and self-interested, the Temple Church itself has become a mere place for business assignations, the returning master of the house readily enters into the dubious practices of his deceitful servant—the formal structure of the play embodies a more regular, orderly, faithful view of the operation of human affairs, depicting a world amenable to explanation, in which events move more or less rationally through various stages of crisis and denouncement to a given end; a world aptly realized in the great figure of a clock.[19]

Jonson's preference for working theatrically within the 'fit bounds' of time and place did not derive from pedantry, or blind adherence to classical practice, or failure to understand the more variable ways in which the dramatic imagination might be called into play. Such 'bounds' worked rather as a powerful stimulus to his comic invention, and his wry and complex vision of the world; a world that ran—almost, yet significantly for the comic dramatist, not quite—like a perfect clock.

---

[18] Deirdre Bair, *Samuel Beckett: A Biography* (New York, 1980), 127–8.

[19] Thomas Burnet in his *Theory of the Earth*, 2 parts (1684–90), pt. 2 (IV. 9) interestingly conflated the analogy of the world-as-theatre with that of the world-as-clock: see Tuveson, *Millenium and Utopia*, ch. 4, 'Nature's Simple Plot'. On the clockwork analogy, see Ian Donaldson, 'The Clockwork Novel: Three Notes on an Eighteenth-Century Analogy', *The Review of English Studies*, NS 21 / 81 (1970), 14–22.

7

Unknown Ends
Volpone

AT the end of the fourth act of Jonson's late comedy, *The Magnetic Lady* (1632), the restless spectator Damplay is confident that he knows how the play will conclude. 'Why, here his *Play* might have ended, if hee would ha' let it', he declares, 'and have spar'd us the vexation of a *fift Act* yet to come, which every one here knowes the issue of already, or may in part conjecture.' The Boy, who speaks for Jonson in these discussions, suggests to Damplay that he wait awhile.

Stay, and see his last *Act*, his *Catastrophe*, how hee will perplexe that, or spring some fresh cheat, to entertaine the *Spectators*, with a convenient delight, till some unexpected, and new encounter breake out to rectifie all, and make good the *Conclusion*. (Chorus after Act IV, 21–4, 27–31)

In the Boy's precocious commentaries throughout *The Magnetic Lady*, Jonson, 'finding himselfe now neare the close, or shutting up of his Circle', makes a final statement about the assumptions and strategies that had governed a lifetime's work in the theatre, and the 'bounds' and limitations within which he had chosen to operate as a dramatist.[1] 'Perplexe', 'cheat', 'unexpected' are suggestive terms in relation to Jonson's dramatic practice, which traded always in complexity, secrecy, and surprise. The endings of Jonson's plays are seldom predictable, and Damplay is soon to discover that his guesses about the resolution of *The Magnetic Lady* are entirely mistaken. In their final acts, Jonson's plays grow denser, busier, more perplexing, as the action moves through unforeseen complications to equally unforeseen conclusions.

Jonson attached particular importance to the endings of his comedies, as he did to the endings of his other writings. 'Our composition must bee more accurate in the beginning and end, then in

---

[1] For the figure of the circle, see Ch. 3; on the notion of dramatic 'bounds', see Ch. 6 above.

the midst', he wrote in *Discoveries*, translating a passage of Vives, 'and in the end more, then in the beginning; for through the midst the streame beares us' (1957–1960). Jonson's audience were at times less compelled by this principle than he was himself. 'Stay, and see his last *Act*. . . .': the Boy's words are addressed not simply to Damplay, but to the actual audience at Blackfriars watching this performance of *The Magnetic Lady* in 1632. For as Jonson had good cause to know, his audiences did not always stay to see his last act. *Sejanus*, with its masterly last act, was hissed from the stage in 1604. *Catiline* seems to have run into similar trouble from a restive audience when it was per-formed in 1611.[2] It is perhaps significant that in *Bartholomew Fair*, Jonson's next play staged in 1614, the puppet play is broken up by the Puritan elder Zeal-of-the-Land Busy before it reaches its conclusion; as the comedy itself concludes, Bartholomew Cokes asks that the re-mainder of the puppet play be privately performed that evening in the sanctuary of Justice Overdo's house: 'bring the *Actors* along, wee'll ha' the rest o' the *Play* at home' (V. vi. 114–15).

    The performance in 1629 of *The New Inn*, with its highly elabor-ate conclusion, was similarly fraught with trouble. At the opening of the final act, the Host of the New Inn, alias Lord Frampul, fears that the various schemes which he has been contriving throughout the piece have all miscarried. 'I had thought . . .', he says, 'like a noble Poet, to have had / My last act best: but all failes i' the plot' (V. i. 24–7). Jonson here performs a deliberate feinting movement which is similar in its effect to that moment in *The Magnetic Lady* when Damplay is allowed to grumble about the predictability of that com-edy's fifth act. A virtuoso sequence of comic revelations is about to unfold. Lord Beaumont announces that he has married a young woman named Laetitia, and is told in turn that his wife is in fact a boy, the Host's son, who has dressed as a woman as part of a friendly game. An ancient whiskey-tippling Irish nurse reveals, to Lord Beaumont's relief, that this boy dressed as a girl is in fact a girl dressed as a boy dressed as a girl. Pulling the black patch from her eye, the nurse then reveals that she herself is none other than Lady Frampul, the Host's own long-lost wife, who has been living un-detected at the New Inn these past seven years. 'And all are con-tented', says Jonson in his summary of the play's action (The Argument, 128), but the audience unfortunately was not. In his

---

[2] Herford and Simpson, ix. 190, 240.

dedication to the text of the play published in 1631 Jonson refers in wounded tones to the way in which the piece was performed and received, and to the audience's temerity in 'rising between the Actes, in oblique lines'.[3] The boldness of Jonson's design in *The New Inn* has found admirers in recent years, and a stage revival has shown the play to be a stronger and more touching piece than had once been recognized.[4] The ending of the comedy is the product of Jonson's enterprise, not of his declining powers. But Jonson is (with justification) nervous about these late experiments in comic resolution. The critical discussions between Damplay, Probee, and the Boy in *The Magnetic Lady* are strategically placed by Jonson *between the acts*, at those most vulnerable of moments when an audience might rise, ominously, in oblique lines, and head for home. And it is before the busy fifth act that they are peremptorily told, in a speech ostensibly addressed to Damplay, to stay in their seats, for the best is yet to come.

'This last Act is best of all', claims the dramatist Mr Bayes in the Duke of Buckingham's burlesque play, *The Rehearsal*, brandishing the manuscript of his new drama; but when the players, having worked through the first four acts in rehearsal, have read the argument of his fifth act, they decide they have seen and done quite enough already, and that it is now high time to go off to dinner. Mr Bayes vows to take his revenge both upon the players and upon the town, 'for I'l Lampoon 'em all. And since they will not admit of my Plays, they shall know what a Satyrist I am. And so farewell to this Stage, I gad, for ever.'[5] Buckingham did not intend Mr Bayes as a humorous portrait of Ben Jonson, but had *The Rehearsal* been written in 1629 and not (as it was) in 1675, Mr Bayes might well have been seen as the disappointed author of *The New Inn*. In remembering Jonson's prodigious and unrivalled skills as a contriver of dramatic plot, it is salutary also to recall that those skills at times, to Jonson's own bewilderment and distress, appear to have outrun the capacities and tolerance of his audiences.

---

[3] Cf. Jonson's scathing reference to 'the *Faeces*, or grounds of your people, that sit in the oblique caves and wedges of your house', *The Magnetic Lady*, Induction, 32–3. The word 'oblique' usually carries a negative charge in Jonson's writing: in *Sejanus*, Cremutius Cordus is accused of libelling Tiberius 'By oblique glance of his licentious pen' (III. 404). In Ovid, *Metamorphoses*, ii. 787, the figure of Envy looks *obliquo*, askance; cf. Jonson, *The Underwood*, 73. 2, *Ungathered Verse*, 2. 7.

[4] See esp. Anne Barton's *Ben Jonson: Dramatist* (Cambridge, 1984), ch. 11.

[5] George Villiers, Duke of Buckingham, *The Rehearsal*, ed. Edward Arber, The English Reprints (1868).

Jonson's late comedies, with their romancy accidents and en-counters, unions and reunions, have suggestively been described in recent years as 'Shakespearian'.[6] Yet the term is apt only up to a point. For Shakespeare—even the Shakespeare of *Cymbeline*—seldom cheats and perplexes his audiences as Jonson does: seldom plots for victory. His narrative style is more casual, more loosely woven, than Jonson's, and the outcome of his plays is generally more predictable. Coleridge in 1813 noted as the first of 'The Character-istics of Shakespeare' the encouragement of 'Expectation in prefer-ence to surprize'.[7] With his relatively open and lucid comic plots, Shakespeare can afford to take certain liberties towards the end, cut-ting across the corners once the final destination is in view.

Jonson's openness is of quite another kind. He characteristically chooses to present himself as a person who is direct and fully know-able, his motives and actions 'all so cleare, and led by reasons flame' (*The Underwood*, 47. 69). He is explicit about the details of his own stagecraft, ready to open the back of the clock and show the cogs in motion, as in the choruses to *The Magnetic Lady*. Yet what he dis-plays at the moment just examined is, paradoxically, his love of mys-tery, of shifting his narrative in deceptive, fox-like ways. These contradictory habits of revealing and concealing, of direction and indirection, are central to Jonson's creative temperament. One part of Jonson seems to have yearned for openness and simplicity, while another was stimulated by concealment and complexity.

The consequent strain is at times apparent. In lines written for the marriage in December 1613 of King James's favourite Robert Carr, Earl of Somerset, and the divorced Countess of Essex (for example), which Jonson prudently decided not to include in any of his poetic collections, he speaks of those who 'weare true wedding robes, and are true freindes / That bid, God give thee joy, and have no endes' (*Ungathered Verse*, 18. 5–6). 'No endes': that is to say, no ulterior motives, nothing that lies behind or beyond that simple wish, 'God give thee joy'. 'No endes' glances at, and quickly away from, the sinister circumstances of the marriage, and the uneasy nature of the current courtly well-wishing. Carr's friend Sir Thomas Overbury, who opposed this match, had been dispatched to the Tower by Carr's own contrivance earlier in the year, and there poisoned, by the

---

[6] Barton, *Ben Jonson*, ch. 12.
[7] *Shakespearean Criticism*, ed. T. M. Raysor, 2 vols. (1960), i. 199.

countess's contrivance, a few months later. There were many tangled ends in this whole unpleasant affair, and the true facts of the case were at this stage far from clear, even, it would seem, to Jonson himself. The motives of those who appeared (as he did) to rejoice over the union may not have been entirely above suspicion. Jonson's bland benediction fleetingly recognizes this truth, which it attempts simultaneously to stabilize and simplify; he deliberately chooses not to explore those very complexities which, in the theatre, would fully have engaged his imagination.[8]

For Jonson's dramas are deeply concerned with hidden 'endes' of precisely the kind that peeped out at the Somerset wedding. To think of the actions of Brainworm and Mosca and Face and Subtle, Sejanus and Tiberius and Macro and Catiline, Zeal-of-the-Land Busy and Sir Paul Eitherside is to think at once (and again) of duplicity, and the immense fascination which this held for Jonson. Such characters, like the artist who created them, are notable plotters. Their aims and motives are concealed; their moral designs, like the narrative designs of Jonson himself, move deviously, mysteriously, unpredictably towards unknown ends. The great plots of Jonsonian comedy thus serve as metaphors and models of the mental, psychological, and moral state of the characters who inhabit them. This correspondence is most strikingly evident in Jonson's greatest comedy, *Volpone*.

❧

To each of the clients who visits his master's house in Venice, Mosca professes in turn a different aim, a different end, always insisting that his true function is to serve his client's ends. 'I would not doe that thing might crosse / Your ends, on whom I have my whole dependance, sir', he says to Corvino (II. vi. 40–1). He tells Bonario that his father Corbaccio is planning to disinherit him, adding that he proffers such information not out of self-interest

> but, as
> I claime an interest in the generall state
> Of goodnesse, and true vertue, which I heare
> T'abound in you: and, for which mere respect,
> Without a second ayme, sir, I have done it.
>
> (III. ii. 46–50)

---

[8] On the Overbury affair, see Ch. 8, and n. 13.

Mosca assures Voltore that he works wholly in his interests: 'My only ayme was, to dig you a fortune / Out of these two old rotten sepulchers' (III. ix. 38–9). 'You see, sir, how I worke / Unto your ends', he says confidingly to the lawyer later in the play (IV. vi. 91–2); and, turning at once to Lady Would-be, 'My purpose is, to urge / My patron to reforme his will . . . you shall be now / Put in the first' (IV. vi. 96–7, 99–100).

Clients and tricksters alike speak solemnly in this play of their purposes, aims, ends, and speculate constantly about the purposes, aims, ends of others. Voltore in the courtroom alleges that Corbaccio's 'setled purpose' was to disinherit his son, Bonario; that Bonario's 'purpose' in entering Volpone's house was therefore to murder Corbaccio, and 'to stop / His fathers ends' (IV. v. 64, 72, 88–9). Later Voltore will confess to the court that he himself gave false evidence to the court 'out of most covetous endes' (V. x. 9). This is most certainly true, but Voltore's 'ends' in making the confession are as devious and as covetous as they were before. And Sir Politic Would-be, ever one to copy Venetian fashions and reduce them to absurdity, declares, 'I should be loath to draw the subtill ayre / Of such a place, without my thousand aymes' (IV. i. 66–7).

The play thus returns insistently to questions of motivation and intent, to the gap between what is said and what is purposed. This is classic Jonsonian territory, already explored in masterly fashion in *Sejanus*: 'the space, the space / Between the breast and lips' (III. 96–8). The broader humour of the play derives from the obvious and farcical 'space' between the professions and intentions of the legacy hunters. But the conduct and ultimate aims of Volpone and Mosca themselves are altogether more mysterious, forming a metaphysical and narrative puzzle at the centre of the play. What are these two men, collectively and individually, really after? How far can each perceive the other's ends? What (if anything) lies *beyond* the space in which they delight to play? Take this moment, for example, from the first act of the play, as Mosca and Volpone await the arrival of the clients. Voltore's knock is heard.

VOLPONE My caps my caps good MOSCA, fetch him in.
MOSCA Stay, sir, your ointment for your eyes.
VOLPONE   That's true;
   Dispatch, dispatch: I long to have possession
   Of my new present.

MOSCA   That, and thousands more,
    I hope, to see you lord of.
VOLPONE   Thankes, kind MOSCA.
MOSCA And that, when I am lost in blended dust,
    And hundred such, as I am, in succession—
VOLPONE Nay, that were too much, MOSCA.
MOSCA   You shall live,
    Still, to delude these *harpyies*.
VOLPONE   Loving MOSCA . . .
                              (I. ii. 114–22)

Mosca and Volpone are acting here partly in collusion, sharing private jokes (picturing their victims as harpies) and a common excitement about the game they are about to play with Voltore. But
Mosca's comically inflated language suggests that something rather
more, and less, than shared play-acting is afoot: for Mosca is of
course flattering Volpone in much the same manner in which he will
flatter Voltore. He sees himself as no more than one of Volpone's
many possessions, one in an unending line of sycophantic servants; a
'hundred such' will in turn succeed Mosca 'when I am lost in blended
dust'. Volpone himself, in Mosca's superlative figure of flattery, will
never die, but 'live, Still, to delude these *harpyies*', as he evidently
will delude death itself. Though Volpone is drawn to mild disclaimer
('Nay, that were too much, MOSCA'), the prospect none the less delights him: 'Loving MOSCA!'. Volpone is easily persuaded to imagine
himself going on for ever; so deeply addictive are the games in which
he is engaged that he cannot imagine they will ever cease. As the
comedy will progressively reveal, Volpone has no single goal, merely
the obsession to keep playing: an impulse that is reflected in the
structure of the play itself, which keeps moving towards closure, then
breaking out again.
    Volpone's temperament is like that of Catiline, whose insatiable
ambition knows no limit, no place to stop:

> That restlesse ill, that still doth build
>   Upon successe; and ends not in aspiring:
> But there begins. And ne'er is fill'd,
>   While ought remaines that seemes but worth desiring.
>
>   (*Catiline*, Chorus after Act III, 864–7)

Such a mind-set distorts perception, enlarging what is far off, re-
ducing what is near at hand:

> Wherein the thought, unlike the eye
>   To which things farre, seeme smaller then they are,
> Deemes all contentment plac'd on high:
>   And thinkes there's nothing great, but what is farre.
>
> (868–71)

Such distortions and obstructions of vision are a central preoccupation in *Volpone*. What can be seen, what lies hidden? Absorbed in future prospects, Volpone fails to observe that 'loving MOSCA' is not
loving at all. Like others in the play, he fails to notice what goes on
under his nose. Corvino, watching his wife like a hawk, nevertheless
contrives to lead her to the bed of the very man who wants to seduce
her. Sir Politic Would-be, preaching to his companion Peregrine the
supreme necessity of noting everything that goes on around him,
sees plots and conspiracies in the most innocent of everyday transactions, yet fails to penetrate the real plots that are played out before
his very eyes. Corbaccio, 'Old glazen-eyes' (v. iii. 25), can, in a literal
sense, barely see the world around him, but his fellow legacy-hunters
are scarcely more perceptive than he. Gold, as Jonson had written
some years previously, 'strikes the quickest-sighted Judgement
blinde' (*Ungathered Verse*, 3, 'Riches', 16). 'Too much light blinds
'hem, I thinke', says Mosca later in the play,

> Each of 'hem
> Is so possest, and stuft with his owne hopes,
> That any thing, unto the contrary,
> Never so true, or never so apparent,
> Never so palpable, they will resist it—
>
> (v. ii. 23–7)

Volpone perceives the general truth of this statement, but misses its
possible application to himself. 'Loving MOSCA!': even as Volpone
utters these words, Mosca himself, in a perfectly timed piece of theatrical business, is applying unguents to Volpone's eyes, to make it
appear that Volpone's eyesight is failing: 'mine eyes are bad',
Volpone will murmur as Voltore approaches (I. iii. 17).

   While we as spectators are allowed to see more clearly than the
characters within the play, it is essential to Jonson's narrative
method, and to the nature of the world he projects, that we cannot
see everything. Dryden described this method accurately:

If then the parts are managed so regularly that the beauty of the whole be
kept entire, and that the variety become not a perplexed and confused mass

of accidents, you will find it infinitely pleasing to be led in a labyrinth of design, where you see some of your way before you, yet discern not the end till
you arrive at it.[9]

The unknown 'end' here is at once narrative and motivational.
Watching Jonson's plays, it may be difficult to perceive not merely
how they will conclude, but why certain characters act in the way
they do: the designs of both are partly hidden. The responses of the
Avocatori to the complex fabrications of the conspirators in the
Scrutineo later in *Volpone* are a heightened version of the bewilderment which the spectators of the play itself may feel as the complex
plot twists this way and that: 'This same's a labyrinth!'; 'What maze
is this!; 'These be strange turnes!'; 'This is subtler, yet!' (V. x. 42, V.
xii. 43, IV. v. 59, V. xii. 47).

❧

In the second act of the play an altogether new drama is unfolding in
a corner of the piazza. The English traveller Sir Politic Would-be and
his new acquaintance Peregrine watch this drama, and puzzle over its
significance. What is this little performance about? What are the
motives of this seeming mountebank, and what is his ultimate end?
Sir Politic, with his genius for spotting duplicity everywhere, is
(ironically) now wholly entranced, taking the supposed Scoto of
Mantua at his own eloquent word. Peregrine is sceptical, but his
scepticism, as it happens, is equally misplaced. They listen, each
with his own convictions, to Volpone's patter.

VOLPONE *And gentlemen, honorable gentlemen, know, that for this time,
our banke, being thus remov'd from the clamours of the* canaglia, *shall
be the* scene *of pleasure, and delight: For, I Have nothing to sell, little or
nothing to sell.*

SIR POLITIC I told you, sir, his end.

PEREGRINE   You did so, sir.

VOLPONE *I protest, I, and my sixe servants, are not able to make of this
precious liquor, so fast, as it is fetch'd away from my lodging, by gentlemen of your city; strangers of the* terra-firma; *worshipfull merchants; I,
and senators too: who, ever since my arrivall, have detayned me to their
uses, by their splendidous liberalities. And worthily. For what availes*

---

9 'Of Dramatic Poesy: An Essay' (1668), in John Dryden, *Of Dramatic Poesy and Other
Critical Essays*, ed. George Watson, 2 vols. (1962), i. 61.

your rich man to have his magazines *stuft with* moscadelli, *or of the purest grape, when his physitians prescribe him (on paine of death) to drinke nothing but water, cocted with* anise-seeds? *O, health! health! the blessing of the rich! the riches of the poore! who can buy thee at too deare a rate, since there is no enjoying this world, without thee? Be not then so sparing of your purses, honorable gentlemen, as to abridge the naturall course of life—*

PEREGRINE You see his end?

SIR POLITIC   I, is't not good?

(II. ii. 69–89)

VOLPONE *And gentlemen, honourable gentlemen, I will undertake (by vertue of chymicall art) out of the honourable hat, that covers your head, to extract the foure elements: that is to say, the fire, ayre, water, and earth, and return you your felt without burne, or staine. For, whil'st others have beene at the* balloo, *I have beene at my booke: and am now past the craggie pathes of studie, and come to the flowrie plaines of honour, and reputation.*

SIR POLITIC I do assure you, sir, that is his ayme.

VOLPONE *But, to our price.*

PEREGRINE   And that withall, sir POL.

(II. ii. 163–72)

'You see his end?' asks Peregrine caustically, implying that it is the crowd's money that Scoto is really after; 'I, is't not good?', remarks Sir Politic innocently, concentrating upon Scoto's apparent concern for the physical well-being of the general public, and the general truth of the adage that health is worth more than riches. But neither Peregrine nor Sir Politic can really see Volpone's 'end'. The man who has been seen in Act I handling diamonds and silver plate is not really interested in the small change of the Venetian riff-raff. For this is not really, as Peregrine suspects, a charlatan, but a charlatan charlatan, a man playing the part of a man playing the part of an honest man, urging the crowd as he does to beware of cheap imitations—for '*very many have assay'd, like apes in imitation of that, which is really and essentially in mee, to make of this oyle*' (II. ii. 149–50). Volpone is not out to make money this time, but rather to catch a glimpse of Corvino's wife Celia, and it is for this 'end' that the elaborate charade has been set up in the street outside Corvino's house.

Yet it is not clear that Volpone is in complete command of the situation. There is a suspicion that the entire show has been organized by Mosca for an 'end' of his own. This is the first time in the play that Volpone has been lured out of the safety of his own house and into

the street; it is the first move in the 'fox trap' that will spring on
Volpone in Act V, leaving Mosca in possession of the keys, the house,
and the goods of his master. Celia is in fact partly a creation of
Mosca's, conjured up at the end of Act I by the power of language.
Mosca has been talking of the dreaded Lady Would-be, who 'hath
not yet the face, to be dishonest', and casually adds:

> But had she signior CORVINO's wives face—
> VOLPONE Has she so rare a face?
> MOSCA   O, sir, the wonder,
> The blazing star of *Italie*! a wench.
> O' the first yeere! a beautie, ripe, as harvest!
> Whose skin is whiter then a swan, all over!
> The silver, snow, or lillies! a soft lip,
> Would tempt you to eternitie of kissing!
> And flesh, that melteth, in the touch, to bloud!
> Bright as your gold! and lovely, as your gold!
> VOLPONE Why had I not knowne this, before?
> MOSCA   Alas, sir.
> My selfe, but yesterday, discover'd it.
> VOLPONE How might I see her?
> MOSCA   O, not possible;
> Shee's kept as warily, as is your gold:
> Never do's come abroad, never takes ayre,
> But at a windore. All her lookes are sweet,
> As the first grapes, or cherries: and are watch'd
> As neere, as they are.
> VOLPONE   I must see her—
> MOSCA   Sir.
> There is a guard, of ten spies thick, upon her;
> All his whole houshold: each of which is set
> Upon his fellow, and have all their charge,
> When he goes out, when he comes in, examin'd.
> VOLPONE I will goe see her, though but at her windore.
> MOSCA In some disguise, then.
> VOLPONE   That is true. I must
> Maintayne mine own shape, still, the same: we'll thinke.

> (I. v. 105–29)

Volpone falls in love with the description of Celia before he ever sees
her. Mosca figures Celia's beauty as 'sweet / As the first grapes, or
cherries', words that may recall Volpone's own description a little
earlier in the play of his manner of luring his victims on,

> still bearing them in hand
> Letting the cherry knock against their lips,
> And, draw it, by their mouths, and back againe.
>
> (I. i. 88–90)

Celia is now such a cherry, knocking against Volpone's mouth; Mosca is now controlling, now playing with, his master—improvising, elaborating, tempting—just as his master has played with the legacy-hunters. Thus it is not merely for Volpone's sake but for a further 'end' of Mosca's own contriving that the scene outside Celia's house is being staged.

What is it about Celia that so excites Volpone? It does not seem to be simply a matter of her physical desirability. What appears to arouse Volpone is rather the thought that Celia is so difficult of access; that he will need to exercise all his ingenuity, all his skills of deception and intrigue, to obtain her. He does not really want her, as they say, 'for herself', for he has no inkling of what her selfhood might consist in; nor could he be said to want her for, or with, himself, either. And what kind of self does he eventually offer her? When in the third act of the play Volpone contrives to have Celia led to his bedroom and left alone with him, he tells her nothing about himself other than that he delights in escaping from self. He claims no constancy and singleness of purpose, describing instead his reputation as an actor and the 'severall shapes' and 'varying figures' he has adopted for her sake (III. vii. 148, 152). What he offers Celia is the promise of incessant, vertiginous change, of continual self-projection into feigned and alien identity, running through and wearying 'all the fables of the gods'.

> Then will I have thee in more moderne formes,
> Attired like some sprightly dame of *France*,
> Brave *Tuscan* lady, or proud *Spanish* beauty;
> Sometimes, unto the *Persian Sophies* wife;
> Or the grand-*Signiors* mistresse; and, for change,
> To one of our most art-full courtizans,
> Or some quick *Negro*, or cold *Russian*;
> And I will meet thee, in as many shapes:
> Where we may, so, trans-fuse our wandring soules,
> Out at our lippes, and score up summes of pleasures.
>
> *That the curious shall not know,*
> *How to tell them, as they flow;*

> *And the envious, when they find*
> *What their number is, be pind.*

                              (III. vii. 226–39)

The number of lovers' pleasures, like the number of guises, is seen by
Volpone as infinite; despite the Catullan note of warning in his earlier song (*'Time will not be ours, for ever'*), he sees no end to this
mode of dalliance and courtship, just as he has seen no end to his
acquisition of riches.

>   Yet, I glory
>   More in the cunning purchase of my wealth,
>   Then in the glad possession

Volpone has said earlier in the play (I. i. 30–2), and the glad possession of Celia seems to be of secondary interest to him once he has her
in the bedroom. So preoccupied is Volpone by reverie, fantasy, and
song, by his imagining of other, hypothetical encounters with Celia
tricked out as other women, that the present opportunity for a real
encounter with her somehow eludes him. For this reason, the long
scene between them in the third act may seem, in a sense, to be curiously unthreatening.

'You see his end?' Such a seemingly simple question doesn't admit
of an easy answer. For Volpone is not just intent upon amassing
wealth, or luring Celia into his bed, or achieving any other such
clearly definable goal. It is the process, not the end, that fascinates
him: the infinite and exhilarating play of possibility. Mosca's private
purposes may be more sharply defined, but to an audience—as to his
master—these purposes are still not visible. This is Dryden's
labyrinth, where 'you see some of your way before you, yet discern
not the end till you arrive at it'.

                              ⧈

Labyrinths are traditionally associated with another and different
figure which Jonson often uses to describe his plots: the manipulation of a thread.[10] 'A good *Play*', observes the Boy in *The Magnetic
Lady*, 'is like a skeene of silke: which, if you take by the right end, you
may wind off, at pleasure, on the bottome, or card of your discourse,

---

[10]   Cf. *Discoveries*, 1997–9; *Epigrams*, 95. 15–16; *The New Inn*, IV. iv. 9.

in a tale or so; how you will: But if you will light on the wrong end, you will pull all into a knot, or elfe-locke; which nothing but the sheers, or a candle will undoe, or separate' (Induction, 136–41). By the end of the fourth act, Damplay, unsure whether he dislikes this play because its plot is too obvious or too obscure, finds the piece 'almost pucker'd, and pull'd into that knot, by your Poet, which I cannot easily, with all the strength of my imagination, untie'. 'Like enough', responds the Boy, 'nor is it in your office to be troubled or perplexed with it, but to sit still, and expect. The more your imagination busies it selfe, the more it is intangled, especially if . . . you happen on the wrong end' (Chorus after Act IV, 2–9). Knotting and plotting often come together in Jonson's imagination. Early in *Volpone*, Mosca tells the advocate Voltore that his master admires the ability of lawyers to 'make knots, and undoe them' (I. iii. 57), and many of the complications of the play's subsequent action are due indeed to the skilful ravellings and unravellings of Volpone, Mosca, and Voltore. 'The knot is now undone, by miracle!' exclaims the first Avocatore at the play's final denouement (v. xii. 95).

In *Volpone* Jonson creates a number of 'wrong ends', moments when the action of the play seems about to conclude, then unexpectedly moves off in another direction; threads that appear to lead us out of the labyrinth, but terminate simply in a knot. Dryden, while praising Jonson's supreme skill in dramatic plotting, was uneasy about this aspect of *Volpone*. The plots of *The Alchemist* and *The Silent Woman* seemed to Dryden superlatively contrived; yet he found the plot of *Volpone* not quite perfect: 'for there appear to be two actions in the play; the first naturally ending with the fourth act; the second forc'd from it in the fifth'.[11] Just when the comedy seems to reach its natural conclusion, the action starts up all over again. At the end of the fourth act of the play, in a bold defence to the charge of attempted rape, Volpone has been carried into the Venetian courtroom in the guise of a man at the very point of death, too frail and impotent even to have threatened the act of which he stands accused: Mosca daringly invites the court to apply its instruments of torture to the dying man to see if this frailty is a sham. The move is brilliantly successful: the Avocatori are fooled, the charges against Volpone are dismissed, the innocent Bonario and Celia are brought under condemnation, and Volpone's fraudulent status as a dying man is

---

[11] 'Of Dramatic Poesy', i. 61.

legitimated. Stephen Greenblatt has described this turn of events as constituting the 'false ending' of Volpone, and suggested that Jonson is here employing a structural device that can be paralleled in other plays of the period.[12]

At the beginning of the fifth act Volpone is discovered at home, oddly shaken by his latest victory in the Scrutineo; confronting, as Greenblatt suggestively remarks, a kind of existential void, a moment at which he has no more roles to assume, when his very sense of selfhood is thus paradoxically threatened; for what Volpone *is* seemingly depends upon the games he plays.

> Well, I am here; and all this brunt is past.
> I ne're was in dislike with my disguise,
> Till this fled moment; here, 'twas good, in private,
> But in your publike, *Cave*, whil'st I breathe.

> (v. i. 1–4)

'Breathe', from exertion and lack of exertion; make a pause, and quicken into life again: for Volpone has been playing the part of a man who is almost at his last breath. And the play itself momentarily breathes, pauses, for this is the furthest reach of Volpone's and Mosca's audacity.

Jonson's dramatic endings, Lawrence Danson has argued, are intimately connected to his concept of selfhood and self-discovery. His endings differ from Shakespeare's, just as his characters differ. Shakespearian comedy often culminates in the characters' understanding and acceptance of new relationships and new departures, while Jonson's comedy frequently ends with their exposure, punishment, and deflation. The characters themselves, as well as the plays they inhabit, seem suddenly and strangely to stop. Wholly dependent upon the social relationships they maintain and the frauds or affectations they practise, they find, once unmasked, that there is literally nowhere to go. Jonson may bring his characters 'out of their humor', but cannot describe them beyond that point, 'for out of their humor they cease to exist'.[13] At the opening of the fifth act, Volpone is at the brink of such a metaphysical collapse, triggered not from without

---

[12] 'The False Ending in *Volpone*', *Journal of English and Germanic Philology*, 75 (1976), 90–104.

[13] Lawrence Danson, 'Jonsonian Comedy and the Discovery of the Social Self', *PMLA: Publications of the Modern Language Association*, 99 (1984), 179–93.

but within, by his and Mosca's own ambitious, heart-stopping con-
trivances.

MOSCA   We must, here, be fixt;
  Here, we must rest; this is our master-peece:
  We cannot thinke, to goe beyond this.

(V. ii. 12–14)

Yet neither Volpone nor Mosca can 'rest' or 'be fixt' even at their
most triumphant moments. 'Nay, wee so insist in imitating others, as
wee cannot (when it is necessary) returne to our selves', Jonson
wrote in *Discoveries*.[14] Neither Volpone nor Mosca now has a self to
return to, to rest or be fixed in; they can only move forward, and the
play accordingly moves forward with them. Like the children in
Cocteau's *Les Enfants terribles*, daring each other to perform ever
more hazardous and more public thefts, Mosca and Volpone urge
each other to take one more step, defy each other not to enjoy the
risks that they are deliberately running. 'You are not taken with it,
enough, me thinkes?' Mosca remarks, catching the weariness in
Volpone's voice as they discuss their latest coup; and Volpone attempts to rally:

  O, more, then if I had enjoy'd the wench:
  The pleasure of all woman-kind's not like it.

(V. ii. 10–11)

'It'—an 'it' which lies at the very centre of the play—is the art of impersonation and deception: an art which for Volpone and Mosca is
more thrilling than sex itself. This *it* is the ultimate end for which
Volpone plays.
  'How now, sir?', Mosca has asked at his entry in this scene,

          do's the day looke cleare againe?
  Are we recover'd? and wrought out of error,
  Into our way? to see our path, before us?

(V. ii. 1–3)

The notion of a true moral pathway which Mosca ironically invokes
at this moment has both classical and biblical precedent, which
serves merely to point up the waywardness, the mysteriousness, of

---

[14] Lines 1093–9; see Ch. 3 above.

the 'path' which Mosca and Volpone are now choosing to follow.[15] What path lies before them? How clear *is* the day? How far into the labyrinth can they see? For *Volpone* the play is to end not at this moment but in the courtroom, where the Avocatori will administer harsh penalties to the tricksters and their collaborating victims, in a bizarre sequence of events which neither the characters nor we as audience anticipate. And in this strange final movement to the piece, as Dryden remarked, 'the poet gained the end he aimed at, the punishment of vice, and the reward of virtue'.[16] In his Epistle addressed to the Universities of Oxford and Cambridge prefixed to the 1607 quarto edition of *Volpone*, Jonson himself spoke of this, his ultimate 'end' or 'ayme' in writing the comedy, a moral end more important to him than the formal end traditionally associated with comedy. 'Doctrine', wrote Jonson, 'is the principall end of *poesie*, to inform men, in the best reason of living'.

And though my catastrophe *may, in the strict rigour of* comick *law, meet with censure, as turning back to my promise; I desire the learned, and charitable critick to have so much faith in me, to think it was done off industrie: For, with what ease I could have varied it, neerer his scale (but that I feare to boast my owne faculty) I could here insert. But my special ayme being to put the snaffle in their mouths, that crie out, we never punish vice in our enter-ludes, &c. I tooke the more liberty . . .*   (108–17)

It is significant perhaps that Jonson's explanation of his own moral and formal ends in writing Volpone is itself *fixed* in the full authority and stability of the printed text, in an epistle addressed 'to the learned and charitable critick' at the universities of Oxford and Cambridge, and strategically placed at the very beginning of the 1607 quarto. In the theatre, the restive or ignorant playgoer might, like Damplay, seize on 'the wrong end' of the comedy, failing to observe its larger narrative and moral design; failing, perhaps, even to stay in the playhouse until its conclusion.

[15] The biblical concept of the true and narrow pathway is also found in much classical writing. Jonson returns frequently to the idea. Cf. Knowell in *Every Man In His Humour* (folio), II. v. 42–3. 'This is one path! but there are millions more / In which we spoile our owne with leading them' (remembering Juvenal, *Satires*, xiv. 36–7); Busy in *Bartholomew Fair*, III. ii. 26, 'So, walke on in the middle way', etc. (deviously invoking Matt. 7: 14: 'strait is the gate and narrow is the way'); *Epigrams*, 119, 'To Sir Ralph Sheldon': 'That to the vulgar canst thy selfe apply, / Treading a better path, not contrary; / And, in their errors maze, thine owne way know' (varying Seneca, *Epistles*, v. 3); *The Forest*, 13, on Lady Aubigny, who lives 'Farre from the maze of custome, error, strife', and those who 'cannot see / Right, the right way' (60, 67–8): echoing Seneca, *Epistles*, xxiii. 7–8.
[16] 'Of Dramatic Poesy', i. 61.

Some readers have felt the ending of *Volpone* to be excessive, as if Jonson were turning punitively against an impulse in his own creative nature, attempting forcibly to resolve some final, wavering irresolution in his own attitude towards the play's two major characters.[17] It is as though—to pick up terms used in an earlier chapter—the gathered self had decided to teach the loose self some ultimate lesson, fixing it finally to the floor:

> Thou art to lie in prison, crampt with irons,
> Till thou bee'st sicke, and lame indeed.

> (v. xii. 123–4)

All of the play's principal characters are either incarcerated or firmly *sent home*.[18] The comedy concludes, notoriously, with no reconciliations, no sudden fortunes, no marriages and no betrothals, no feasts or dances or reunions or lovers' meetings. Celia is formally parted from her husband Corvino, and—to Coleridge's distress[19]—she and Bonario go their different ways.

Is this bilking of comedic expectation, this final swerve towards loss, solitude, separation, itself artistically a loss, a 'wrong end' for the play to have taken? I think not. The fascination of the ending, like that of the play's overall plotting, lies precisely in its unforeseeability. What cannot be foreseen at the end of the play is more than particular twists and turns of plot: it is the startling manner in which the play in the last act jumps the comic boundaries altogether, and enters alien territory. Yeats recognized the power and singularity of this last movement of the play when he saw *Volpone* in performance in 1921. '*Volpone* was even finer than I expected', he wrote to the producer, Allan Wade,

I could think of nothing else for hours after I left the theatre. The great surprise to me was the pathos of the two young people, united not in love but in innocence, and going in the end their separate way. The pathos was so much greater because their suffering was an accident, neither sought nor noticed by the impersonal greed that caused it.[20]

---

[17] See esp. S. L. Goldberg, 'Folly into Crime: The Catastrophe of *Volpone*', *Modern Language Quarterly*, 20 (1959), 233–42. John Creaser defends the ending of the play in the introduction to his edition of *Volpone* in the London Medieval and Renaissance series (1978).

[18] See Ch. 5 above.

[19] Coleridge, *Literary Remains*, 1836, quoted in Jonas A. Barish (ed.), '*Volpone*': A *Casebook* (1972), 51.

[20] *The Letters of W. B. Yeats*, ed. Allan Wade (1954), 665.

Shortly before his death Yeats discussed Jonson's play again. Attempting to explain his antipathy to a modern play which 'displayed a series of base actions without anything to show that the author disapproved or expected us to do so', Yeats turned by way of contrast to *Volpone*, arguing this time that the ending of the play carried not only an affective but a moral force:

The wicked should be punished, the innocent rewarded, marriage bells sound for no evil man, unless an author calls his characters before a more private tribunal and has so much intellect and culture that we respect it as though it were our own. In Jonson's 'Volpone', one of the greatest satiric comedies, Volpone goes to his doom but innocence is not rewarded, the young people who have gone through so much suffering together leave in the end for their fathers' houses with no hint of marriage, and this excites us because it makes us share in Jonson's cold implacability. His tribunal is private, that of Shakespeare public.[21]

'Public' in the sense that Shakespeare was ready to comply with the larger generic expectations and conventions of the popular theatre and its audiences, writing 'as you like it'. Jonson went his own unpredictable way, following his own more sombre notions of dramatic propriety, judging his own plays first, and allowing others to judge, if they wished, after him. As he wrote significantly of another, earlier piece: 'By (G——), 'tis good, and if you like't, you may' (*Cynthia's Revels*, Epilogue, 20).

[21] W. B. Yeats, *On the Boiler* (Dublin, 1939), 32–3.

8

Politic Picklocks
Reading Jonson Historically

A CENTRAL problem in the methodology of both the new and 'old' historicism turns on the nature of the link that is assumed to exist between historical description and literary interpretation. The monolithic accounts of Elizabethan systems of belief assembled by so-called old historicists such as E. M. W. Tillyard (it is common these days to complain) often seem quite at variance with the diverse and at times rebellious energies of the literary texts which they are apparently devised to illuminate. Even in the work of a more sophisticated old historicist such as L. C. Knights the supposedly related activities of historical and literary investigation seem often to tug in contrary directions. The divergence is apparent, for example, in the very structure of Knights's influential study, *Drama and Society in the Age of Jonson*, the first half of which offers a stolid, Tawney-derived historical account of economic conditions in England during the late Elizabethan, early Jacobean period (entitled 'The Background'), while the second half ('The Dramatists') advances livelier readings of the work of individual authors. The connections here between foreground and 'background', text and context, 'drama' and 'society', literature and history are quite loosely articulated and theoretically undeveloped.[1] A disjunction of a different kind is often evident in the work of a new historicist such as Stephen Greenblatt, as he turns from a closely worked meditation upon a particular and highly intriguing historical incident—often quirky in nature, but assumed also to be in some way exemplary—to ponder the particularities of a literary text. The transition is generally athletic and exhilarating in its unexpectedness: a leap from the

---

[1] *Drama and Society in the Age of Jonson* (1937). For a more detailed analysis of the methodologies of this book see Don E. Wayne, '*Drama and Society in the Age of Jonson*: An Alternative View', in Leonard Barkan (ed.), *Renaissance Drama*, vol. xiii (Evanston, 1982), 103–29.

historical platform across a void to the literary cross-bar, upon which further agile feats are soon to be performed. This is a thoroughly postmodern manœuvre, challenging precisely on account of its discontinuity, undertaken as coolly as flipping across the television channels, defying (though not perhaps wholly obliterating) old-fashioned expectations of argumentative sequentiality.[2]

Can 'history' and 'literature' as interpretative processes ever be more closely aligned, more logically interdependent, less bumpily discontinuous? There is another, even older, kind of historicism which maintains they can be, positing a relationship between history and literature which is as intimate and necessary as that of the key to the lock. The art practised in this school was known in the seventeenth century as *application*: the interpretation of literary texts with detailed reference to the social and political events of the times to which, it is supposed, they cryptically yet provably refer. The work of Ben Jonson, more densely topical and allusive than that of Shakespeare, is particularly seductive to interpretation of this kind. Those who have tried to 'apply' characters and incidents in Jonson's dramatic writing to real-life characters and incidents of his day, however, have not always succeeded in persuading others of the plausibility of their conjectures. I want to review both the attractions and the risks of this kind of approach to Jonson's writing: an approach which broadly assumes the existence of a one-to-one relationship between historical events and characters and their dramatic counterparts, and uses history as a tool to burgle the supposedly hidden meaning of the text, to pick the locks of literature. I shall then propose a rather different way in which the relationship of 'history' and 'literature' might be viewed, and Jonson's work be read historically.

❧

In *Jonson's Romish Plot* (1967) B. N. De Luna argued that Ben Jonson's tragedy of *Catiline*, performed and published in 1611, was a veiled allegory or (as she termed it) 'classical parallelograph' of recent events in England; and that in Jonson's drama about the Catilinarian conspiracy of 65 BC the discerning Jacobean spectator would have detected a series of detailed allusions to the conspiracy

---

[2] For a recent critique of new historicist (and cultural materialist) methodologies, see Graham Bradshaw, *Misrepresentations: Shakespeare and the Materialists* (1993).

of Guy Fawkes and his followers to blow up the English Houses of Parliament with gunpowder in November 1605. De Luna's 'parallelograph' is quite elaborately worked out. She believes that the character of Gabinius Cimber in Jonson's play represents Guy Fawkes, that Catiline represents Fawkes's fellow conspirator Robert Catesby, that the character of Cicero represents Sir Robert Cecil, that Cato stands for Sir Edward Coke, Quintus Curius for Ben Jonson himself, and so on.[3] The book was sceptically reviewed in the learned journals, and privately regarded by many readers as a madcap venture, doomed to take its place eventually on the dustier library shelves alongside such works as *The Great Cryptogram* and *Did the Jesuits Write Shakespeare?*

Jonson's Romish Plot might perhaps have been differently received had the book been published in the mid 1990s rather than the late 1960s, now that the work of Annabel Patterson, Richard Dutton, Janet Clare, Richard Burt, and others has enlarged our understanding of the operation of Renaissance theatrical censorship, and the way in which plays of this period may often consequently be interpreted.[4] In 1967 De Luna's book looked too speculative and chancy to please traditional scholars, and was a complete non-starter for the new critics, challenging as it did the assumed autonomy of the literary text. De Luna regarded Jonson's work not as a self-sufficient, well-wrought artefact but as a kind of transparent screen, fully comprehensible only when looked *through* as well as *at*, pondered in relation to a set of historical events—or, to be precise, two sets of historical events—which had prompted its composition. Her notion of the parallelograph invited the reader's mind to run simultaneously on twin tracks not simply in relation to Rome and England, or to ancient and modern political conspiracies, but—more radically and disturbingly—in relation to text and context, without determining the primacy of the one over the other. This was not at the time a popular line to take.

[3] B. N. De Luna, *Jonson's Romish Plot: A Study of 'Catiline' and its Historical Context* (Oxford, 1967).

[4] Annabel Patterson, *Censorship and Interpretation: The Conditions of Writing and Reading in Early Modern England* (Madison, Wis., 1984); Richard Dutton, *Mastering the Revels: The Regulation and Censorship of English Renaissance Drama* (Basingstoke, 1991); Janet Clare, *'Art Made Tongue-Tied by Authority': Elizabethan and Jacobean Dramatic Censorship* (Manchester, 1990); Richard Burt, *Licensed by Authority: Ben Jonson and the Discourses of Censorship* (Ithaca, 1993). See also Jerzy Limon, *Dangerous Matter: English Drama and Politics in 1623/24* (Cambridge, 1986).

The pronouncements soon to arrive from Paris about the death of the author and the pleasure of the text did nothing during the immediately subsequent years to make this kind of interpretative position more congenial. Barthes and his colleagues in France, like earlier proponents of the new criticism in England and America, were reacting against precisely that kind of intensive historical scholarship which De Luna's book appeared to represent: scholarship that implied that the text could not be enjoyed without the possession of anterior knowledge which seemed to ramify endlessly away into the circumstantial detail of social, political, and domestic history.

Yet there is nothing intrinsically absurd or disreputable (it seems possible now to insist) about De Luna's general wish to bring biographical and historical knowledge to the understanding of a literary text. If much recent theory has discountenanced this practice, it may be partly in reaction to the methodologies of an earlier generation of scholars who worked quite speculatively in the middle ground between history, biography, and literature, with generally simplistic notions about the nature of literary representation. In the more Conan Doylish of these studies, literature is regarded as if it were the scene of some recent large-scale crime, littered with clues—fingerprints, bloodstains, dropped wallets, spent bullets—all capable of undergoing forensic examination, and of supporting some Holmesian hunch which might ultimately lead to the apprehension of a culprit, the narration of a real-life story more absorbing than the fictional one which had lightly covered it. 'Many of the old plays written prior to the outbreak of the Civil War', declared one scholar in 1931, 'seem greatly to resemble the modern detective story, because, to understand them, it becomes necessary to follow up the clues—more or less obvious—they give.'[5]

Here is a typical example of this sort of investigative scholarship, with its chasing up of more or less obvious clues, from a somewhat earlier period. Robert Cartwright's *Shakespere and Jonson: Dramatic, versus Wit-Combats*, published in 1864, is premised on the assumption that some kind of violent quarrel took place between Shakespeare and Jonson, provoked by Jonson, who persistently ignored Shakespeare's repeated attempts at reconciliation. The evidence for this imagined falling-out was to be found, so Cartwright

---

[5] W. Landsdown Goldsworthy, *Ben Jonson and the First Folio* (1931), preface.

believed, within the plays which the two dramatists wrote, which indeed appear in his account to be concerned with practically nothing
else. Each dramatist, according to Cartwright, wrote obsessively
about the other. Jonson depicted Shakespeare as Ovid in *Poetaster*,
as Fungoso in *Every Man Out of His Humour*, as Stephen and
Wellbred both in *Every Man In His Humour*, as Sir Politic Would-be
and Volpone in *Volpone*, and Sejanus in *Sejanus*, as Sir John Daw in
The Silent Woman, as Sir Epicure Mammon and also as Dapper
in *The Alchemist*, as Littlewit in *Bartholomew Fair*, as Fitzdottrel in
The Devil is an Ass, as Fly in *The New Inn*, and in other roles besides.
Shakespeare meanwhile depicted Jonson as Apemantus in *Timon of
Athens*, as Don John in *Much Ado About Nothing*, as Oliver in *As
You Like It*, as Aguecheek in *Twelfth Night*, as Edmund in *King Lear*,
as Aufidius in *Coriolanus*, and as Autolycus in *The Winter's Tale*. All
of these characters of Shakespeare's *were* Ben Jonson, just as all of
Jonson's characters *were* William Shakespeare: that was their simple
representational function, their ultimate ontological and dramatic
status. So exciting does the hunt for identification become that
Cartwright fails to confront the possibility that Sir Andrew
Aguecheek may actually not *represent* anyone at all, but simply *be*
Sir Andrew Aguecheek.

Though B. N. De Luna's revelations are less startling than Robert
Cartwright's, her procedures seem based at times on disconcertingly
similar assumptions about the nature of dramatic representation.
Her investigations occasionally have an obsessive air, and at times
she presses the evidence further than it can reasonably be taken. Yet
her book presents much evidence that, in a general sense, is still compelling, while her larger thesis cannot lightly be dismissed. What
then is to be made of such a work?

Jonson himself would strongly have disliked its manner of approach, but then Jonson's dislike for such readings of his work itself
repays analysis. 'Application, is now, growne a trade with many', he
wrote caustically in the Epistle Dedicatory to *Volpone*,

*and there are, that professe to have a key for the decyphering of every thing:
but let wise and noble persons take heed how they bee too credulous, or give
leave to these invading interpreters, to be overfamiliar with their fames, who
cunningly, and often, utter their owne virulent malice, under other mens
simplest meanings.* (65–70)

From early plays such as *Cynthia's Revels* through to late work such
as *The Magnetic Lady*, Jonson consistently attacked what he called

'the solemne vice of interpretation, that deformes the figure of many a fair *Scene*, by drawing it awry' (*The Magnetic Lady*, Chorus after Act II, 34–5). In the Articles of Agreement that are formally drawn up between the author and the audience in the Induction to *Bartholomew Fair*, Jonson inserted a crucial clause:

it is finally agreed, by the foresaid hearers, and *spectators*, that they neyther in themselves conceale, nor suffer by them to be concealed any *State-decipherer*, or politique *Picklocke* of the *Scene*, so solemnly ridiculous, as to search out, who was meant by the *Ginger-bread-woman*, who by the *Hobby-horse-man*, who by the *Costard-monger*, nay, who by their *Wares*. Or that will pretend to affirme (on his owne *inspired ignorance*) what *Mirror of Magistrates* is meant by the *Justice*, what *great-Lady* by the *Pigge-woman*, what *conceal'd States-man*, by the *Seller* of *Mouse-trappes*, and so of the rest. But that such person, or persons so found, be left discovered to the mercy of the *Author*, as a forfeiture to the *Stage*, and your laughter, aforesaid. (135–48)

Does Jonson protest over-much? It is worth remembering that several of his closest friends (John Selden, Hugh Holland, Sir Henry Goodyere, John Donne) had suspected that the character of Lantern Leatherhead in *Bartholomew Fair*—originally called, it would seem, 'Inigo Lantern'—was a satirical portrait of Inigo Jones. The character of Justice Adam Overdo in the same play has been shown to be closely based on that of a former Lord Mayor of London, Thomas Middleton, and to incorporate characteristics of two contemporary pamphleteers, Richard Johnson and George Whetstone. The cut-purse scene in Act III of the play recalls the exploits of a real-life cutpurse named John Selman who had been executed just two years before the play's original performance. The relationship between the incorrigible Bartholomew Cokes and his irascible 'governor' Humphrey Wasp has been plausibly compared with that of the high-spirited son of Sir Walter Ralegh and his tutor in France—none other than Jonson himself.[6] Jonson's plays constantly shadow and invoke real-life characters and events in this manner, and it does not seem logically implausible or methodologically inconsistent that major

---

[6]   On Lantern Leatherhead and Inigo Jones, see Herford and Simpson, ii. 146–8, x. 213; David Riggs, *Ben Jonson: A Life* (Cambridge, Mass., 1989), 193 ff.; R. C. Bald, *John Donne: A Life* (Oxford, 1970), 197. On Overdo, Middleton, *et al.*, see David McPherson, 'The Origins of Overdo', *Modern Language Quarterly*, 37 (1976), 221–33; on Selman, see Herford and Simpson, x. 200; on Ralegh and Jonson, see *Conversations with Drummond*, 295–305, and Herford and Simpson, xi. 141–2. See also William W. E. Slights, *Ben Jonson and the Art of Secrecy* (Toronto, 1994), ch. 7.

political characters, events, and controversies of the day should also therefore be glanced at in his drama.[7] In the privacy of Hawthornden in 1618/19 Jonson freely admitted to William Drummond that he and Marston had represented each other's characters on stage during the so-called War of the Theatres.[8] Jonson's frequent pose of wounded innocence, of bitter incredulity that 'invading interpreters' should trace connections between the events and people of his plays and those of the world in which he lived, does not sit easily with his actual dramatic practice, and needs itself to be subjected to more measured interpretation.

Jonson had every reason to be sensitive on these matters, having been brought repeatedly before the civil authorities for suspected libellous or treasonable references in his plays. He had been committed to the Marshelsea prison for his part in the now lost play, *The Isle of Dogs*, which he had written with Thomas Nashe; he had been summoned before the Lord Chief Justice to answer questions about *Poetaster*, and before the Privy Council on charges concerning *Sejanus*. He was imprisoned along with Marston and Chapman on account of their jointly written comedy *Eastward Ho!* which had made fun of royal policies and Scottish accents, and he was to have further skirmishes with the law over *The Devil is an Ass* and *The Magnetic Lady*. In *Poetaster* Jonson alludes to the practice of 'sinister application' which has led to trouble of this sort, and to the 'false lapwing cries' of informers and misinterpreters of his work.[9] But Jonson's many protestations on this theme must themselves be understood as lapwing cries, deliberate attempts to divert attention from what he is actually up to.

Yet the question of interpretation is not easy. While Jonson repeatedly protests that he 'flies from all particularities in persons', that he taxes 'vices generally', he may well be speaking the truth: there were not only prudential reasons for avoiding topicality and mere one-to-one literalism in his writing, but good artistic reasons too, strengthened by classical precedent.[10] Nevertheless, during his

---

[7] James Tulip, 'Comedy as Equivocation: An Approach to the Reference of *Volpone*', *Southern Review*, 5 (1972), 91–101, and Richard Dutton, *Ben Jonson: To the First Folio* (Cambridge, 1983), ch. 6, have independently suggested that in the character of Sir Politic Would-be Jonson may be glancing at Sir Robert Cecil.

[8] *Conversations with Drummond*, 284–6.

[9] *Poetaster*, V. iii. 124, IV. vii. 50.

[10] Thus Martial declares it his aim 'to spare the person, to denounce the vice' (*parcere personis, dicere de vitiis*), X. xxxiii. 10. Cf. Jonson, *Poetaster*, Apologetical Dialogue, 71–2;

twelve years living as a Catholic under strict Protestant surveillance Jonson had also become very familiar with numerous rhetorical strategies of self-defence.[11] Though he protested his love of honesty, though he was always keen to maintain the terms on which the interpretation of his work should proceed, his own statements about the tendencies of that work cannot always be accepted at their face value.

⁓⁕⁓

If Jonson's untrustworthiness in these matters creates one sort of problem for would-be interpreters of his work, another and perhaps more intriguing problem arises at times in relation to chronology. A number of passages in his work look very much as if they are meant to refer to contemporary figures and events, but a calculation of the relevant dates appears to make such an interpretation impossible. The difficulties that arise here may shed some light on what is amiss with the simple one-to-one representational model of historical explication just discussed.

Here is an example of the kind of problem I have in mind. In the final act of Jonson's comedy *The Silent Woman*, the misogynistic, noise-hating Morose despairingly attempts to secure a divorce from the woman he has just misguidedly married—who turns out in the concluding moments of the play to be no woman at all, but a boy in disguise. The barber Cutbeard, dressed as a canon lawyer, and Captain Otter, dressed as a divine, learnedly discuss the possibilities of Morose's obtaining a divorce, larding their discussion with numerous Latin tags. Labouring through eleven possible grounds for divorce, they arrive at last at the twelfth and final cause, *si forte coire nequibus* ('if it chances that you are unable to have a sexual relationship').

OTTER I, that is *impedimentum gravissimum*. It doth utterly annull, and annihilate, that. If you have *manifestam frigiditatem*, you are well, sir.

(v. iii. 171–3)

Discoveries, 2304 ff.; Dedication of *Epigrams* to William, Earl of Pembroke; and in particular the discussion between Probee, Damplay, and the Boy in the Chorus following Act II of *The Magnetic Lady*. See further Edward B. Partridge, 'Jonson's *Epigrammes*: The Named and the Nameless', *Studies in the Literary Imagination*, 6 (1973), 153–98.

[11] See Ch. 4 above.

Seeing this as a path of escape from his troubles, Morose makes a momentous announcement to his wife and the assembled company of women.

MOROSE I am no man, ladies.

ALL How!

MOROSE Utterly un-abled in nature, by reason of *frigidity*, to performe the duties, or any the least office of a husband. . . .

EPICOENE Tut, a device, a device, this, it smells rankly, ladies. A mere comment of his owne.

TRUEWIT Why, if you suspect that, ladies, you may have him search'd.

DAW As the custome is, by a jurie of physitians. . . .

MOROSE O me, must I under-goe that!

MISTRESS OTTER No, let women search him, madame: we can do it our selves.

(V. iv. 44–7, 52–6, 58–60)

In his annotation to the play, Jonson's nineteenth-century editor William Gifford commented as follows on the exchange between Cutbeard and Captain Otter:

It is scarcely possible to read this humorous discussion without adverting to one of a serious kind, which took place on the divorce of the Lord Essex. If it were not ascertained beyond a doubt that the *Silent Woman* appeared on the stage in 1609, four years at least prior to the date of that most infamous transaction, it would be difficult to persuade the reader that a strong burlesque of it was not here intended. The bishops Neal and Andrews [who were involved in the Essex divorce proceedings] are the very counterparts of Otter and Cutbeard; nor does Morose himself display more anxiety for the fortunate termination of his extraordinary suit than the credulous and ever-meddling James exhibited on that occasion for the success of his unworthy favourite.[12]

In 1606 Frances Howard, the 13-year-old daughter of the Earl of Suffolk, was married to the Earl of Essex, who was then aged 15. Jonson wrote a masque, *Hymenaei*, to celebrate the occasion. It was agreed that the marriage would not be consummated until the couple were of age. Straight after the marriage Essex was sent off on foreign travels and did not return until 1609. He was coolly received by his bride, who had by this time fallen in love with James's latest favourite, Robert Carr. In 1613 she sued for divorce from Essex on the grounds that he was impotent and unable to consummate the marriage. The case was tried before two commissioners appointed by

[12] *The Works of Ben Jonson*, ed. William Gifford, 9 vols. (1816), note to *Epicoene*, V. i.

James, and when they divided evenly he appointed two more commissioners who could be depended upon to provide the desired result. Frances Howard was examined by a panel of four ladies and two midwives who finally attested to her virginity, though there was a widespread rumour at the time that another young gentlewoman had been substituted for the Countess of Essex when these tests were made. Thomas Overbury, who had advised Robert Carr not to proceed with this whole affair, was removed to the Tower apparently at Carr's instigation, and subsequently poisoned, apparently at the instigation of Frances Howard. Robert Carr and Frances Howard were married in December 1613, and Jonson—a friend of Overbury, but almost certainly unaware of the precise cause of his recent death— wrote *A Challenge at Tilt* and *An Irish Masque* to be performed on this occasion, along with a poem of congratulation addressed to Robert Carr, now newly created Earl of Somerset.[13]

Can the scene between Otter and Cutbeard in *The Silent Woman* have anything to do with this extraordinary affair? For a start, the dates, as Gifford recognized, simply do not fit. *The Silent Woman* was performed in December 1609 or January 1610. The earliest extant text, however, is that of the 1616 folio, and one scholar has gone so far as to argue that the play was reworked some time between 1613 and 1616 in order to incorporate what he calls 'hilarious parodies of the grim history of Frances Howard, Countess of Essex, Countess of Somerset'.[14] This seems highly implausible. To begin with, Jonson himself clearly declares that the play has not been revised, and does not contain personal allusions.

> For he knowes, *Poet* never credit gain'd
>   By writing truths, but things (like truths) well fain'd.
> If any, yet, will (with particular slight
>   Of application) wrest what he doth write;
> And that he meant or him, or her, will say:
>   They make a libell, which he made a play.
>
> (Second Prologue, 9–14)[15]

---

[13] See Ch. 7 above; William McElwee, *The Murder of Sir Thomas Overbury* (New York, 1952); Beatrice White, *Cast of Ravens* (1965); David Lindley, *The Trials of Frances Howard: Fact and Fiction at the Court of King James* (1993); *Ungathered Verse*, 18.

[14] Thomas Kranidas, 'Possible Revisions or Additions in Jonson's *Epicoene*', *Anglia*, 83 (1965), 451–3.

[15] 'There is not a line, or syllable in it changed from the simplicity of the first Copy', Jonson declares in his dedication of *The Silent Woman* to Sir Francis Stewart.

This prologue, as a side-note reveals, was 'Occasion'd by some persons impertinent exception' to the comedy, which had already run into trouble with the authorities on account of a passage which was thought to refer slightingly to James I's cousin, Lady Arbella Stuart.[16] Perhaps the denials of the prologue, then, can be dismissed as mere foxing on Jonson's part, to cover his self-incriminating tracks. But it is scarcely credible that Jonson would then have dared or wished to insert further highly dangerous references into the published text of a play which had already caused him problems enough, especially when the text was to form part of the 1616 folio, to which Jonson attached such high value. The scholar who advances the theory about a late revision of *The Silent Woman* never confronts this larger issue, nor does he observe how deeply the notion of impotence is woven into the play as a whole, nor speculate how the play might originally have concluded before these alleged revisions occurred. His single aim is to establish a one-to-one correspondence, a precise parodic allusion.

What one can safely say is that by the time *The Silent Woman* was published in 1616 the scene between Otter and Cutbeard would in all likelihood have reminded readers of the recent Essex divorce case, taking on at this moment a novel layer of contemporary significance. Annabel Patterson has argued in a similar way that by the mid-1620s Jonson's tragedy *Sejanus*, first performed in 1603, must have *looked as if* it were referring to the fall of James's favourite George Villiers, Duke of Buckingham, who was not, however, impeached until 1626; and that Jonson's poem on Ralegh's *History of the World*, written in 1614, must likewise have acquired a new and deeper meaning when read in the knowledge of Ralegh's execution four years later. Such topicality is acquired, so to speak, retrospectively, through the simple passage of time.[17]

This is a familiar process, of which I can give a recent example. Visiting China in 1990 when the memory of the events in Tiananmen Square was still fresh, I was taken to see a performance of Lao She's play *Teahouse* at the Beijing People's Art Theatre. The play was officially approved as a politically orthodox classic of the 1950s in which the author, as the programme note curiously declared, 'condemns and buries three crucial periods in China's recent history, and

---

[16] Herford and Simpson, v. 144–7.
[17] Patterson, *Censorship and Interpretation*, 57–66, 134–52.

transpires his hopes and loves for the new society of which he was an active and ardent participant'. The piece had developed a new and contrary significance, however, as a result of the recent events in Beijing, as the audience was quick to recognize. It follows the fortunes of a group of teahouse proprietors and *habitués* from 1898 and the last days of the Ching dynasty ('they can't last much longer'—loud applause) through to the Kuaonmintang years, where the same spies are operating ('we serve whoever is in authority'—laughter) to the post-World War II period, when students appear on stage wounded after street clashes with the military. At this extraordinary moment in the performance, the theatre exploded with cheers and whistles. Despite official pronouncements to the contrary, the audience of 1990 knew very well what this play was really about.[18]

For plays to be capable of undergoing topical reactivation of this kind, there must be (I suggest) some significant general similarity of historical circumstance between the time of original composition and that of subsequent performance, such that a new event or series of events can trigger a new moment of recognition and identification. The continuities may at times relate to social structures and practice. The fact that impotence and failure to consummate a marriage formed one of the major, and very few available, grounds for divorce in early modern England is probably of greater usefulness to an understanding of the final act of *The Silent Woman*, for example, than the particular details of the Essex divorce scandal.[19]

The continuities may (again) be political: a certain kind of regime, a certain variety of repression or method of surveillance prompting, initially, a fictional response, and later a real-life episode which (not surprisingly) resembles it. The Gunpowder Plot was not a unique event within Jonson's lifetime: almost every year of the final decade of Elizabeth's reign and of the first decade of James's reign had brought to light a political conspiracy of one kind or another, and the Catilinarian conspiracy could serve as an archetype for almost

---

[18] In a similar way Voltaire's tragedy of *Brutus*, not perceived as greatly relevant to the times when first presented in 1730, caused great excitement when revived in Paris by the Comédie Française on 17 November 1790, recent events in the city having invested its theme with a startling topicality. See Robert L. Herbert, *David, Voltaire, 'Brutus', and the French Revolution* (1972).

[19] Lawrence Stone, *The Road to Divorce: England 1530–1987* (Oxford, 1992), 191; id., *The Family, Sex, and Marriage in England 1500–1800* (1977), 37 and 691 n. 49 (on the long-standing custom of female juries testing the virginity of wives in cases of alleged non-consummation).

any of them. Jonson could scarcely have failed to observe the general similarities that existed between the Gunpowder Plot and that of Catiline and his followers, but that does not imply that he meant to depict the former with any kind of precision in the tragedy of *Catiline*. Until quite recently it was believed that Jonson's *Sejanus* ran into trouble with the authorities because the fall of Sejanus was seen to reflect upon the fall of Elizabeth's favourite, the Earl of Essex. Philip Ayres has, however, now argued that Jonson's troubles with the Privy Council had nothing whatever to do with Essex, whose fall by 1603 was already ancient history; but that the story of Sejanus might instead have been linked with the trial earlier in 1603 of Sir Walter Ralegh, who had been accused and found guilty of conspiring, in the cause of Spain, to murder James I, and of taking Spanish bribes.[20] By the 1620s, as already noted, that archetype could be applied equally well to the fall of Buckingham, and indeed the parallel between Buckingham and Sejanus was invoked by Sir John Eliot during the impeachment proceedings in the House of Commons.[21] These were, in short, the kind of times in which Ben Jonson lived, and the kind of events which recurred within them, lending his plays on occasions a greater measure of adventitious topicality than he might, or could possibly, ever have intended.

∻

The link between Jonson's imaginative writing and the events of his personal life has prompted similar speculation over the years, the practice of 'application' persisting surprisingly into (and beyond) the age of deconstruction. Alvin B. Kernan in an ingenious reading of Act II, Scene ii of *Volpone* some years ago pointed to a series of resemblances between the life of the mountebank Scoto of Mantua and that of Jonson himself, suggesting that 'under the cover of

---

[20] Philip Ayres, 'Jonson, Northampton, and the "Treason" in *Sejanus*', *Modern Philology*, 80 (1983), 356–63, and introduction to his Revels edition of *Sejanus His Fall* (Manchester, 1990), 16–22. Ayres's contention that Essex's rebellion 'was not a burning issue' when *Sejanus* was first performed is, however, questionable: in 1604 Daniel's tragedy *Philotas* was judged by the Privy Council 'to be a reflection of the dangerous matter of the dead Earl of Essex'. 'Shortly they will play me in what forms they list upon the stage', Essex himself had predicted to Elizabeth four years earlier. See C. J. Sisson, *Lost Plays of Shakespeare's Age* (Cambridge, 1936), 3; Dutton, *Mastering the Revels*, ch. 7. and (on problems arising from dating the original performance of *Sejanus* early in 1603), 11–12.

[21] Patterson, *Censorship and Interpretation*, 64–5.

16th-century Venice, Jonson is talking about 17th-century London and his own life as a playwright', and his arguments have been accepted unquestioningly by most (though not all) subsequent editors of the play.[22] David Riggs in his recent biography of Jonson extends Kernan's reading, going on to propose a number of other correspondences between the dramatist and his own characters.[23] These proposals stand in stark contrast to recent formalist theories which minimize the significance of such links between author and text. Is there a middle path between these contrasting interpretative practices; a way of reading that is at once more sceptical and more tenacious in assessing the possible impact of the particular events of Jonson's life upon his imaginative writing?

Consider, for example, the first (quarto) version of *Every Man In His Humour* (performed in 1598): how, if at all, does this comedy reflect the known and presumed experiences of Jonson's early life? David Riggs reads the play as romantic autobiography, taking Young Lorenzo to be the *alter ego* of Jonson himself, with whom Lorenzo shares a love of poetry and of amorous adventuring. Many years later, Riggs recalls, Jonson was to confess to William Drummond that he had enjoyed adulterous escapades in his youth. 'Is it mere coincidence', Riggs asks, 'that the sexual comedy in *Every Man in His Humour* revolves around a jealous merchant who believes that Jonson's poet–hero is having an affair with his wife?'

Although the act of adultery never occurs in the play, it pervades the fantasy life both of the paranoid husband and of Young Lorenzo's suspicious father. Indeed, these characters become so preoccupied with Young Lorenzo's supposed philandering that he is able to elope with the merchant's sister-in-law. The illicit wishes that had formerly led Jonson to commit adultery were satisfied on a vicarious level in his comedy of 1598. His alter ego reduces the merchant to the status of a cuckold, wins his independence from his father, and carries off the bride of his choice, yet remains a paragon of bland rationality throughout the play.[24]

But it would be just as plausible to maintain that the braggart captain Bobadilla was Jonson's *alter ego* in the play—as perhaps in a sense he was. For the 1598 version of the comedy clearly reflects in a humorous, tangential way the experiences of a young man who had

[22] *Volpone*, ed. Alvin B. Kernan, The Yale Ben Jonson (New Haven, 1962), 214–16. For a sceptical view of this equation, see John Creaser's edition of *Volpone* in the London Mediaeval and Renaissance series (1978), 231–2.

[23] *Ben Jonson*, 137 ff., 102, 304 ff., and *passim*.   [24] Ibid. 44.

seen military service in the Low Countries. The clever servant Musco disguises himself as an old soldier who boasts about former campaigns, offering to show his scars in return for money, and to sell his rapier. Jonson was to ridicule this type of bogus veteran again in *Poetaster*, and to defend himself against the sensitive charge of libelling the military by reminding his readers that he too had once belonged to that 'great profession', 'And did not shame it with my actions, then'.[25]

One of Jonson's more distinguished 'actions' is bizarrely and fleetingly recalled in the fantasies of the blustering Bobadilla. Bobadilla devises an imaginative scheme to save money and lives by challenging the enemy, in the company of nineteen other like-minded swordsmen, to a series of single combats which, in a mere 200 days, would swiftly demolish all of the adversary's forces. Twenty years later, gossiping at Hawthornden, Jonson was to report to William Drummond that 'In his servuce in the Low Countries, he had in the face of both the Campes Killed ane Enimie & taken opima spolia from him' (*Conversations with Drummond*, 244–6). To resolve a battle through the single combat of chosen champions was a known but rare practice in this period. In 1567 there was a proposal that Bothwell, as Mary Stewart's champion, might fight single-handed at Carberry against one of the confederate lords, and in 1591 the Earl of Essex challenged Villars, head of the beseiged garrison at Rouen, to a similarly decisive single combat. Neither of these fights in the end took place. Less high-ranking officers and even privates were at times, however, permitted to fight in this manner: thus Jonson might have pursued his personal engagement in the Netherlands, for which presumably he was a ready volunteer. Was Jonson, in Bobadilla's preposterous fantasy of slaughtering an entire enemy one by one in single combat with the help of nineteen like-minded champions, consciously recalling in an amused, burlesque manner his own moment of personal triumph in the Low Countries just a few years earlier?[26]

---

[25] *Poetaster*, Apologetical Dialogue, 136–7; *Epigrams*, 108. 6–7.

[26] On the custom of single combatants fighting on behalf of their contesting armies, see V. G. Kiernan, *The Duel in European History: Honour and the Reign of Aristocracy* (Oxford, 1988), 58–9. Dekker, in his address 'To the World' (18–21) prefixed to *Satiromastix* (1602), refers to Horace–Jonson making himself believe '*that his* Burgonian *wit might desperately challenge all commers, and that none durst take up the foyles against him*'. The reference, according to Cyrus Hoy, is to John Barrose, the Burgonian fencer who came to England and challenged all the fencers of England, and 'was hanged without

Much dramatic material no doubt derives, directly or indirectly, from personal experiences and encounters of this general kind, but in tracing the possible links between life and art it is important also to notice the transformations, reductions, and enlargements that art—especially comic art—achieves, and the obstacles that stand in the way of such direct, one-to-one identifications. Bobadilla, of course, is no hero; though much preoccupied with military schemes and the exercise of a bed-staff, he is alarmed when challenged by Giuliana and asked to draw his weapon, protesting pathetically that he has been bound to keep the peace, and later explaining to his companions that '(by heaven) sure I was strooke with a Plannet then, for I had no power to touch my weapon' (v. ii. 125–6). In *Every Man In His Humour* Jonson creates a charmed and comic world in which hurts are constantly threatened yet never finally inflicted; in which weapons stick in their scabbards, and cannot be drawn; or are flourished, as by Doctor Clement over Musco in the final act of the play, yet never descend.

CLEMENT . . . so come on sir varlet, I must cut of your legges sirha; nay
    stand up, ile use you kindly; I must cut of your legges I say.
MUSCO Oh good sir I beseech you, nay good maister doctor, oh good sir.
CLEMENT I must do it; there is no remedie;
    I must cut of your legges sirha.
    I must cut of your eares, you rascall I must do it;
    I must cut of your nose, I must cut of your head.

(v. iii. 103–11)

No part of the body is cut, no blood is ever spilt in *Every Man In His Humour*, a comedy which 'sport[s] with humane follies, not with crimes', never crossing—in the manner of *Volpone*—into the world of graver transgressions and harsher penalties.[27]

Speaking many years later to William Drummond about the ill-fated comedy *Eastward Ho!*, Jonson recalled that its authors, Chapman, Marston, and he, had all been imprisoned, and 'the report was that they should then had their ears cutt & noses', but these

Ludgate, for killing an officer of the Cities which had arrested him for debt, such was his desperatenesse, and brought such reward as might be an example to other the like' (John Stow, *Annales* (1605), 1308), July 1598: *Introductions, Notes, and Commentaries to Texts in Fredson Bowers' Edition of 'The Dramatic Works of Thomas Dekker'*, ed. Cyrus Hoy, 4 vols. (Cambridge, 1982), i. 201–2. But the reference is also to Jonson's own combativeness, which is here ironically conflated, it would seem, with that of Bobadilla.

[27] *Every Man In His Humour* (folio), Prologue, 24.

threats were never fulfilled. It would be tempting to see this episode reflected in the final scene of *Every Man In His Humour*. That of course is impossible, for the episode which Jonson reported to Drummond occurred eight years after the original staging of *Every Man In His Humour*. The resemblances between life and art are (again) quite general and fortuitous. However exceptional the threats may seem to modern readers, physical mutilation was a common juridical penalty of the day, as Jonson knew all too well.[28]

Yet art and life were to perform a curious dance for Jonson in the period immediately following *Every Man In His Humour*. That comedy was first performed in the autumn of 1598 by the Lord Chamberlain's Men at the Curtain Theatre. The first known reference to the play comes in a letter from Tobie Mathew to Dudley Carleton of 20 September 1598. Two days later, on 22 September 1598, Jonson was indicted on a charge of manslaughter for killing a fellow actor named Gabriel Spencer, who was buried on 24 September 1598. The scuffle occurred in a duel, as Jonson later explained to Drummond: 'being appealed to the fields he had Killed his adversarie, which had hurt him in the arme & whose sword was 10 Inches Longer than his, for the which he was Emprisoned and almost at the Gallowes'. Jonson was to escape being hanged through pleading benefit of clergy, but was branded on the thumb for this offence, and bore the mark and the memory of the episode to his grave.[29]

The contrasts here are eloquent. Inside the Curtain Theatre, Bobadilla dodges a duel and saves his skin, while in the fields beyond the theatre his creator accepts a challenge and kills his adversary. In Jonson's comedy, a long sword sweeps innocuously through the air, and is sheathed harmlessly in its scabbard; in the world in which Jonson actually lived, his own short sword strikes home to kill an adversary (an actor trained, no doubt, in swordplay). Justice is dispensed—skittishly, severely—at the end of either episode. Yet any precise connections here are entirely accidental: the dates once again—this time, by a couple of days—make it unthinkable that the comedy in any exact way reflects an incident in Jonson's life. It is the more general connections which are none the less striking, between the kind of world Jonson imagines in this comedy and the kind of

---

[28] *Conversations with Drummond*, 273–7.
[29] Herford and Simpson, i. 181–9, 219–20, ix. 168; *Conversations with Drummond*, 246–9; G. E. Bentley, *The Profession of Dramatist in Shakespeare's Time 1590–1642* (Princeton, 1986), 48–9; and Ch. 12 below.

world in which he actually lived. 'History' does not act upon 'literature' here like a seal upon wax, like a key to a lock. Art and life interfold and overlap in a more complex manner than an older generation of literary detectives believed, yet also more intimately and intricately than much recent theory—and some recent historicist practice—would seemingly allow.

9

The Story of Charis

'A CELEBRATION OF CHARIS IN TEN LYRIC PIECES' (*The Under-wood*, 2) is one of the most attractive and seemingly most accessible of all Ben Jonson's poetic works. Subtle, humorous, enchanting, these often admired lyrics appear at a casual reading to present few problems of exegesis or interpretation. Yet the sequence has provoked sharply divergent readings over recent years. There is continuing disagreement amongst critics about its tone and seriousness, about the contexts—intellectual, historical, and literary—within which it may need to be understood, and even about the main outlines of the narrative which these seemingly simple lyrics unfold.

Part of the problem in reading the 'Charis' poems lies precisely in that tension between their narrative and lyric functions: between a view of the poem as constituting (on the one hand) a single, continuous, and organically related whole—'*the Storie*' which the poet announces in the opening poem—and (on the other hand) ten discrete 'lyric pieces' to be independently savoured and understood. A somewhat similar tension is to be found within the 'ten pieces' on Lady Venetia Digby which make up the sequence 'Eupheme', placed in apparent counter-balance to the 'Charis' poems near the end of *The Underwood* (no. 84) in the 1640–1 folio, and within those larger groups of poems, the *Epigrams* and *The Forest*, in Jonson's 1616 folio.[1] In all of these cases, poems written at different times and for different occasions are lightly but significantly organized within a new structural grouping whose continuities and contiguities encourage subtly different readings from those which the poems might have

---

[1] It is not known whether Jonson himself was entirely responsible for the ordering of the poems in the posthumously published *Underwood*; it is possible that some adjustments to the sequence were made by his executor, Sir Kenelm Digby. On the ordering of the poems in the 1616 folio, see in particular Edward Partridge, 'Jonson's *Epigrammes*: The Named and the Nameless', *Studies in the Literary Imagination*, 6 (1973), 153–98, and Alastair Fowler, 'The *Silva* Tradition in Jonson's *The Forrest*', in Maynard Mack and George deForest Lord (eds.), *Poetic Traditions of the English Renaissance* (New Haven, 1982), 163–80.

attracted in their original literary or social contexts. Jonson's early poetic tributes to Robert, Earl of Salisbury (*Epigrams*, 63, 64)—to take a much-discussed case[2]—are innocuous enough if read as self-contained poems of praise, but that praise is sharply modified if we read them in the carefully organized sequence of *Epigrams* in the 1616 folio, where they are followed by a strategically placed poem 'To My Muse' (*Epigrams*, 65), beginning

> Away, and leave me, thou thing most abhord,
> That hast betray'd me to a worthlesse lord . . .

Jonson's Catullan translation, 'Come, my Celia', seems (likewise) to possess a subtly different character when sung in the third act of *Volpone* by the Magnifico of Venice in the course of his attempt to seduce Corvino's wife Celia, and when recontextualized as the fifth song of *The Forest*, where it is placed in company with a number of poems solemnly addressed to noble ladies. In a similar way, the verses beginning 'Doe but looke on her eyes' have a different flavour when sung during Wittipol's wooing of Frances Fitzdottrel, wife of the doltish Fabian Fitzdottrel, in the second act of *The Devil is an Ass*, and when incorporated into the mythological pageantry of the fourth lyric in 'A Celebration of Charis', and read in relation to the multiple shifts and balances of the sequence as a whole.

'A Celebration of Charis' was probably put together in the 1620s, but some of the lyrics, including the song from *The Devil is an Ass*, were evidently written at various times during the preceding decade.[3] The lyrics are assembled in a seemingly casual fashion, to form a narrative that is continuous yet at the same time intermittent. There are leaps and gaps in the story of Charis, which often moves by

---

[2] B. N. De Luna, *Jonson's Romish Plot: A Study of 'Catiline' and its Historical Context* (Oxford, 1967), 71; Robert C. Evans, *Ben Jonson and the Poetics of Patronage* (Lewisburg, Pa., 1989), ch. 4 n. 5 (pp. 285–6); James A. Riddell, 'The Arrangement of Ben Jonson's *Epigrammes*', *SEL: Studies in English Literature 1500–1900*, 27 (1987), 53–70, esp. 55–6. On this general question see also Richard C. Newton, 'Making Books From Leaves: Poets Become Editors', in Gerald P. Tyson and Sylvia S. Wagonheim (eds.), *Print and Culture in the Renaissance* (Newark, NJ, 1986), 246–64, esp. 257 ff.

[3] Herford and Simpson (xi. 49) reckon the first of the lyrics to have been written in 1623 (a literal reading of 'fifty years'), and the remaining pieces 'after 1612, when Jonson made up his lyrics for *The Forest*, and before 1616, when *The Devil is an Ass*, containing II. 4. 11–30, was acted at the Blackfriars'. Why all of these remaining lyrics had to be completed before the performance of *The Devil is an Ass* the editors do not explain. The seventh lyric was amongst 'the most common place of his repetition' when Jonson visited Drummond in 1618/19: *Conversations with Drummond*, 89, 96–101. The reference to Anne of Denmark's dancing in vi. 28 indicates a date before her death in March 1619.

hints, implications, and seemingly contradictory transitions rather than by the denser and more comprehensive narrative method which Jonson characteristically favours in his plays. The story, which is much concerned with guessing, speculation, and mistaking, must itself be completed by a measure of guesswork on the reader's part: a fact that helps to account for the highly discrepant interpretations which the sequence has attracted in recent years.

And it is only in recent years that much attention has been paid to the nature of this story, or to the structural organization of the sequence as a whole. Historically, 'A Celebration of Charis' was known and enjoyed chiefly on account of its individual lyrics, in particular of 'Her Triumph', which seems always to have been the best-loved poem in the group. Its early popularity is suggested by a number of manuscript versions and variants that survive from the seventeenth century. The song was parodied by Suckling, imitated by Shirley, and later shamelessly appropriated by Garrick for his operatic version of *The Tempest* in 1756: a recontextualization that Jonson himself, with his well-known views on those who beget 'Tales and Tempests', might have viewed a little wryly.[4] It was popular even in the nineteenth century, when Jonson's literary reputation was at its lowest ebb. Hazlitt paused in the midst of his fluent disparagement of Jonson in his *Lectures on the Dramatic Literature of the Age of Elizabeth* in 1820 to express a liking for Jonson's 'detached poetry' and his 'fugitive and lighter pieces', including 'Her Triumph'; though his praise is interestingly tempered by a suspicion that even these lyrics—and in particular the famous song celebrating Charis—are marred by some stubbornly prosaic or unromantic element:

but still often in the happiest of them, there is a specific gravity in the author's pen, that sinks him to the bottom of his subject, though buoyed up for a time with art and painted plumes, and produces a strange mixture of the mechanical and fanciful, of poetry and prose, in his songs and odes. For instance, one of his most airy effusions is the Triumph of his Mistress: yet there are some lines in it that seem inserted almost by way of burlesque.[5]

---

[4] Sir John Suckling, *Non-Dramatic Works*, ed. Thomas Clayton (Oxford, 1971), 29–30; James Shirley, *The Poems, &c* (1646), 9 (once incorrectly ascribed to Thomas Carew: see his *Poems*, ed. Rhodes Dunlap (Oxford, 1949), 197); David Garrick, *Plays*, ed. H. W. Pedicord and F. L. Bergmann, 7 vols. (Carbondale, Ill., 1980–2), iii. 294; 'Tales and Tempests': *Bartholomew Fair*, Induction, 130.

[5] *The Complete Works of William Hazlitt*, ed. P. P. Howe, after the edition of A. R. Waller and Arnold Glover, 21 vols. (1931), vi. 239–40.

About 'His Discourse with Cupid' Hazlitt was more enthusiastic, though he regarded this lyric also as a detached piece rather than as part of a poetic sequence: it 'is infinitely delicate and *piquant*, and without one single blemish', he wrote; 'it is a perfect "nest of spicery" '.[6] The poem is a *nest*, as Venus's breasts are said to be within the lyric itself: a location delightful in, and sufficient to, itself, from which there is no incentive to move. Charles Cowden Clarke in 1871 echoed Hazlitt's description of this lyric ('so exquisite a thing as to have been aptly termed "a nest of spicery" '), and also praised 'Her Triumph': 'Every glee-singer knows those pompous lines, "See the chariot at hand", sounding the glories of his mistress, and which are as sonorous without as with music.'[7] While other lyrics from the sequence enjoyed some popularity during the nineteenth century, it was 'Her Triumph' that established itself as the standard Jonsonian anthology piece in Victorian times (along with 'Drinke to me, onely, with thine eyes' and 'It is not growing like a tree', from the Cary–Morison ode).[8] The lyric has continued to find its way into anthologies right up to the present day, where it can still be read as an example of what Hazlitt called 'detached poetry'.[9] Thus decontextualized, it is thought to achieve what Jonson's Oxford editors describe as a 'romantic note . . . sadly lacking, as a rule, in Jonson's portrayal of love'.[10]

When in the late Victorian period some interest in the narrative and sequential aspects of the 'Charis' poems was at last displayed, it was by scholars intent upon finding a historical explanation for that

[6] Ibid. 241. 'Nest of spicery' is from *Richard III*, IV. iv. 424 (Richard, speaking to Queen Elizabeth about her daughter's womb).

[7] 'On the Comic Writers of England: II—Ben Jonson', *The Gentleman's Magazine* (May 1871), 635.

[8] The seventh lyric was admired by 'Barry Cornwall' (B. W. Procter) in his *Memoir of the Life and Writing of Ben Jonson* (1838), p. xxxix, and by Nathan Drake, *Shakspeare and his Times*, 2 vols. (1817), i. 631. On nineteenth-century anthologies and their part in the formation of Jonson's poetic reputation, see my article, 'Jonson's Ode to Sir Lucius Cary and Sir H. Morison', *Studies in the Literary Imagination*, 6 (1973), 139–52.

[9] 'Her Triumph' was thus anthologized (to give just a few examples) in *English Lyrics* (1883); *The Oxford Book of English Verse 1250–1939*, ed. Sir Arthur Quiller-Couch (Oxford, 1900); *Lyrics from the Dramatists of the Elizabethan Age*, ed. A. H. Bullen (1901); *The Pageant of Poetry* (1916); *English Verse*, ed. W. Peacock, 5 vols. (1929), ii; *Seventeenth-Century Poetry*, ed. John Hayward (1948); *Elizabethan Lyrics*, ed. Norman Ault (New York, 1949); *The Penguin Book of English Verse*, ed. John Hayward (Harmondsworth, 1956); *English Masterpieces*, ed. Leonard Dean, iii: *Renaissance Poetry* (Englewood Cliffs, 1961); *Poets of the Early Seventeenth Century*, ed. Bernard and Elizabeth Davis (1967); *Everyman's Book of English Verse*, ed. John Wain (1981).

[10] Herford and Simpson, xi. 49.

perceived 'romantic note'. 'A Celebration of Charis', like Shakespeare's sonnets and *Astrophil and Stella*, was viewed as an exercise in semi-fictional autobiography; the 'story' that was looked for was a story about Jonson himself. If the poems were scrutinized with sufficient care, it was believed, the thin veil of fiction would fall away, and the historical truth stand revealed. The lover who is dramatized within the Charis sequence is a bearded, 50 year-old poet named 'Ben', a transparent representation, it was assumed, of Jonson himself. Charis was thought to represent some actual lady of the court circle. F. G. Fleay in 1891 suggested that she was Lady Elizabeth Hatton (wife of the jurist Sir Edward Coke), with whom he believed Jonson had had a romantic entanglement commemorated in these lyrics.[11] The fact that one of the lyrics from the Charis sequence had previously appeared in *The Devil is an Ass*, like the fact that phrases and images similar to those found throughout the sequence recur elsewhere in Jonson's work, simply encouraged Fleay to pursue his 'story' more widely, collecting apparently substantiating hints and clues from Jonson's masques, comedies, and other poetic writings. As the search spread, the hypothesis became increasingly attenuated and implausible. In the end, Fleay's biographical speculations turned out to be neither provable nor disprovable; they served simply to distract attention from the dramatic life of the sequence, and the (perhaps entirely fictitious) narrative which it presents.

Over the past thirty years various attempts have been made to find a different sort of narrative, thematic, or methodological coherence in 'A Celebration of Charis'. Paul M. Cubeta, conceivably provoked by the 'nest of spicery' school of appreciation, argued in 1958 that Jonson's poetic purposes in the sequence were largely satirical and parodic. Throughout the ten lyrics, Cubeta suggested, Jonson makes fun of the conventions of Petrarchan love poetry, and also makes fun of himself; in the rare moments when parody is suspended (as briefly in 'Her Triumph'), the tone is still that of 'high comic irony', for Jonson is bent upon exposing Charis in all her 'affection and vanity'. The 'celebration' of Charis is thus akin to Pope's 'celebration' of Belinda in *The Rape of the Lock*, being deeply undermined by irony.[12] G. J. Weinberger was later to extend this reading, suggesting that the entire sequence, including 'Her Triumph', was to be

---

[11] *A Biographical Chronicle of the English Drama 1559–1642*, 2 vols. (1891), i. 324–5.
[12] ' "A Celebration of Charis": An Evaluation of Jonsonian Poetic Strategy', *ELH: A Journal of English Literary History*, 25 (1958), 163–80.

interpreted as a mock-encomium of a lady undeserving of such high estimation.[13] Wesley Trimpi in 1962 offered a very different interpretation, arguing that the poems should be seen not as humorous anti-Petrarchan exercises but as more serious explorations of the nature of love and beauty and the good life, modelled upon Neoplatonic *discorsi*. Trimpi viewed Charis herself not as an object of satire but as a lady of intelligence and discernment, sturdy enough to tease her poetic admirer, but not unworthy of the adulation he offers. Charis's description of the ideal lover in the ninth lyric, Trimpi argued, enshrines courtly and ethical notions which Jonson himself would have admired. Such irony as can be found in the sequence, he argued, is not at Charis's expense; it turns rather on the fact that Charis, in stating her preference for an ideal young courtier, thereby rejects the uncourtly, middle-aged poet who is most ardent to possess her.[14] Richard S. Peterson, viewing the sequence in yet another light, denied that Charis *does* reject the poet, arguing that the final lines of the ninth lyric ('But of one, if short he came, / I can rest me where I am') imply Charis's recognition that her ideal lover is unattainable, and that she will stay instead with the poet. Peterson argued that Jonson in these lyrics is reworking the theme of pleasure reconciled to virtue, which he had treated in his court masque of 1618. At the outset of the sequence, the lady seems bent upon virtue, while the poet is pursuing pleasure, but finally they strike a happy compromise.[15]

Most of these interpretations, in attempting to relate the 'Charis' poems to a learned or poetic tradition, seem in danger of running their theses a little hard, and missing what is perhaps the most attractive feature of the sequence: its extraordinary flexibility and

[13] 'Jonson's Mock-Encomiastic "Celebration of Charis" ', *Genre*, 4 (1971), 305–28.

[14] *Ben Jonson's Poems: A Study of the Plain Style* (Stanford, 1962), 210–27.

[15] 'Virtue Reconciled to Pleasure: Jonson's "A Celebration of Charis" ', *Studies in the Literary Imagination*, 6 (1973), 219–68. Peterson's interpretation of the significance of the closing lines in the ninth lyric has been independently supported by Anne Ferry, *All in War With Time: Love Poetry of Shakespeare, Donne, Jonson, Marvell* (Cambridge, Mass., 1975), 162. For other accounts of the sequence see Sara van den Berg, 'The Play of Wit and Love: Demetrius *On Style* and Jonson's "A Celebration of Charis" ', *ELH: A Journal of English Literary History*, 41 (1974), 26–36; S. P. Zitner, 'The Revenge on Charis', in G. R. Hibbard (ed.), *The Elizabethan Theatre*, vol. iv (1974), 127–42; R. V. Leclercq, 'The Reciprocal Harmony of Jonson's "A Celebration of Charis" ', *Texas Studies in Language and Literature*, 16 (1975), 627–50; and Raymond B. Waddington, ' "A Celebration of Charis": Socratic Lover and Silenic Speaker', in Claude J. Summers and Ted-Larry Pebworthy (eds.), *Classic and Cavalier: Essays on Jonson and the Sons of Ben* (Pittsburgh, 1982), 121–38.

variety. Throughout the 'Charis' poems, Jonson shifts deftly and rapidly through a range of poetic forms, voices, and moods, modulating with wonderful suppleness from satire to celebration, from pathos to playfulness, switching emotional registers and angles of vision in order to create a complex total picture of the developing and dwindling relationship between Charis and her adoring lover.

These contrasts and variations go well beyond what is suggested by any notion of a 'love debate': *debating* is scarcely what the characters get up to, nor do the lyrics themselves address and answer each other in anything resembling a dialectical manner. The lyrics are variously spoken and variously directed. The first, second, and third are in the voice of the poet, who is at once the presenter and principal actor in this little drama. The story he tells is of events which have already occurred; it appears to be leading to a conclusion that is already known to him. In the closing lines of the third lyric, however, the narration moves suddenly into the present tense ('Looser-like, now, all my wreake / Is, that I have leave to speake', etc.), and the fourth lyric, 'Her Triumph', dramatically describes an occurrence that is happening *now*, even as we watch and listen: 'See the Chariot at hand here of Love, / Wherein my Lady rideth!' The fifth, sixth, and seventh lyrics seem to ignore us, the bystanders and witnesses of this story, being addressed instead to Cupid and to Charis. The most intimate of these, the seventh ('*Begging another, on colour of mending the former*'), bases its plea indeed on the assumption that the lovers are now alone: 'Here's none to spie, or see.' The eighth lyric briefly remembers our presence, returning for a dozen lines to the original narrative mode before turning once again to Charis and addressing her directly. Other listeners are now present: the lover's tone is accordingly less intimate and more peremptory than in the preceding song. The ninth lyric is addressed by Charis to the poet, once more in the presence of others; it is a public answer to a public challenge, studiously casual in manner, teasingly non-committal in its declarations. The tenth lyric is spoken by another lady '*present at the hearing*' in a witty aside directed to Charis or members of her retinue. This courtly circle grouped around Charis has seemingly replaced the original audience to which 'Ben' addresses his early lyrics.

This is not exactly the conclusion that we might have anticipated at the outset of the sequence. Something surprising has happened to the story along the way. The poet who began with would-be dignity to tell a (past-tense) narrative about himself that he vowed would move us to sorrow and gladness has now been silenced by the emergence of a (present-tense) drama that is more likely to move us to a smile. The last word is delivered not by the infatuated narrator but by a skittish lady of the court. 'Ben' has seemingly been marginalized not only as a lover but also as a poet; to have lost not merely Charis, but control of the story about Charis which he was attempting to narrate.

To follow the changing narrative shape of the Charis sequence in this way is to realize that the poems are not simply concerned with charting the progress of a love affair, as older scholars believed; they also chart the progress of *a story about* that affair. Jonson is writing not only about the adventures of a lover, but also about the adventures of a poet; about the power of love and the power of poetry; and about the humorous, sublime, and troublesome ways in which those two great forces may tangle and intersect.

❧

The love-struck poet in the opening lyric is dignified yet faintly absurd. 'His Excuse for Loving' is an attempt to control our responses to the story that he is about to tell. We are not to wonder, not to laugh; to be ready for sorrow, ready for gladness. The would-be firmness of these injunctions is gently dissolved through the nursery metre of the lines, and the banality of the rhymes:

> If you then will read the Storie,
> First, prepare you to be sorie . . .   (13–14)

These subversive effects are to become more noticeable in the second of the lyrics:

> Farre I was from being stupid,
> For I ran and call'd on *Cupid* . . .   (5–6)

The naked stupidity of the rhyme itself humorously denies the overt proposition of the lines. In a similar way, the very appeal *not* to laugh at the outset of the first lyric paradoxically alerts the reader to the possibility of comicalities to come; a possibility that is nevertheless held in check through a steadying modulation of the lines:

> Poets, though divine, are men:
> Some have lov'd as old agen.
> And it is not always face,
> Clothes, or Fortune gives the grace;
> Or the feature, or the youth:
> But the Language, and the Truth,
> With the Ardor, and the Passion,
> Gives the Lover weight, and fashion.   (5–12)

The last three lines, with their anaphoric repetitions and skilful deployment of vowels ('With the Ardor, and the Passion') themselves demand to be read with a certain deliberation or *weight*: a word which, as Anne Ferry has shown, has a precise, stylistic sense in Jonson's critical vocabulary,[16] yet also passingly reminds us of the poet himself, whose 'weight is twenty Stone within two pound' (*The Underwood*, 56. 11). Art and life, fiction and 'Truth' are wittily cut and blended. 'Fashion' has a similarly humorous double life, for the term could be used either in the lightly modish sense which Charis intends when she later expresses her preference for a lover 'French to boote, at least in fashion' (ix. 7), or with the deeper sense of poetic artistry and endeavour that is to be found in Jonson's lines to the memory of Shakespeare:

> For though the *Poets* matter, Nature be,
>   His Art does give the fashion. And, that he,
> Who casts to write a living line, must sweat,
>   (Such as thine are) and strike the second heat
> Upon the *Muses* anvile: turne the same,
>   (And himselfe with it) that he thinkes to frame . . .
>
>   (*Ungathered Verse*, 26. 57–62)[17]

In a poetic sense, 'Ben' may have exemplary *weight* and *fashion*, but whether Charis seeks this kind of fashion, whether she fancies this (or any other) kind of weight in her lover, remains to be discovered.

The first lyric, ostensibly celebrating the power of Charis, also celebrates the power of poetry itself. The verses we are about to hear will arouse our feelings (the poet assures us) just as Charis has aroused his own. The makers of poetry are both 'divine' and human (5), like the subject of these poems, Charis herself. Charis fulfils the prophecies of poetry, being one

---

[16] *All in War With Time*, 159–61.   [17] Cf. *Discoveries*, 2162, 2192.

> Of whose Beautie it was sung,
> She shall make the old man young,
> Keepe the middle age at stay,
> And let nothing high decay,
> Till she be the reason why,
> All the world for love may die.   (19–24)

She will miraculously halt the progress and incursions of time, just as poetry itself is alleged to do, both for its practitioners and the subjects whom they immortalize.[18] The lyric invites us simultaneously to smile at the naïve trustfulness of the narrator, and to respect his noble praise. 'Of whose Beautie it was sung': the allusion, if it is one, has not been traced. But the hyperbolic tribute to the powers of Charis in these lines is curiously like the hyperbolic tribute to the powers of the poet in the Epistle Dedicatory addressed to the Universities of Oxford and Cambridge which Jonson prefixed to the 1607 quarto edition of *Volpone*—an epistle which functions in one sense like the opening lyric of the 'Charis' sequence, making a similar bid to raise our admiration and control our responses to the narrative that follows.

> *He that is said to be able to informe yong-men to all good disciplines,* *inflame growne-men to all great vertues, keepe old-men in their best and* *supreme state, or as they decline to child-hood, recover them to their first* *strength; that comes forth the interpreter, and arbiter of nature, a teacher of* *things divine, no lesse then humane, a master in manners; and can alone (or* *with a few) effect the businesse of man-kind: this, I take him, is no subject* *for pride, and ignorance to exercise their rayling rhetorique upon.* (23–31)

In 'A Celebration of Charis' these fine truths are humorously tempered by a shrewd awareness of the actual limits of the poet's powers. 'Poets, though divine, are men' is a formula that contains its own comic potential, which the second lyric is soon to exploit.

In the Epistle Dedicatory to *Volpone* Jonson expresses his hope that '*men will impartially, and not a-squint, looke toward the offices,* *and function of a Poet*' (20–1). This stress upon right and wrong ways of seeing is characteristic of Jonson:

> Looke here on *Bretons* worke, the master print:
> Where, such perfections to the life doe rise.
> If they seeme wry, to such as looke asquint,
> The fault's not in the object, but their eyes.
>
> (*Ungathered Verse*, 2. 5–8)

[18] Cf. *The Forest*, 13. 121–4; *The Underwood*, 27.

> Looke up, thou seed of envie, and still bring
>> Thy faint, and narrow eyes, to reade the *King*
> In his great Actions: view whom his large hand
>> Hath rais'd to be the *Port* unto his *Land!*
>
> (*The Underwood*, 73. 1–4)

The poet's task is to encourage right ways of seeing, to lead the reader to a viewpoint from which the truth will be revealed in its proper lineaments and proportions:

> For, as one comming with a laterall viewe,
>> Unto a cunning piece wrought perspective,
> Wants facultie to make a censure true:
>> So with this Authors Readers will it thrive:
>
> Which being eyed directly, I divine,
> His proofe their praise, will meete, as in this line.
>
> (*Ungathered Verse*, 2. 9–14)[19]

There is a certain simplicity about the categories of moral and artistic perception that Jonson here entertains: there are wrong ways of seeing things (enviously, narrowly, faintly, wryly, laterally, obliquely, asquint) and there is the right way (directly, impartially). The notion of truth is primitively conceived: it is something that is just *there* to be seen by anyone who aligns himself with it, opens his eyes, and looks straight ahead. Jonson's verse satires are sometimes characterized by fierce exhortations to *look* at this or that example of iniquity or supposed happiness, and draw the inevitable conclusion: to see the truth. Thus the friend who is being urged to the wars in *The Underwood*, 15, is told to 'Looke on th'ambitious man', 'Looke on the false, and cunning man', 'See the grave, sower, and supercilious Sir', 'See him, that's call'd, and thought the happiest man' (11, 15, 19, 23), and so on, until this repeated act of *looking* leads to a small detonation of satiric energy:

> O, these so ignorant Monsters! light, as proud,
> Who can behold their Manners, and not clowd-
> Like upon them lighten? If nature could
> Not make a verse; Anger; or laughter would,
> To see 'hem aye discoursing with their Glasse,
> How they may make some one that day an Asse;

---

[19] The perspective line in Jonson's court masques achieved their true effect when viewed from the king's chair, which was centrally placed: see Allardyce Nicoll, *Stuart Masques and the Renaissance Stage* (1937), 34; Stephen Orgel, *The Jonsonian Masque* (Cambridge, Mass., 1965), 66.

> Planting their Purles, and Curles spread forth like Net,
> And every Dressing for a Pitfall set
> To catch the flesh in, and to pound a Prick.   (59–67)

These ways of seeing, like the truths they seek to reveal, are relentlessly singular. The women 'discoursing with their Glasse' can be seen only as 'monsters', having no life beyond the immediate rhetorical purposes of the satire. It is impossible to move outside the intense but limited field of vision which the poet creates.

The modes of perception and presentation in 'A Celebration of Charis' are strikingly unlike those just described. Through successive lyrics, Jonson offers a complex set of variable, subjective, and competing views of a situation which shifts and alters even as it is being observed. The poet is no longer figured, as in the Epistle Dedicatory to *Volpone*, as sole '*interpreter and arbiter*' of the narrative that unfolds. Though the lover in the first lyric speaks proudly of 'the Truth' (10) which he, as poet, presents and represents, it quickly becomes apparent that the truth about Charis is larger and more various than his story at first admits.[20] The sequence itself becomes a humorous meditation upon ways of seeing, and the elusive subjectivity of narrative 'truth'.

The title of the second lyric, '*How he saw her*' hints not simply at a time when and place where the poet first beheld Charis, but at his whole manner of seeing (and not seeing) her: perceiving, assessing, adoring, approaching, pursuing, lamenting, wooing, scolding, exalting, writing verses to and about. *Seeing* Charis, the poet at once calls upon the blinded Cupid to see her too, and unties the cloth around Cupid's eyes. His sight restored, Cupid prudently and instantly flees. The poet looks at Charis again, hoping to strike her with love; instead, she throws a look that immobilizes and strikes him blind. It is the blinded poet who comically attempts to share his vision with us: his vision of 'the Truth'. In the third lyric, his eyes and limbs restored, the poet is struck in the heart, yet vows to write on:

> Looser-like, now, all my wreake
> Is, that I have leave to speake,
> And in either Prose, or Song,
> To revenge me with my Tongue,
> Which how Dextrously I doe,
> Heare and make Example too.   (21–6)

[20] Wesley Trimpi's remarks on Jonson's high regard for 'the truth' overlook this point: *Ben Jonson's Poems*, 210.

In the following lyric, 'Her Triumph', the wounded poet urges us (as he had once urged Cupid) to *look* at Charis, to look on those eyes that have already been his undoing, to share his present way of seeing them as agents not of harm but of divine good:

> Doe but looke on her eyes, they doe light
>   All that Loves world compriseth!
> Doe but looke on her Haire, it is bright
>   As Loves starre when it riseth!
> Doe but marke, her forehead's smoother
>   Then words that sooth her!
> And from her arched browes, such a grace
>   Sheds it selfe through the face,
>   As alone there triumphs to the life
> All the Gaine, all the Good, of the Elements strife.   (11–20)

Lines 17 and 18 were ridiculed by Swinburne for their apparent clumsiness; Trimpi and Peterson detect in them a learned reference to the Neoplatonic association of the light that emanates from God and from a lady's eyes.[21] In acknowledging such an allusion, however, it is necessary also to notice the delicate ironies that surround it: 'arched browes' reminds us that Charis's looks, which are now seen to be like grace itself issuing from the Godhead, were observed in the second lyric to be baleful arrows shooting from her eyes: a comparison which is to return later in the sequence (v. 17–19). These ironies do not neutralize the tribute, but they do affect the nature of its authority. The Neoplatonic viewpoint is just one of several that are offered throughout the sequence. Charis is kindly, Charis is cruel; she is a goddess riding majestically by, she is (in the poet's later observation) a woman tattling and idling in her boudoir:

> You shall neither eat, nor sleepe,
> No, nor forth your window peepe,
> With your emissarie eye,
> To fetch in the Formes goe by:
> And pronounce, which band, or lace,
> Better fits him, then his face;
> Nay, I will not let you sit
> 'Fore your Idoll Glasse a whit,
> To say over every purle
> There; or to reforme a curle;
> Or with Secretarie *Sis*

---

[21] A. C. Swinburne, *A Study of Ben Jonson* (1880), 104; Trimpi, *Ben Jonson's Poems*, 219–20; Peterson, 'Virtue Reconciled to Pleasure', 227.

> To consult, if *Fucus* this
> Be as good, as was the last . . .   (viii. 15–27)

The vision of female vanity here is quite different from that offered in 'An Epistle to a Friend, to Persuade Him to the Wars', not
simply in its tone—affectionately teasing, where that was angrily
vituperative—but also in its manner of composition. It is merely one
of the several ways in which the adorable, vexatious Charis is regarded by her lover, whom we in turn can view from several angles
and in several lights. The 'truth' of the relationship is revealed not
through a reliable and continuous narrative dictated by the
lover–poet, but in tantalizing and contrary glimpses afforded from
lyric to lyric throughout the sequence.

Not only does our view of Charis and of her lover change as the
sequence proceeds; so too does our view of the verses which the lover
writes and the tale he tells. The lyrics which at first seemed designed
to celebrate Charis and to tell her story begin to take on another
function, acting as precipitating agents *within* that story, and affect-
ing its course. It is through 'either Prose, or Song' that the poet is permitted at the end of the third lyric to take his 'revenge' upon Charis
(iii. 23–4): his writing is seen as a potential weapon, that he may hurl
at Charis as she has hurled her arrow-looks at him.[22] Yet the ensuing
lyric is his tender and impassioned hymn to Charis: what it celebrates is '*Her* Triumph', not his. Critics have hunted ingeniously to see
the poet's 'revenge' fulfilled elsewhere in the sequence, but this is to
miss the magical effect that is achieved by the transition from the
third lyric to the fourth, as the poet's weapon changes to a bouquet in
mid-flight, and his intended satire, confronting the beauty of Charis,
turns to praise.[23] There is a similar little surprise in the transition
from the fourth lyric to the fifth, where Cupid discovers the poet
writing verses to Charis.

> Sure, said he, if I have Braine,
> This, here sung, can be no other
> By description, but my Mother!   (10–12)

[22] Writing and fighting are often equated in Jonson's work: see my 'Jonson and Anger',
in Claude Rawson (ed.), assisted by Jenny Mezciems, *English Satire and the Satiric
Tradition* (Oxford, 1984), 56–71.

[23] Zitner, 'The Revenge on Charis', 135–6, notes that the third stanza of 'Her Triumph'
compares Charis with things whose beauty is transitory, and argues that the poet's 'revenge' lies in 'his insistence that Charis is as vulnerable to time as the old lover she rejects'.
Weinberger (as discussed later in this chapter) sees the final lyric as 'revengeful' ('Jonson's
Mock-Encomiastic "Celebration of Charis" ', 324).

What is 'here sung' is not 'her Triumph' or indeed any lyric we are to encounter in the sequence; the poetic images that Cupid declares 'your verse discloses' (v. 21) are never fully shown to us: a fact that has puzzled editors, and prompted them to search elsewhere for the missing verses.[24] The humorous point lies precisely, however, in such small confusions, as love generates in the poet more verses than are strictly needed to relate 'the story' of Charis: verses which sometimes lead to further unlooked-for developments in the relationship which the sequence is attempting to describe. Reading these verses about milk and roses, kisses and blisses, Cupid assumes that the poet is in love with Venus herself. The mistake becomes the subject of a 'discourse' which becomes the fifth lyric which in turn is presented to Charis. Such poems are thus converted to gifts and tokens within the courtship itself, whose progress they in turn affect.[25] The sixth lyric praises the comeliness of Charis, and reflects (and bargains) upon its own skill in so doing, 'Clayming a second kisse by Desert'.

> Guesse of these, which is the true;
> And, if such a verse as this,
> May not claime another kisse.   (vi. 34–6)

The seventh and eighth lyrics are each in their different ways acts of persuasion, urging Charis once more to a kiss, then to a declaration. The function of the verse throughout the sequence is thus constantly mobile: it is not in any simple sense that of 'celebration' or of satire or of narrative or of unalloyed lyric, but shifts unpredictably from one mode to another. The lyrics constitute a story that is told to us; they are also part of an amorous game that is played within that story. This multiplicity of poetic function, like the multiplicity of poetic viewpoint, lends the sequence a teasing complexity and self-reflexiveness more often encountered in Jonson's dramatic than in his non-dramatic work.

In the ninth lyric of the sequence the object of adoration is at last permitted to speak in her own voice.

> Of your Trouble, *Ben*, to ease me,
> I will tell what Man would please me,
> I would have him, if I could,
> Noble; or of greater Blood:

---

[24] See e.g. *Poems of Ben Jonson*, ed. G. B. Johnston, The Muses Library (1954), 332. *The Underwood*, 19, is sometimes thought to be the 'missing' lyric.

[25] The effect is Ovidian: cf. e.g. *Amores*, I. xi, I. xii.

> Titles, I confesse, doe take me;
> And a woman God did make me:
> French to boote, at least in fashion,
> And his Manners of that Nation.   (ix. 1–8)

The character of Charis is nicely suggested through the tripping
metre and feminine rhymes, with their significant trailing stress:
'ease me', 'please me'; that Charis consents to ease herself but not
Ben of his 'Trouble' bodes ill for the poet. Charis's sketch of the perfect lover is archly calculated (as others have noticed) to list those
very qualities—of youth, grace, beauty, noble birth—that her
present suitor lacks. Her vision of this ideal lover ironically resembles the poet's vision of the ideal Charis: the skin smooth as
snow, as down, as wool; the hair a nest for Cupid, the eyebrows bent
like Cupid's bow, the eyes like those of Venus and Minerva. Ben's
own poetic figures return here to plague him. The 'fashion' that the
lady fancies is that of the court, not the finer artistry upon which the
poet has prided himself and based his courtship; yet she has a mis-
chievous eye for the tropes and metaphors which he has scattered
throughout the lyrics written in her praise. Charis moves from the
physical qualities she seeks in her man to the moral ones:

> Valiant he should be as fire,
> Shewing danger more then ire.
> Bounteous as the clouds to earth;
> And as honest as his Birth.
> All his actions to be such,
> As to doe no thing too much.
> Nor o're praise, nor yet condemne;
> Nor out-valew, nor contemne;
> Nor doe wrongs, nor wrongs receave;
> Nor tie knots, nor knots unweave;
> And from baseness to be free,
> As he durst love Truth and me.
>   Such a man, with every part,
> I could give my very heart;
> But of one, if short he came,
> I can rest me where I am.   (ix. 41–56)

The sentiments are flawless, and the glancing comment on over-
praise has special point; yet the unstrenuous rhymes ('be such'/'too
much', 'condemne'/'contemne') and even imperturbability of metre
lend the catalogue a faint air of languid facility. The declaration

which set out to 'ease me' and 'please me' leads insouciantly to 'Truth and me', coming to its final point of rest 'where I am'. It is difficult to see how these lines can mean anything other than what they appear to mean: that until the perfect lover materializes, Charis will keep herself to herself, giving no public pledge either to Ben or to any of the numerous other suitors who pursue her (viii. 5–10).

'Truth and me': in her closing words, Charis effortlessly elides the two. Her phrase returns us to the opening lyric, in which the poet declares his love not only for Charis but also for those several qualities—language, truth, ardour, passion—that make him a poet; qualities that he believes may win her, against all odds. His poetry does not in the long run achieve this result. The 'truth' it urges, though passionately felt, seems (like the 'Truth' of which Charis lightly speaks) merely one component in a larger and more various dramatic truth which the sequence as a whole has revealed to us. The truth concerns not merely the nature of love, but also the nature of poetry: what it can do, what it cannot do. Jonson's own great trust in the power of poetry is evident not only in the passage from the Epistle Dedicatory to the two Universities prefixed to *Volpone* that has already been quoted, but throughout his writing.[26] Yet some of his most touching poems turn upon the realization that such power has its limits: that his poetry, for all its grace and dignity, cannot bring to life a dead son, cannot perpetually 'Keepe the middle age at stay', cannot ultimately secure him the lady whom he loves. This wry knowledge is an important part of the final 'truth' of 'A Celebration of Charis', as it is of 'My Picture Left in Scotland' (*The Underwood*, 9).

The 'truth' of the sequence may not be, in any literal and easily legible sense, autobiographical. To read from the inventions of literature to the particularities of life is not as simple a matter as scholars such as Fleay once believed. Yet the 'Charis' poems are clearly concerned with those very puzzles and intractabilities of the relationship between life and literature to which Jonson constantly returns throughout his writing: with a larger dilemma which is at once traditional and of recognizably particular significance to Jonson himself.[27]

---

[26] See e.g. *Discoveries*, 2375 ff.

[27] Jonson may be varying a lament found in Ovid, that the lady accepts her verses, but not his person (*Amores*, III. 8, III. xi a; *Heroides*, xv. 33 ff.). Jonson's treatment of the notion is, however, very much his own.

'Charis' is the singular form of *charites*, the Graces, and the notion of *grace* appropriately recurs throughout the sequence.[28] Traditionally, the three Graces are benevolent; iconographically, they are represented naked and holding hands: two of the figures always advance towards us, while one presents her back. Their hands are joined to show the 'perpetual and never-ceasing intercourse of kindness and benevolence among friends'; the disposition of their figures suggests that for every grace going from us, two graces will always come our way.[29] The final balance of the accounts in 'A Celebration of Charis' cannot be simply drawn up; the notion of winning and losing is lightly played over throughout the sequence, but it is on a note of apparent loss that the story of Charis ends. Ben seems to be pursuing a Grace who is walking away.

The final lyric of the sequence has been described by one critic as

revengeful in its display of the fury of an old lover scorned. Showing 'ire more than danger', Ben concludes the 'Celebration' of Charis by hurling a final, carnal statement in the face of his vain, apparently worthless, pseudo-Platonic mistress by way of putting her in her place in a manner reminiscent of Hamlet's turning on Ophelia. . . .[30]

This is seriously to confuse the real-life author who creates, organizes, and controls 'A Celebration of Charis' with the infatuated and at times humorously incompetent 'Ben' who is depicted as a dramatic character within it. As has already been noted, it is not 'Ben' who concludes the sequence at all, for he is bilked of the last word by a witty lady of the court circle, losing control of his narrative as he has seemingly lost Charis herself. If one were to link this semi-fictional creation to the actual author of the sequence, it would be to note how very uncharacteristic of Jonson himself is this final surrender of authorial control. Though Jonson spoke often of the way in which an author, in submitting his work to the public, 'departed with his right',[31] he was never in fact keen to surrender authorial power, constantly reaching out through his prologues and epilogues, his dedications and his title-pages, his addresses to the reader and his apologetical dialogues, anxious to utter the last, definitive word, to steer his narrative to its final haven, so to align his reader that the true

---

[28] See i. 8, iv. 17–20, v. 51–4, vi. 19–26.

[29] J. Lempriere, *A Classical Dictionary* (Halifax, 1865), s.v. 'Charites'; Edgar Wind, *Pagan Mysteries in the Renaissance* (1958).

[30] Weinberger, 'Jonson's Mock-Encomiastic "Celebration of Charis" ', 324.

[31] *Bartholomew Fair*, Induction, 87; *Epigrams*, 131.2.

beauties and proportions of his work could be observed. In 'A Celebration of Charis', Jonson the actual author is (needless to say) in perfect control to the last, but the narrative situation which he humorously and thoughtfully imagines is one in which 'Ben', the feigned author, a projection of himself, is finally pushed gently but firmly right out of the story he is attempting to tell. It is a witty yet sobering reflection on the limits of the poet's power, not only in the events and wishes of his life, but also in the execution of his art.

10

Fathers and Sons
Jonson, Dryden, and Mac Flecknoe

LITERARY relationships are in some respects like family relationships, as Ben Jonson and John Dryden were each acutely aware. The
notion of a poetic lineage was of particular and absorbing interest to
both men, and it seems natural therefore to ask about the kind of
relationship, the family tie, that may subsist between them. There are
fortuitous but significant similarities in the shape of the two writers'
careers. Both Jonson and Dryden attended Westminster School, and
retained from their schooldays a lifelong interest in classical translation, imitation, and precedent. Both were converted in adult life to
Roman Catholicism, Jonson returning to the Anglican faith after a
dozen years, Dryden persevering in his new religion until death. Both
men for a time received a royal salary and a butt of wine in recognition of their poetic eminence, Jonson being (in fact if not in name)
England's first Poet Laureate in the modern sense, Dryden later succeeding to this (by now officially designated) position.[1] Each
presided over a literary coterie: Jonson, gregariously, at the Mermaid
tavern, Dryden, more soberly, at Will's Coffee House. Each attempted also to shape public opinion through numerous critical
writings which often defended, and set in a longer historical perspective, their own literary practice.

Dryden is generally regarded as the critic who first steered English
allegiances away from the work of Jonson, shaping the popular modern devotion to the work of Shakespeare.[2] Dryden's decisive inter-
vention in the debate concerning the nature of Shakespeare's genius
is well documented, but his complex attitude towards Jonson and
his work has not been well understood. I want to argue that deep

[1] Richard Helgerson, *Self-Crowned Laureates: Spenser, Jonson, Milton, and the
Literary System* (Berkeley, 1983).
[2] See in particular G. E. Bentley, *Shakespeare and Jonson: Their Reputations in the
Seventeenth Century Compared*, 2 vols. (Chicago, 1945), i. 101-2.

affinities in fact existed between Jonson and Dryden, whose true literary relationship was close and familial.

✦

Ben Jonson never knew his own father, that 'grave minister of the gospel' who died a month before Jonson was born. Towards the bricklayer Robert Brett whom his mother married not long afterwards he seems to have felt no special closeness or regard; taunts about the trade at which his stepfather and, more briefly, he himself had worked were to follow him throughout his later life.[3] Jonson sought his true paternity outside the family circle. He regarded Sir Walter Ralegh (so it is said) as his 'father' in literature,[4] and according to John Aubrey placed himself in a similarly filial relationship to the lawyer Sir John Hoskyns: 'Ben Jonson called him *father*. Sir Benet [Hoskyns' son] told me that one time desiring Mr Johnson to adopt him for his sonne, No, said he, I dare not; 'tis honour enough for me to be your Brother: I was your Father's sonne, and 'twas he that polished me.'[5] The great antiquary William Camden, Jonson's teacher at Westminster School, was another powerful and quasi-paternal figure in his intellectual life:

> Camden, most reverent head, to whom I owe
>   All that I am in arts, all that I know,
> (How nothing's that?) . . .
>
>   (*Epigrams*, 14. 1–3)

Jonson was especially interested in the nature of such paternal relationships, and in the various ways in which, for good or ill, one man may shape the conduct, thought, and creative imagination of another. Subtle in *The Alchemist* is hailed by Sir Epicure Mammon as 'father', and in turn addresses Mammon as his 'gentle son': Subtle is a *maker*, if not of the fabled elixir itself, then of the expectations and very characters of those who come beneath his spell.[6] His

---

[3] See Ch. 5 n. 3 above.

[4] See the account of Ralegh given by Sir John Knox Laughton and Sidney Lee in the *Dictionary of National Biography*, xvi. 645; no authority is cited. Jonson gives a less amiable view of Ralegh in the *Conversations with Drummond*, 197.

[5] *Aubrey's Brief Lives*, ed. O. L. Dick (Harmondsworth, 1962), 246.

[6] For Subtle as 'maker', see (for example) *The Alchemist*, I. i. 64–79, II. vi. 25, III. iv. 44–6.

powers are like those of the poet, whom Jonson traditionally describes in *Discoveries* (2348) as 'a Maker, or a fainer'. Poets and fathers are alike in their ability to create, invent, control, and refine ("twas he that polished me'). The analogy is memorably invoked in Jonson's touching lines on his dead son:

> Rest in soft peace, and, ask'd, say here doth lye
> BEN. JONSON his best piece of *poetrie*.

> (*Epigrams*, 45. 9–10)

It returns again in Jonson's lines which stand at the head of Shakespeare's first folio:

> Looke how the fathers face
> Lives in his issue, even so, the race
> Of *Shakespeares* mind, and manners brightly shines
> In his well torned and true-filed lines . . .

> (*Ungathered Verse*, 26. 65–8)

Shakespeare, in Jonson's great tribute, stands alone in his age and in all ages, without peer, progenitor, or heir. Yet Jonson figures Shakespeare paradoxically as a father—not to other poets, but to a literary 'issue', a 'race' of works which live on after his death.

We think of Jonson himself as a literary progenitor of a rather different kind: as the father of a 'tribe' of other writers—imitators, disciples, 'sons of Ben'. At Jonson's death, Sir William Davenant complained, those who survived him were 'As sullen Heires, when wastefull Fathers die': Jonson, the great patriarch, had squandered 'all the Muses Treasure', leaving his poetic progeny bankrupt.[7] By this time the notion of literary fatherhood already had its own well-established lineage. Chaucer had been honoured as 'fader and founder of ornate eloquence' centuries before Dryden described him as 'the father of English poetry', and there were many classical fathers before him: Herodotus, father of history, Homer, father of epic, Ennius, father of Roman literature, Isocrates, father of eloquence.[8] Pindar, pursuing the notion to its logical limits, had hailed

---

[7] Sir William Davenant, 'To Doctor Duppa, Deane of Christ-Church, and Tutor to the Prince', 27, 11, in *The Shorter Poems and Songs From the Plays and Masques*, ed. A. M. Gibbs (Oxford, 1972), 78.

[8] The tribute to Chaucer is from the anonymous *Book of Courtesy* (1477), repr. in John Burrow (ed.), *Geoffrey Chaucer: A Critical Anthology* (Harmondsworth, 1969), 44; Dryden's phrase is in his *Preface to Fables Ancient and Modern*: see *Of Dramatic Poesy and Other Critical Essays*, ed. George Watson, 2 vols. (1962), ii. 280. Cicero speaks filially

Orpheus, son of Apollo, as the father of song.[9] No other writer in English, however, is more firmly associated with the notion of literary paternity than is Ben Jonson; and the very title, 'father', associates Jonson with the great classical forebears whom he admired. Thomas Randolph, writing to thank Jonson '*for his adopting him to be his Son*', knew that he had made his way into a good family:

> I am a kinne to *Hero's* being thine,
> And part of my alliance is divine.
> *Orpheus, Musaeus, Homer*, too; beside
> Thy Brothers by the *Roman* Mothers side;
> As *Ovid, Virgil*, and the *Latin Lyre*,
> That is so like thy *Horace*; the whole quire
> Of Poets are by thy Adoption, all
> My uncles; thou hast given me pow'r to call
> *Phoebus* himselfe my grandsire: by this graunt
> Each Sister of the nine is made my Aunt.[10]

Christopher Ricks has shown in illuminating detail what special power the notion of paternity also held for John Dryden—'the father of literary criticism', as Dr Johnson was to call him—and how questions of lineage, succession, and inheritance deeply pervade his work.[11] And yet, as Ricks reminds us, Dryden also had some scepticism about those 'sons of Ben': 'They can tell a story of Ben Jonson, and perhaps have had fancy enough to give a supper in Apollo that they might be called his sons; and, because they were drawn in to be laughed at in those times, they think themselves now sufficiently entitled to laugh at ours.'[12] Yet Dryden could speak easily none the less in his *Apology for Heroic Poetry* of 'our great forefathers, even from Homer down to Ben', and allows Crites in *An Essay of Dramatic Poesy* to speak loyally of 'Father Ben' as 'the greatest man of the last

---

of Herodotus in *De Legibus*, trans. C. W. Keyes, Loeb Classical Library (1970), I. i. 5, and of Isocrates in *De Oratore*, trans. E. W. Sutton and H. Rackham, Loeb Classical Library, 3 vols. (1967–8), II. iii. 10. For the salute to Homer, see Pliny, *Natural History*, trans. H. Rackham *et al.*, Loeb Classical Library, 10 vols. (1949–62), XXV. v. 11, and Horace, *Epistles*, trans. H. R. Fairclough, Loeb Classical Library (1970), II. i. 50–2 (where Ennius is also styled 'father').

[9] *Pythian Odes*, trans. Sir John Sandys, Loeb Classical Library (1937), iv. 176–7.

[10] *Poems with the Muses Looking-glass: and Amyntas* (1638), 22–3, quoted in Herford and Simpson, xi. 390.

[11] Christopher Ricks, 'Allusion: The Poet as Heir', in R. F. Brissenden and J. C. Eade (eds.), *Studies in the Eighteenth Century*, vol. iii (Canberra, 1976), 209–40. I owe a large general debt to this essay.

[12] 'Defence of the Epilogue', *Of Dramatic Poesy*, i. 181.

age'.[13] Neander puts a different view: 'If I would compare him with Shakespeare, I must acknowledge him the more correct poet, but Shakespeare the greater wit. Shakespeare was the Homer, or father of our dramatic poets; Jonson was the Virgil, the pattern of elaborate writing; I admire him, but I love Shakespeare.'[14] Yet to Jonson, Shakespeare, and Fletcher together, Neander nevertheless pays his wry and collective filial dues: 'We acknowledge them our fathers in wit; but they have ruined their estates themselves before they came to their children's hands.'[15] Like Davenant, Neander fears that the patrimony has been squandered.

Dryden's own attitude to Jonson resembles Neander's rather than Crites'. He is at once generous and guarded; ready enough to concede a general debt to Jonson, but less ready to be sealed himself of the tribe of Ben. Dryden must have been aware that to be a son of Ben would have made him not only (as Randolph had excitedly put it) a nephew to Ovid and Virgil, but also, less happily, a brother to Thomas Shadwell. The stock might well have seemed weakened, the filial honour rendered a little too common.

Shadwell is indeed the real problem here. As we try to think of Dryden's relationship with Jonson, the bulky figure of Shadwell officiously intervenes, zealously praising his father Ben and disparaging the seemingly un-Jonsonian Dryden. Shadwell seems not only to have ignored the deep affinities between Dryden and Jonson, but to have prompted Dryden to ponder the wisdom of such lavish admiration: R. Jack Smith has shown how, as Shadwell became progressively warmer in his remarks about Jonson over the years, Dryden in due proportion became progressively cooler.[16] Much has been written about Dryden's quarrel with Shadwell over the relative merits of 'wit' comedy and the older Jonsonian comedy of humours.[17] Since Shadwell's championing of Jonsonian methods is

---

[13] 'Defence of the Epilogue', *Of Dramatic Poesy*, i. 206, 31.
[14] Ibid. 70.   [15] Ibid. 85.
[16] 'Shadwell's Impact upon John Dryden', *The Review of English Studies*, 20 (1944), 29–44.
[17] D. M. McKeithan, 'The Occasion of *Mac Flecknoe*', *PMLA: Publications of the Modern Language Association*, 47 (1932), 766–71; Michael W. Alssid, 'Shadwell's *Mac Flecknoe*', *SEL: Studies in English Literature 1500–1900*, 7 (1967), 387–402. Michael Wilding has a fine account of the poem 'Allusion and Innuendo in *Mac Flecknoe*', *Essays in Criticism*, 19 (1969), 355–70, more extensively argued in Earl Miner (ed.), *John Dryden* (1972), 191–233; this foreshadows the view of Jonson presented here. See also Jennifer Brady, 'Collaborating with the Forebear: Dryden's Reception of Ben Jonson', *Modern Language Quarterly*, 54 (1993), 345–69, and her 'Dryden and Negotiations of Literary

central to this quarrel, it is understandable that some critics should have been led into seeing *Mac Flecknoe* as a poem antagonistic not merely to Shadwell but also in some sense to Jonson, a poem which marks the climax to a running battle of many years' duration in which Dryden (as one commentator puts it) 'derided Jonson and his principal follower, Thomas Shadwell'.[18] I want to sketch quite a contrary view of the poem. I believe that in *Mac Flecknoe* Dryden uses Jonson as a standard by which Shadwell, for all his Jonsonian pretensions, is judged and found wanting; and that Dryden, turning the knife more exquisitely, disposes of Shadwell in a manner similar to that which Jonson had at times deployed against his own literary opponents. 'I know I honour Ben Jonson more than my little critics', wrote Dryden tersely in 1673, 'because without vanity I may own I understand him better.'[19] The implication of *Mac Flecknoe*, I suggest, is similar. Dryden's poem reveals that the true lineage runs not from Jonson to Shadwell, but from Jonson to Dryden, who may with justice say, 'I understand him better'.

∼❧∽

Mac Flecknoe is a poem about literary fathers and sons. Flecknoe, 'the good old *Syre*' (60), chooses as his successor the most filial, most Flecknoe-like of his sons:

> And pond'ring which of all his Sons was fit
> To Reign, and wage immortal War with Wit;
> Cry'd, 'tis resolv'd; for Nature pleads that He
> Should onely rule, who most resembles me:
> *Sh*——alone my perfect image bears,
> Mature in dullness from his tender years.
> *Sh*——alone, of all my Sons, is he
> Who stands confirm'd in full stupidity.   (11–18)[20]

Succession and Precession', in Earl Miner and Jennifer Brady (eds.), *Literary Transmission and Authority: Dryden and Other Writers* (Cambridge, 1993), 27–54.

[18] B. J. Frye, introduction to his casebook, *John Dryden: 'Mac Flecknoe'* (Columbus, Oh., 1970), 7.

[19] 'To My Most Honoured Friend Sir Charles Sedley, Baronet' (prefixed to *The Assignation*), *Of Dramatic Poesy*, i. 188.

[20] Quotations from Dryden's poems are taken from *The Poems of John Dryden*, ed. James Kinsley, 4 vols. (Oxford, 1958). The best commentary on the poem is now that of Paul Hammond, *The Poems of John Dryden*, 4 vols. [in progress] (1995–   ), i. 306–36.

Like David in *Absalom and Achitophel*, Flecknoe has sired many sons, and has one favourite. Throughout the poem it is suggested that both Flecknoe and Shadwell are hugely prolific and yet at the same time paradoxically barren.

> Success let others teach, learn thou from me
> Pangs without birth, and fruitless Industry.   (147–8)

There is an enjoyable contradiction about the fact that a father should be speaking to his own son in this way about his own sterility.

> But Worlds of *Misers* from his pen should flow;
> *Humorists* and *Hypocrites* it should produce,
> Whole *Raymond* families, and Tribes of *Bruce*.   (91–3)

'Worlds of *Misers*': the phrase beautifully suggests both lavishness and constraint, spending and keeping. The only families which Shadwell is capable of producing are those made up of his own, predictably repetitious, dramatic characters: 'Whole *Raymond* families, and Tribes of *Bruce*'. The tribes of Bruce are of Shadwell's own making, and bear no resemblance to the tribe of Ben. The fools of Shadwell's comedies are 'Not Copies drawn, but Issue of thy own'; 'All full of thee, and differing but in name' (160, 162). The metaphor which Jonson had once used in rich tribute to Shakespeare ('Looke how the fathers face / Lives in his issue . . .') is given now to Flecknoe to convey a similar, but impoverished, truth about Shadwell's fatuous, identical brainchildren, all models of their father. Flecknoe chooses for the site of Shadwell's throne a 'Nursery' for actors which turns out on closer inspection to be a mausoleum, a 'Monument of vanisht minds'. The site is—significantly—unvisited by Shadwell's hero, Ben Jonson:

> Great *Fletcher* never treads in Buskins here,
> Nor greater *Johnson* dares in Socks appear.   (79–80)

The place is associated instead with Jonson's old rival and antagonist, Thomas Dekker—that 'rogue', as Jonson had called him, that 'dresser of plaies'—who is presented now as a forerunner and prophet of Thomas Shadwell.[21]

---

[21] *Conversations with Drummond*, 51; *Poetaster*, III. iv. 322. See also G. Blakemore Evans, 'Dryden's *Mac Flecknoe* and Dekker's *Satiromastix*', *Modern Language Notes*, 76 (1961), 598–600.

Dryden's tactics are to sever one by one Shadwell's flimsy claims to Jonsonian kinship, and to affiliate him firmly instead with the line of Flecknoe:

> Sir *Formal*, though unsought, attends thy quill,
> And does thy *Northern Dedications* fill,
> Nor let false friends seduce thy mind to fame,
> By arrogating *Johnson's* Hostile name.
> Let Father *Fleckno* fire thy mind with praise,
> And uncle *Ogleby* thy envy raise.
> Thou art my blood, where *Johnson* has no part;
> What share have we in Nature or in Art?
> Where did his wit on learning fix a brand,
> And rail at Arts he did not understand? . . .
>
> Nor let thy mountain belly make pretence
> Of likeness; thine's a tympany of sense.   (169–78, 193–4)

Shadwell's '*Northern Dedications*' were addressed to William Cavendish and his wife Margaret, Duke and Duchess of Newcastle. Newcastle had been a patron of poets other than Shadwell: James Shirley, for example, Dryden himself, and in an earlier period, Ben Jonson—who wrote two entertainments for Newcastle, two poems to celebrate his prowess in fencing and horsemanship, two epitaphs in commemoration of his parents, and a moving appeal for financial help. Newcastle was in turn an admirer and imitator of Jonson's dramatic style.[22] Shadwell was delighted at the thought of being thus united with Jonson through a common patron. '*Welbeck* is indeed the only place where the best Poets can find a good reception', he purred in his dedication to *Epsom-Wells* (for Jonson himself had been received at Welbeck). '*The Interest of all Poets*', he wrote again (to the Duchess of Newcastle) in his dedication to *The Humorists*, '*is to fly for protection to* Welbecke; *which will never fail to be their Sanctuary*. . .'. Addressing the duke in the Dedication to *The Virtuoso*, Shadwell pointed out that the same people who disapproved of his own plays also happened, by a curious chance, to disapprove of those of Ben Jonson, '*who was incomparably the best Dramatick Poet that ever was, or, I believe, ever will be*. . .'.[23]

---

[22] Anne Barton describes the Jonsonian turns of Newcastle's comic writing in *Ben Jonson: Dramatist* (Cambridge, 1984), ch. 14.

[23] All quotations are from *The Complete Works of Thomas Shadwell*, ed. Montague Summers, 5 vols. (1927).

Dryden implies that these fulsome dedications are not so much in the style of Father Ben as in that of one of Shadwell's own dramatic 'children', Sir Formal Trifle, the wordy orator of *The Virtuoso*. Shadwell's true relationships are other than he professes; Jonson is not kin to him, but 'Hostile'.

> Let Father *Fleckno* fire thy mind with praise,
> And Uncle *Ogleby* thy envy raise.

Dryden is alluding here (as is well known) to Virgil's lines on Ascanius in *Aeneid*, iii. 342–3:

> ecquid in antiquam virtutem animosque virilis
> et pater Aeneas et avunculus excitat Hector?

(Do his father Aeneas and his uncle Hector arouse him at all to ancestral valour and to manly spirit?)

But the reference is also to the distinct notion of literary parenthood, which held such appeal for Shadwell; who now is shown sadly to be not Mac Jonson, but Mac Flecknoe.

> Thou art my blood, where *Johnson* has no part;
> What share have we in Nature or in Art?

Of Shakespeare, Jonson had written in 1623:

> Yet must I not give Nature all: Thy Art
> My gentle *Shakespeare*, must enjoy a part.
>
> (*Ungathered Verse*, 26. 55–6)

In the course of the seventeenth century, 'nature' and 'art' became central terms in the developing debate concerning the quality of Shakespeare's genius and that of Jonson; it became commonplace to associate Shakespeare with 'nature', Jonson with 'art'.[24] Richard Flecknoe in *A Short Discourse of the English Stage* in 1664 had actually written of Jonson, 'Comparing him with *Shakespear*, you shall see the difference betwixt Nature and Art';[25] while in 1667 Dryden himself wrote in his prologue to *The Tempest*:

[24] See T. W. Baldwin, *William Shakespere's Small Latine and Lesse Greeke*, 2 vols. (Urbana, 1944), i. 13 ff., 41; *The Critical Works of John Dennis*, ed. E. N. Hooker, 2 vols. (Baltimore, 1943), ii. 428–31.

[25] *The Short Discourse* is appended to *Love's Kingdom*, 1664; the passage quoted is printed in Herford and Simpson, xi. 512.

> *Shakespear*, who (taught by none) did first impart
> To *Fletcher* Wit, to labouring *Johnson* Art.
> He Monarch-like gave those his subjects law,
> And is that Nature which they paint and draw. (5–8)

'What share have we in Nature or in Art?': the question gently pushes both Shadwell and Flecknoe into a limbo out of nature, beyond the reach of art; it also clearly dissociates the two men from the traditions of Shakespeare and of Ben Jonson.

Dryden's allusions to Jonson in *Mac Flecknoe* are often close and specific:

> Where did his wit on learning fix a brand,
> And rail at Arts he did not understand?

'Thy Forehead is too narrow for my Brand', Jonson had written disdainfully of Inigo Jones, whom he had elsewhere castigated for his lack of learning. The notion of *branding*, common in Jonson's work, reaches back to Martial ('Frons haec stigmate non meo notanda est').[26] Shadwell's brand, unlike Jonson's and Martial's, is applied without discrimination or understanding. Throughout his work Jonson constantly stresses the need for literary *understanding*; a poem on this theme stands at the head of his *Epigrams* in the 1616 folio; and when Jonson in the Induction to *Bartholomew Fair* tilts in passing at 'the understanding Gentlemen o' the ground' (49), he means that these gentlemen are 'understanding' merely in the sense that they stand beneath the level of the stage. Dryden's language in *Mac Flecknoe* itself suggests an exceptional understanding of Jonson's writing: 'I understand him better'. Again:

> Nor let thy mountain belly make pretence
> Of likeness; thine's a tympany of sense.

Shadwell prided himself on resembling his admired master both in bulk and feature.[27] Dryden alludes not merely to Jonson's well-known corpulence, but to the dramatist's own allusion to that corpulence, in 'My Picture Left in Scotland':

[26] 'Your brow is not one to be marked by my brand': Martial, XII. lxi. 11; and see Ch. 12 n. 20 below.

[27] See Summers's introduction to his edition of Shadwell, vol. i, p. lxix. Shadwell's vanity is like that of Davenant, who 'when he was pleasant over a glasse of wine with his most intimate friends' would hint that Shakespeare might have been his father: 'say, that it seemed to him that he writt with the very spirit that did Shakespeare, and seemed contented to be thought his Son', *Aubrey's Brief Lives*, 177.

I now thinke, Love is rather deafe, then blind,
   For else it could not be,
         That she,
Whom I adore so much, should so slight me,
   And cast my love behind:
I'm sure my language to her, was as sweet,
   And every close did meet
   In sentence, of as subtile feet,
         As hath the youngest Hee,
That sits in shadow of *Apollo* 's tree.

Oh, but my conscious feares,
   That flie my thoughts betweene
   Tell me that she hath seene
   My hundred of gray haires,
   Told seven and fortie years,
Read so much wast, as she cannot imbrace
My mountaine belly, and my rockie face,
And all these through her eyes, have stopt her eares.
               (*The Underwood*, 9)

Jonson's poem is about the limits of the poet's art: however sweet and subtle his verses, they will not win his lady, who judges by her eyes and not her ears. Hence it is not his poem which is left with her in Scotland, but his picture, the unflattering image of a fat and middle-aged poet. Here as so often in his work Jonson laments the preference given to 'eyes' over 'ears': to things seen, rather than things heard and understood. (One thinks of the significant phrase Jonson wrote at the head of his masque *Love's Triumph Through Callipolis*: 'To make the Spectators understanders.') In *Mac Flecknoe* Dryden implies that Shadwell, on the other hand, prides himself upon those very outward forms of which Jonson had such mistrust: upon the 'mountaine belly' which Shadwell naïvely supposed authenticated his kinship with Jonson. (Pepys amusingly notes how Shadwell, sitting next to him at a performance of Jonson's *The Silent Woman* at the Theatre Royal in 1668, was 'big with admiration of it'.[28]) True likeness and kinship, Dryden implies, do not rest upon appearances, on things seen, but on what is found within. And within, Shadwell is merely hollow, 'a tympany of sense'. Jonson had coincidentally lampooned his great collaborator and rival in a similar figure, presenting him as a 'drum' (*Epigrams*, 129. 7).

[28] *The Diary of Samuel Pepys*, ed. R. C. Latham and W. Matthews, 11 vols. (1971–95), ix. 310: entry for 19 Sept. 1668.

'A tympany of sense': Shadwell's drum-like belly produces mere noise, mere nonsense. *Sense* and *nonsense* are central terms in Dryden's poem, and it seems likely that these words too are used with a memory of Jonsonian contexts and significance. The word 'nonsense' is first found in English in the work of Ben Jonson.[29] It occurs in a side-note in *Bartholomew Fair* (IV. iv. 27), explaining the game of 'vapours' played in the fourth act (*'which is* non sense. *Every man to oppose the last man that spoke: whether it concern'd him, or no'*), and again in *Discoveries* (1868–70): 'Many Writers perplexe their Readers, and Hearers with meere *Non-sense*. Their writings need sunshine.' 'Nonsense' gains great currency as a word after the Restoration, and is frequently used by Shadwell himself. In his Preface to *The Humorists* in 1671 Shadwell laments the fact that the rabble are 'more pleased with the extravagant and unnatural actions, the trifles and fripperies of a Play, or the trappings and ornaments of Nonsense, than with all the wit in the world'. In the epilogue to the same play he confesses lamely (after a routine flourish concerning the genius of 'Noble BEN!'):

> Yet if you hiss, he knows not where the harm is,
> He'll not defend his Nonsense *Vi & Armis*.

Tom Towers, writing on 'The Lineage of Shadwell', has suggested why Dryden should have given Shadwell in *Mac Flecknoe* four 'predecessors'—Heywood, Dekker, Shirley, and Ogilby. All these writers, as Towers shows, had been associated with a kind of drama which relied largely upon spectacle; and Shadwell himself had recently devised the lavishly spectacular *Psyche* for presentation at Dorset Garden, a theatre well suited to such scenic extravagances. 'Like Jonson before him', Towers writes, 'Dryden fears the written play may be lost among the wonderful scenes and machines.' Towers further notes that 'Jonson had broken with Inigo Jones over exactly the same issue'.[30] The hint is valuable; and it is worth recalling that Jonson's quarrel with Inigo Jones over the relative importance of the court masque reached its climax in 1631 with a satire which Dryden would certainly have known, 'An Expostulation with Inigo Jones':

---

[29] See my essay, 'Language, Noise, and Nonsense: *The Alchemist*', in Earl Miner (ed.), *Seventeenth-Century Imagery* (Berkeley, 1971), 69–82.

[30] 'The Lineage of Shadwell: An Approach to *Mac Flecknoe*', *SEL: Studies in English Literature 1500–1900*, 3 (1963), 323–34. Rachel Trickett, *The Honest Muse* (Oxford, 1967), 54–8, associates such spectacle specifically with the city.

O Showes! Showes! Mighty Showes!
The Eloquence of Masques! What need of prose
Or Verse, or Sense t'express Immortal you?
You are the Spectacles of State! Tis true
Court Hieroglyphicks! & all Artes affoord
In the mere perspective of an Inch Board!
You aske noe more then certeyne politique Eyes,
Eyes that can pierce into the Misteryes
Of many Coulors! read them! & reveale
Mythology there painted on slit deal!
Oh, to make Boardes to speake! There is a taske
Painting & Carpentry are the Soul of Masque.

(*Ungathered Verse*, 34. 39–50)

Jonson here characteristically laments the primacy given to 'eyes' over understanding. The 'politique Eyes' of the court audience are proud to 'pierce' the mysteries of Jones's masques, but such mysteries are wholly superficial, running no deeper than 'the mere perspective of an Inch Board'. What is neglected is the more profound art of the poet: 'What need of . . . Sense'? 'Sense' is a very precise word in Jonson's vocabulary. 'In all speech', he writes in *Discoveries* (1884–9), 'words and sense, are as the body, and the soule. The sense is as the life and soule of Language, without which all words are dead. Sense is wrought out of experience, the knowledge of humane life, and actions, or of the liberall Arts . . . .' Inigo Jones's scenes and machines, lacking such life and soul, are literally *non-sense*.

Shadwell in *Mac Flecknoe* is similarly presented as a foe to sense and champion of nonsense. He has a 'want of sense', makes no 'truce with Sense', is a 'flayle of Sense', 'a tympany of sense' and finally and deservedly inherits all the realms of nonsense (156, 117, 89, 194). Like Inigo Jones, he has given his energies to 'Mighty Showes'. In writing *Psyche* in 1674/5, Shadwell was uneasily aware that he was not treading in the best Jonsonian traditions. '*In a thing written in five weeks, as this was*', he declares in his Preface, '*there must needs be many Errors, which I desire true Criticks to pass by* . . . .' (True critics may not need to be reminded of what neither Shadwell nor his modern commentators point out, that Jonson had taken exactly the same period to write *Volpone*: ''Tis knowne, five weekes fully pen'd it', *Volpone*, Prologue, 16.) And Shadwell continues:

I doubt not but that the Candid Reader will forgive the faults, when he considers, that the great Design was to entertain the Town with variety of

Musick, curious Dancing, splendid Scenes and Machines: And that I do not,
nor ever did, intend to value my self upon the writing of this Play. For I had
rather be Author of one Scene of Comedy, like some of Ben. Johnson's, then
of all the best Plays of this kind that have been, or ever shall be written. . . .

The contradiction which Dryden delightedly explores in *Mac*
Flecknoe is just this: that Shadwell, the arch-Jonsonian, should have
resorted to devising elaborately spectacular entertainments of a
kind which—as Dryden and Shadwell both well knew—Jonson himself would heartily have despised. It is in this context that Dryden can
write with telling precision that 'Sh——never deviates into sense'.

Dryden's presentation of Shadwell in *Mac Flecknoe* is in many
ways reminiscent of Jonson's presentation of Inigo Jones in the
'Expostulation'. Shadwell, like Jones, is at once a servant and a
product of 'the money-gett, Mechanick Age' (52), a risibly busy but
thoughtless engineer of dance, music, and spectacle, whose activities
have become as mechanical as his stage-devices:

> Sometimes as Prince of thy Harmonious band
> Thou weild'st thy Papers in thy threshing hand.
> *St. Andre*'s feet ne'er kept more equal time,
> Not ev'n the feet of thy own *Psyche*'s rhime . . .   (51–4)

Dryden introduces into *Mac Flecknoe* some of Shadwell's own stage-
machinery from *The Virtuoso*, just as Jonson had introduced into
'An Expostulation' some of Jones's machinery from his recent
masque, *Chloridia*. In Dryden's poem, Shadwell's own creations
Bruce and Longvil accelerate the advent of his reign by dropping the
still-declaiming Flecknoe through a recognizably Shadwellian stage
trapdoor; in Jonson's poem, Jones seems to elevate his own fame as
he had recently elevated Lady Fame in an admired piece of invisible
masquing machinery. Jones wears a wooden stage-dagger, Shadwell
bears *Love's Kingdom*, 'At once his Sceptre and his rule of Sway'
(123).

In some respects, Dryden's manner of satire and Jonson's are
worlds apart: Dryden is cool, urbane, amused, indirect, where
Jonson is passionate, blunt, contemptuous, and direct.[31] Yet
Dryden's poem is nevertheless informed by Jonsonian judgements
and attitudes. One might say that throughout *Mac Flecknoe* Dryden
is, in a sense, 'playing Jonson', while casting the unfortunate and

[31] See my essay, 'Jonson and Anger', in Claude Rawson (ed.), assisted by Jenny
Mezciems, *English Satire and the Satiric Tradition* (Oxford, 1984), 56–71.

obsessively Jonsonian Shadwell into various roles and positions formerly occupied by Jonson's satirical adversaries. It was not the first time Dryden had assumed such a role: only a few years before the composition of *Mac Flecknoe*, he had written in the Preface to *Notes and Observations on the Empress of Morocco* (1673)—this time in collaboration with Shadwell, in an assault upon Elkanah Settle: 'I knew indeed that to Write against him, was to do him too great an Honour: But I considered Ben. Johnson had done it before to Decker, our Authors Predecessor, who he chastis'd in his Poetaster under the Character of Crispinus; and brought him in Vomiting up his Fustian and Non-sense.'[32]

⊷❀⊶

Allusions to Jonson's work, both acknowledged and concealed, pervade all of Dryden's writing; their very frequency shows that Dryden had an exceptionally intimate knowledge of Jonson's work: a testimony in itself to the power of Jonson's influence on Dryden, even where the context of Dryden's remarks is uncomplimentary. There is a curious moment early in Dryden's *Discourse Concerning the Original and Progress of Satire* in which he dismisses Jonson's poem to the memory of Shakespeare as 'an insolent, sparing, and invidious panegyric', only half a dozen lines after praising the lyric verses of Charles, Earl of Dorset, in a phrase boldly plundered from Jonson's poem: 'they are the delight and wonder of this age, and will be the envy of the next'.[33] (Jonson: 'Soule of the Age! / The applause! delight! the wonder of our Stage!' *Ungathered Verse*, 26. 17–18. There was nothing sparing about Dryden's praise of Dorset.) It is doubly odd that Dryden should introduce the notion of Dorset's verses arousing future 'envy' while dismissing Jonson's 'invidious panegyric', for Jonson's poem begins with an explicit denial of invidiousness: 'To draw no envy (*Shakespeare*) on thy name . . . .' Dryden was later to make the same sort of denial in his epistle to Congreve: 'We cannot envy you because we love' (34). 'Envy' is a word that recurs

[32] Dryden, *The Works*, ed. E. N. Hooker and H. T. Swenberg Jr, vol. xvii: *Prose 1668–1691* (Berkeley, 1971), 84. (Dekker is in fact represented in *Poetaster* as the character Demetrius; Crispinus represents John Marston.) Settle indignantly complained of Dryden's '*strutting, and impudently comparing himself to* Ben Johnson': Dryden, *Notes and Observations on The Empress of Morocco Revised* (1674), Preface.

[33] *Of Dramatic Poesy*, ii. 75.

with significant frequency in the writings of both Jonson and
Dryden. Both men, even as they formally denied the existence of
envy in their relationships with other writers, were all too aware of
the strains as well as the stimulus such relationships might create.
Dryden's attitude to Ben Jonson was not unlike Jonson's own attitude to Shakespeare: generous in acknowledging the existence of
genius, but careful too to make critical reservations in order to leave,
so to speak, some creative distance.

Christopher Ricks, in a penetrating study of Dryden's literary
relationships, has put this matter shrewdly in speaking of Dryen's
dealings with Milton:

Dryden's respect for Milton was not less real, but it was necessarily more imperilled, its animation overlapping with animus. So his greatest allusion to
Milton, *Absalom and Achitophel*, implies a repudiation of Milton's politics
while gaining energy from Milton's poetic energy; the partial repudiation
left room for Dryden to breathe.[34]

Dryden was closer in spirit to Jonson, his great predecessor, than he
was to Milton, his great contemporary, and Ricks's general perception has particular force as we ponder Dryden's total attitude to
Jonson: partial repudiation again left Dryden room to breathe. ''Tis
as much commendation as a man can bear to own him excellent',
Dryden wrote, of Milton; 'all beyond it is idolatry.' [35] 'For I lov'd the
man, and doe honour his memory (on this side Idolatry) as much as
any', Jonson had written of Shakespeare (*Discoveries*, 654–5). Both
Dryden and Jonson were acutely conscious of the risks of idolatry,
and knew that the strongest relationships are those in which admiration is tempered by criticism, by an awareness that writers and their
times—like fathers and sons and their times—necessarily have their
differences as well as their similarities. 'I do not admire him blindly,
and without looking into his imperfections', said Dryden of
Jonson.[36] The spirit of thoughtless filial devotion shown by Shadwell
and his like was not only ludicrous in its servility to the past: more
damagingly, it impeded the truest kind of poetic continuity from age
to age.

'Tis not with an ultimate intention to pay reverence to the *manes* of
Shakespeare, Fletcher, and Ben Jonson that they commend their writings,

[34] 'Allusion', 235.
[35] Preface to *Sylvae* (1685), *Of Dramatic Poesy*, ii. 32.
[36] Preface to *An Evening's Love* (1671), ibid. i. 148.

but to throw dirt on the writers of this age: their declaration is one thing, and their practice is another. By a seeming veneration to our fathers, they would thrust out us, their lawful issue, and govern us themselves, under a specious pretence of reformation.[37]

Jonson himself seems not have felt (as Dryden from time to time apparently did feel) overshadowed or pre-empted by the achievements of the great literary figures of the immediate past. In Jonson's writing there is little sense that—to use Neander's words from Dryden's *Essay of Dramatic Poesy*—'all comes sullied and wasted to us';[38] little sense of literary fathers cramping the style of an aspiring son; little groaning under the burden of the past. To Jonson, it seemed only natural for the would-be poet to model himself upon an exemplary figure from the past; yet he reflected also on the dangers of thoughtless imitation:

The third requisite in our *Poet*, or Maker, is *Imitation*, to bee able to convert the substance, or Riches of an other *Poet*, to his owne use. To make choise of one excellent man above the rest, and so to follow him, till he grow very *Hee*: or, so like him, as the Copie may be mistaken for the Principall. Not, as a Creature, that swallowes, what it takes in, crude, raw, or indigested; but, that feedes with an Appetite, and hath a Stomacke to concoct, divide, and turne all into nourishment. Not, to imitate servilely, as *Horace* saith, and catch at vices, for vertue: but, to draw forth out of the best, and choisest flowers, with the Bee, and turne all into Honey, worke it into one relish, and savour: make our *Imitation* sweet: observe, how the best writers have imitated, and follow them. (*Discoveries*, 2466–80)[39]

'So like him, as the Copie may be mistaken for the Principall': it is almost as though Shadwell set out to obey this injunction to the letter, without comprehending the larger spirit of the passage as a whole.

Jonson knew furthermore that sons could not lightly assume they had inherited the qualities of their parents. Writing to the sons of his friend Sir Kenelm Digby in the early 1630s, Jonson made the point lightly but tellingly:

[37] 'To the Right Honourable Lord Radcliffe', prefixed to *Examen Poeticum* (1693), ibid. ii. 159.

[38] Ibid. i. 85.

[39] The passage is itself a double imitation, being taken from a Renaissance commentator who is in turn remembering Seneca's Epistle lxxxiv: see *Ad Lucilium Epistulae Morales*, trans. Richard M. Gummere, 3 vols. (1917–25), ii. 278–81. Seneca (but not Jonson) continues: 'Even if there shall appear in you a likeness to him who, by reason of your admiration, has left a deep impress on you, I would have you resemble him as a child resembles his father, and not as a picture resembles its original; for a picture is a lifeless thing.'

Boast not these Titles of your Ancestors;
  (Brave Youths), they'are their possessions, none of yours:
When your owne Vertues, equall'd have their Names,
  'Twill be but faire, to leane upon their *Fames*;
For they are strong Supporters: But, till then,
  The greatest are but growing Gentlemen.

(The Underwood, 84. 8. 1–6)

In this guardedness about the nature of literary inheritance (moral, intellectual, creative), Jonson and Dryden are at one. For all his qualified criticism of Ben Jonson—or, more accurately, *because* of that criticism—Dryden seems to have earned the Jonsonian inheritance in a way that Shadwell did not. As T. S. Eliot noted years ago, Dryden was 'precisely, a poetic practitioner who learned from Jonson', and his writing was 'a living criticism of Jonson's work'.[40] 'A living criticism': it is in that deeper sense that Dryden may be recognized as Jonson's truest successor in the age that followed his death.

---

[40] 'Ben Jonson', in *Selected Essays*, 3rd, enlarged, edn. (1951), 147.

11

'Not of an Age'
Jonson, Shakespeare, and the Verdicts of Posterity

'HE was not of an age, but for all time!', declared Ben Jonson in his poem 'To the Memory of My Beloved, The Author, Mr William Shakespeare, and What He Hath Left Us', that stands at the head of Shakespeare's 1623 First Folio. These were brave words in 1623: no one until then had so positively asserted the perennial and enduring nature of Shakespeare's genius, hailing him so boldly as a writer *for all time*. By the late eighteenth century Jonson's phrase had changed from a lively prediction to an uncontested truism. Shakespeare had by now self-evidently stood the test of time, and appeared to belong to more ages than one. In the late twentieth century the tribute has become once more debatable: Shakespeare is no longer viewed as a timeless and transhistorical genius, but as a textual phenomenon that is constantly reconstructed, constantly reinvented, constantly reinterpreted by every age according to its needs, priorities, and preconceptions. At the end of his memorial poem, Jonson figures Shakespeare as a fixed star, shining chidingly and cheeringly from the heavens throughout all time. For Gary Taylor, Shakespeare is no longer a star but a black hole, an insatiable vortex, 'spinning, sucking, growing', a source and centre of massive critical turbulence. In this new and sharply relativist vision, Shakespeare has become, as Derek Longhurst puts it in the title of a recent revisionist essay, ' "Not for all time, but for an Age" '.[1]

The variations in Ben Jonson's own literary reputation, as I wish to show, have been similarly linked to changing historicist assumptions, his writings having been at various times valued and devalued on account of their supposed relationship to the age in which Jonson

---

[1] Gary Taylor, *Reinventing Shakespeare* (1991), 410–11; Derek Longhurst, ' "Not for all time, but for an Age": An Approach to Shakespeare Studies', in Peter Widdowson (ed.), *Re-Reading English* (1982), 150–63.

lived—and of the supposed relationship of that age to the historical present. The author who vowed to show 'an Image of the times', to 'oppose a mirrour' to the audiences who viewed his plays, who was hailed in turn at his death as the 'Mirror of our *Age*!', was judged by the late seventeenth and early eighteenth centuries to have reflected all too faithfully the manners and mores of his bygone times.[2] Historicized (so to speak) out of existence, Jonson was to be seen as an author fit chiefly for antiquarian study; a poet of his age, perhaps, but scarcely *for all time*.

The shape of this story is in part chiasmic, with Jonson's star sinking as Shakespeare's climbs ever higher in the skies. Nothing so exciting or voracious as a black hole, Jonson was to move quietly into a part of the literary heavens where, for years to come, he would not be much admired or even much observed. The story is also circular; for the *age* which Jonson and Shakespeare were thought (variously) to have represented and transcended was largely an imaginary construct, fabricated out of the very writings of the authors themselves. The story thus concerns the conjunction of 'history' and 'literature', and the use (and misuse) of literary texts as historical evidence.

⋘✦⋙

> Soule of the Age!
> The applause! delight! the wonder of our Stage!
> My *Shakespeare*, rise . . .

(Ungathered Verse, 26. 17–19)

When Ben Jonson's great poem of tribute was published in 1623, Shakespeare had been dead for seven years. The age of which Shakespeare is the soul is the present age, as well as that in which he literally lived. The word 'Soule' is carefully chosen: Jonson uses it elsewhere quite precisely in relation to literary texts. In the 1606 quarto of *Hymenaei* he distinguishes the text of that masque, that will survive to posterity, from its spectacular and scenic elements, devised by Inigo Jones, that are transitory and ephemeral:

It is a noble and just advantage, that the things subjected to *understanding* have of those which are objected to *sense*, that the one sort are but

---

[2] *Every Man In His Humour* (folio), Prologue, 23; *Every Man Out Of His Humour*, Induction, 118 (cf. III. vi. 202–7); Edmund Waller, 'Upon Ben: Johnson', Herford and Simpson, xi. 447.

momentarie, and meerely taking, the other impressing, and lasting: Else the glorie of all these *solemnities* had perish'd like a blaze, and gone out in the *beholders* eyes. So short-lived are the *bodies* of all things, in comparison of their *soules*. And though *bodies* oft-times have the ill luck to be sensually preferr'd, they find afterwards, the good fortune (when *soules* live) to be utterly forgotten. (1–10)

Shakespeare is the soul of his age, then, in the sense that he represents that element which will endure and carry to posterity. There is consequently a faint air of paradox but no actual contradiction when Jonson moves to his supreme tribute to Shakespeare, to the phrase that is now carved in stone on the exterior of the Folger Shakespeare Library: 'He was not of an age, but for all time!' (43). Shakespeare is the soul of the age, but is not of an age: the double truth is nicely poised.[3]

By the Restoration, the age of Shakespeare and of Jonson already seemed remote; those placid, far-off days before the Civil War were now 'the last age', 'the age before the flood'.[4] With the growing sense of temporal distance came a new sense of cultural progressivism. Dryden, in his Epilogue to the second part of *The Conquest of Granada* in 1672, measures the advance of English manners and English dramatic writing since the final years of Queen Elizabeth and the early years of King James, 'When men were dull, and conversation low'. To the more cultivated audiences of the Restoration, the comedy of Jonson seemed dated, laboured, gross.

> Then, Comedy was faultless, but 'twas course:
> *Cobbs* Tankard was a jest, and *Otter's* horse . . .
>
> Wit's now arriv'd to a more high degree;
> Our native Language more refin'd and free.
> Our Ladies and our men now speak more wit
> In conversation, than those Poets writ.   (4–6, 23–6)

Dryden's own good fortune is now 'To please an Age more Gallant than the last' (34).[5]

---

[3] Anthony Miller has pointed to Ciceronian borrowings in the poem, and suggested that in the phrase 'not of an age, but for all time!' Jonson may be recalling and outdoing Cicero's praise of each of the ancient poets and orators he hails as *princeps temporibus illis*: 'Jonson's Praise of Shakespeare and Cicero's *De Oratore*, III. vii', *Notes and Queries*, NS 38/236 (March 1991), 82–3. For other criticism, see Ch. 2 n. 36 above.

[4] See e. g. 'To my Dear Friend Mr Congreve, on his COMEDY, call'd The Double Dealer', in *The Poems of John Dryden*, ed. James Kinsley, 4 vols. (Oxford, 1958), ii. 852–4.

[5] Ibid. i. 134–5.

It is tempting to regard this Epilogue as itself no more than an act of strategic gallantry towards those audiences whose gallantry it ingratiatingly salutes. Dryden's compliment rests upon the premiss that dramatists are of necessity the products and mirrors of the societies for which they collusively and mimetically write. Whether, and how, a writer such as Shakespeare may transcend his age is a question that is never seriously addressed; indeed, it is a necessary part of Dryden's strategy in the Epilogue to keep the very name of Shakespeare, which might threaten the cogency of his proposition, safely out of sight. Instead he concentrates his attention upon Jonson, firmly relegating him to the dull mechanic age for which he conformingly wrote. There is none the less a noticeable ambivalence about the way in which Dryden seems at once to concede and to deny the supremacy of his dramatic predecessors. That ambivalence is more clearly evident in Dryden's essay written in defence of the Epilogue later in the same year, 'On the Dramatic Poetry of the Last Age'.[6] In this more measured and generous, yet still determinedly progressivist account, Dryden acknowledges the greatness of Jonson and Shakespeare, but attempts to demonstrate in a more detailed way how deeply their work is flawed by the cultural backwardness of the age in which they lived. Many of his examples may seem, to modern eyes, somewhat unpersuasive. Both writers, we are told, resorted on occasions to puns and wordplay; Jonson at times finished a sentence with a preposition, and was known occasionally to use a Latinism at the expense of a common English word; both Shakespeare and Jonson employed from time to time the double comparative; some of Shakespeare's plots seem nowadays ridiculous and incoherent. Neither writer had the benefit of listening to polite conversation at the court of Charles II, and their dramatic dialogue suffered accordingly.

What is remarkable about this account is the way in which it attempts to substantiate a general view of an entire historical period—one might almost say, a general view of the processes of history—from a handful of literary texts; indeed, from certain aspects of those texts which to readers in another age might seem of very slight significance. Small changes in linguistic and grammatical usage that have occurred between the age of Shakespeare and the age

---

[6] *Of Dramatic Poesy and Other Critical Essays*, ed. George Watson, 2 vols. (1962), i. 169–83.

of Dryden are taken as evidence of a larger process of cultural refinement. The late Elizabethan/early Jacobean period is historically constructed as a culturally primitive age which nevertheless produced by a process of inexplicable paradox the greatest dramatists the English stage has ever known.

G. E. Bentley has argued that, up until the time of Dryden, it was Jonson and not Shakespeare who was widely regarded as England's 'arch poet', her supreme literary genius; and that, when Shakespeare's reputation began at last to move ahead of Jonson's in the 1690s, this was largely owing to the testimony of Dryden himself.[7] The next century was to witness the rapid and spectacular rise of Shakespeare's reputation, and a corresponding plummeting in the fortunes of Ben Jonson.[8] These two phenomena are intimately and complicatedly related, the greatness of Shakespeare being often explained throughout the eighteenth century by contrastive reference to the supposed weaknesses of Jonson, which are in turn regularly highlighted by reference to the seemingly opposite practice of Shakespeare. I want to concentrate here upon one aspect of this complex realignment of literary reputations by looking at the way in which the promotion of Shakespeare's reputation necessitated his being detached more and more from the supposedly primitive age in which he lived, idealized to a transcendental role, seen as belonging to *no age*; while the subordination of Jonson necessitated, conversely, that he be increasingly associated with and relegated to the age in which he lived, seen as its product, its chronicler, and ultimately its victim.

This process begins with the routine explanation that such faults as Shakespeare possessed could be attributed to the times in which he lived, and that he himself in his own person somehow stood free of guilt. Initially this indulgence was granted to three major writers, Shakespeare, Jonson, and Fletcher; progressively it was to be reduced. 'Their Slips were more the Age's Fault than theirs', wrote Robert Gould in his poem *The Play-House: A Satyr* in 1695:

---

[7] See Ch. 2 n. 14, above.

[8] Brian Vickers's six-volume *Shakespeare* (1974–81) and D. H. Craig's *Ben Jonson* (1990) in the Routledge Critical Heritage series provide indispensable documentation here. The secondary literature on this realignment is extensive. See R. G. Noyes, *Ben Jonson on the English Stage, 1660–1776* (Cambridge, Mass., 1935); R. W. Babcock, *The Genesis of Shakespeare Idolatry, 1766–1799* (Chapel Hill, 1931); Stuart Tave, *The Amiable Humorist* (Chicago, 1960); Jonathan Bate, *Shakespearean Constitutions* (Oxford, 1989); Margreta de Grazia, *Shakespeare Verbatim* (Oxford, 1991); and esp. Howard Felperin, *The Uses of the Canon* (Oxford, 1990), ch. 1.

Where *Fletcher*'s loose, 'twas Writ to serve the *Stage*,
And *Shakespeare* play'd with Words to please a Quibbling Age.[9]

Much was to be said about this quibbling age in the years to come. 'As for his Jingling sometimes, and playing upon Words, it was the common Vice of the Age he liv'd in', wrote Nicholas Rowe in his edition of the works of Shakespeare in 1709 (viciously completing his sentence with a preposition).[10] Charles Gildon the following year agreed with Rowe: Shakespeare's faults were to be ascribed to 'the Ignorance of the Age he liv'd in'.[11] Elijah Fenton expressed his opinion in couplets in 1711.

> *Shakespeare* the Genius of our Isle, whose Mind—
> The universal Mirror of Mankind—
> Express'd all Images, enrich'd the Stage
> But stoop'd too low to please a barb'rous Age.
> When his Immortal Bays began to grow
> Rude was the Language, and the Humour Low.[12]

The processes of bardolatry and transcendentalism are here already visible. Shakespeare is now not merely 'the Genius of our Isle', but 'the universal Mirror of Mankind'. Yet Shakespeare mirrored also, it would seem, the language and humour of the barbarous age in which he lived. His genius appears to have survived in despite of this regrettable contact; it is not seen in any sense to have been nourished by the age. 'The Faults of Shakespeare, which are rather those of the Age in which he liv'd', pronounced John Dennis in 1719, 'are his perpetual Rambles, and his apparent Duplicity (in some of his Plays) or Triplicity of Action, and the frequent breaking the Continuity of the Scenes.'[13] As for 'the poor witticisms and conceits' of Shakespeare, Sir Thomas Hanmer explained in his edition of Shakespeare in 1744, 'it is to be remember'd that he wrote for the Stage, rude and unpolished as it then was; and the vicious taste of the age must stand condemn'd for them.'[14] Shakespeare's 'jingles, puns, and quibbles',

---

[9] Robert Gould, *Works* (1709), quoted in Vickers, *Shakespeare*, i. 416.
[10] Quoted ibid. ii. 197.
[11] *An Essay on the Art, Rise, and Progress of the Stage in Greece, Rome, and England*, quoted ibid. 217–18.
[12] *An Epistle to Mr Southerne, From Kent*, quoted ibid. 265.
[13] Letter to Judas Iscariot, Esq.: 'On the Degeneracy of the Publick Taste', quoted ibid. 350; cf. ii. 282.
[14] Quoted ibid. iii. 119.

judged Zachary Grey a few years later, 'were certainly owing to the false taste of the times in which he lived'.[15]

In all these examples it is clear that two things are happening. First, an agreed historical view of the late Tudor and early Stuart age is being consolidated from literary evidence: the evidence of puns, double plots, indecorous witticisms, which, taken together, are thought sufficient to stamp the age as vicious and barbarous. No other literary, cultural, or social factors are brought into consideration; how the age produced so many distinguished writers and artists is allowed to remain a mystery. Secondly, a rescue operation is being mounted on behalf of Shakespeare, who is gradually prised away from the age in which he unhappily lived, and 'universalized' in such a way as to accommodate his work to eighteenth-century tastes and dispositions. Elizabeth Montagu in 1769 perfectly demonstrates these two co-ordinated rhetorical strategies:

Shakespeare wrote at a time when learning was tinctured with pedantry, wit was unpolished and mirth ill-bred. The court of Elizabeth spoke a scientific jargon, and a certain obscurity of style was universally affected. James brought an addition of pedantry, accompanied by indecent and indelicate manners and language. By contagion, or from complaisance to the taste of the public, Shakespeare falls sometimes into the fashionable mode of writing. But this is only by fits, for many parts of all his plays are written with the most noble, elegant, and uncorrupted simplicity. Such is his merit that the more just and refined the taste of the nation has become the more he has encreased in reputation. He was approved by his own age, admired by the next, and is revered, and almost adored by the present.[16]

Dr Johnson by a more strenuous process of argumentation arrived at a similar position. His editing of the works of Shakespeare is premissed on the belief that, with the passage of time, Shakespeare's language, his allusions, his very systems of belief have become in many ways obscure, demanding editorial explication. 'In order to make a true estimate of the abilities and merit of a Writer', he declares in his *Miscellaneous Observations on the Tragedy of 'Macbeth'*, 'it is always necessary to examine the genius of his age, and the opinions of his contemporaries.' Thus, to understand *Macbeth* one must attempt to understand what Shakespeare and his

---

[15] Zachary Grey et al., Preface to *Critical, Historical, and Explanatory Notes on Shakespeare*, 2 vols. (1754); Vickers, *Shakespeare*, iv. 148.

[16] *An Essay on the Writings and Genius of Shakespeare*, quoted in Vickers, *Shakespeare*, iii. 329.

contemporaries may have felt on the subject of witchcraft.[17] Johnson speaks frankly of the 'barbarity' of Shakespeare's age. Yet Shakespeare's chief distinction, in Samuel Johnson's view, is that he ultimately transcends that age.

Shakespeare is above all writers, at least above all modern writers, the poet of nature; the poet that holds up to his readers a faithful mirrour of manners and of life. His characters are not modified by the customs of particular places, unpractised by the rest of the world; by the peculiarities of studies or professions, which can operate but upon small numbers; or by the accidents of transient fashions or temporary opinions: they are the genuine progeny of common humanity, such as the world will always supply, and observation will always find. His persons act and speak by the influence of those general passions and principles by which all minds are agitated, and the whole system of life is continued in motion. In the writings of other poets a character is too often an individual; in those of Shakespeare it is commonly a species.[18]

Shakespeare in Samuel Johnson's analysis is presented as the poet of nature, not of a particular society; his work is seen to belong not merely to his age but to 'common humanity', to exemplify what Johnson roundly calls 'the whole system of life'.

It remained for Coleridge to take the universalizing process one step further, dehistoricizing Shakespeare in a way that Dr Johnson had not. 'Shakespeare', wrote Coleridge in 1834, 'is of no age—nor, I may add, of any religion, or party, or profession. The body and substance of his works came out of the unfathomable depths of his own oceanic mind: his observation and reading, which was considerable, supplied him with the drapery of his figures.'[19] And again:

Least of all poets colored in any particulars by the spirit or customs of his age, [so] that the spirit of all that it had pronounced intrinsically and permanently good concentrated and perfected itself in his mind. Thus we have neither the chivalry of the North, nothing indeed in any peculiar sense of the word, and as little of the genii and winged griffins of the East; in an age of religious and political heat nothing sectarian in religion or politics; in an age of misers so flagrant in all the dramas of his contemporaries and successors, no miser characters; in an age of witchcraft and astrology, no

---

[17] *Johnson on Shakespeare*, ed. Arthur Sherbo, vol. vii of the Yale Edition of the Works of Samuel Johnson (New Haven, 1968), 3.

[18] 'Preface to Shakespeare' (1765), in *Johnson on Shakespeare*, 62.

[19] *Table Talk* (1835), 15 Mar. 1834, in James Thornton (ed.), *Table Talk from Ben Jonson to Leigh Hunt* (1934), 251–2.

witches (for we must [not] be deluded by stage directions); but the female character, the craving for presight (Macbeth), all that must ever be elements of the social state, etc.[20]

The difference between Johnson's position and that of Coleridge is nicely indicated by that passing comment on the delusive nature of stage directions. For Johnson, it was necessary to remember that while Shakespeare spoke to modern sensibilities he also lived in an age in which people believed quite literally in the existence of witches. For Coleridge, the weird sisters of *Macbeth* are not witches but transhistorical beings, manifestations of 'the female character', equally comprehensible, equally mysterious, in any age, the recurrent products of human society.

❧

While Shakespeare was being thus abstracted, generalized, and de-contextualized, Ben Jonson was undergoing a contrary course of treatment. By the 1690s other critics were echoing Dryden's complaint that Jonson's plays seemed products of a bygone age. His characters were based on well-known types and personalities of that age, and yet, said one commentator, 'Such Representations are like a Painters taking a Picture after the Life in the Apparel then Worn, which becomes Ungraceful or Ridiculous in the next Age, when the Fashion is out.'[21] Jonson was seen as having opportunistically exploited such fashions for satirical purposes within his plays. The character of Volpone, wrote one critic in the 1730s, was no doubt based upon some figure of the day, but the allusion, like others, is now lost on modern audiences.

'Tis highly probable that this Method of *Ben*'s might be of great Service, as to the immediate Fortune of his Plays, tho' at this Day it doubtless leaves us in the Dark, as to many Particulars which, if we had an exact Character of him against whom the Satyr is pointed, would become Beauties instead of being thought Defects . . . such is the Variety of Characters presented in the Space of a few Years on the publick Theatre of Life, that in a short time the most striking grow antiquated, and the public by gazing continually on what passes in their own Times, lose all Ideas of what passed before. Hence it follows that not only *Johnson*'s Plays, but all the Tribe of Writers who

---

[20] *Shakespearean Criticism*, ed. T. M. Raysor, 2 vols. (1960), i. 216–17.

[21] The opinion of 'Julio' in James Wright's *Country Conversations* (1694); quoted in Noyes, *Ben Jonson on the English Stage*, 26.

followed him, fail of moving a Modern Audience upon the Stage, or of entertaining them in their Closets.[22]

Having witnessed a revival of Jonson's comedy *The Silent Woman* in 1752 the theatre historian Thomas Davies regretted that 'the frequent allusions to forgotten customs and characters render it impossible to be ever revived with any probability of success. To understand Jonson's comedies perfectly', he went on, 'we should have before us a satirical history of the age in which he lived.'[23] History must now be brought to the service and understanding of dramatic literature. The difference between Shakespeare and Jonson, declared B. Walwyn in 1782, is that 'the portraits of Shakespeare are made to last till Doomsday, while the lustring and fashionable shadows of the day drawn by Ben Jonson grow obsolete in the wearing of them'.[24] It remained for Nathan Drake in 1817 to put the final nail in Jonson's coffin, by recalling and reversing the famous tribute which Jonson had once paid affectionately to Shakespeare:

When Jonson, in his noble and generous eulogium on Shakespeare, tells us, that

'He was not of an age, but for all time,'

he seized a characteristic of which the reverse, in some degree, applies to himself; for had he paid less attention to the *minutiae* of his own age, and dedicated himself more to universal habits and feelings, his popularity would have nearly equalled that of the poet whom he loved and praised.[25]

There are several ironies in this developing contrast between the generalized, universalized, eternalized Shakespeare and the particularized, ephemeral, transitory Jonson. For one thing, Jonson himself in his own lifetime had placed great faith in the judgement of posterity; however spurned or neglected his works might be in his own age, he never ceased to believe that their true value would be recognized in the years to come. When his Roman tragedy *Catiline* was hissed from the stage in 1611, Jonson defiantly published the text of the play,

---

[22] Anon., *Memoirs of the Life of Robert Wilks, Esq.*, 1732, pp. vii–viii, quoted in Noyes, *Ben Jonson on the English Stage*, 29.
[23] *Dramatic Miscellanies*, 2 vols. (1784), ii. 101–2.
[24] *An Essay on Comedy*, quoted in Vickers, *Shakespeare*, vi. 327.
[25] *Shakspeare and his Times*, 2 vols. (1817), ii. 580. Commenting on Jonson's tribute to Shakespeare, 'Horatio' in the *Gentleman's Magazine*, 42 (1772), 522, had reached a similar verdict: 'Ben's reputation was partly confined to the age in which he lived, and that which immediately succeeded to it. He delighted to catch the Cynthia of the minute; to paint the follies of the times, which are as uncertain as the forms of court-address, and as changeable as the fashions of our cloaths.'

commending it to William Herbert, Earl of Pembroke, with a characteristic dedication: '*In so thick, and darke an ignorance, as now
almost covers the age, I crave leave to stand neare your light: and, by
that, to bee read. Posteritie may pay your benefit the honor, &
thanks: when it shall know, that you dare, in these Jig-given times, to
countenance a legitimate Poeme*' (1–6).

It was a strategic necessity in the eighteenth-century rescue of
Shakespeare to insist that Shakespeare had done all that he could to
reform the evil theatrical and linguistic practices of his day, and distance himself from them. 'While the stage was thus over-run with
ignorance, impertinence, and the lowest quibble, our immortal
Shakespeare arose', wrote William Guthrie in 1747. 'But supposing
him to have produced a commission from that heaven whence he derived his genius, for the reformation of the stage, what could he do in
the circumstances he was under? He did all that man and more that
any man but himself could do.'[26] The truth is, however, that
Shakespeare did not see it as his divine mission to berate and reform
the age or the stage, while Jonson undeniably did. It is Jonson who
speaks of these jig-given times, of darkness and ignorance covering
the age; it is Jonson who asserts, in the Epistle Dedicatory to
Volpone, that the manners and natures of the writers of these days
are inverted, that the age is one 'wherein *Poetrie*, and the Professors
of it heare so ill, on all sides, there will a reason bee look'd for in the
subject' (11–12); it is Jonson who roundly declares, in his 'Ode to
Himself' written after the failure of *The New Inn*, 'Come, leave the
lothed stage, / And the more lothsome age'. The first line of this ode
has attracted more attention than the second; but how, one may ask,
does Jonson, in this remarkable phrase, expect to leave the loath-
some *age*, other than by death? The answer is: through his verse,
which Jonson vows will 'hit the starres' (58). It is as a star that Jonson
finally pictures Shakespeare in the poem to his memory, through his
rage or influence chiding or cheering the drooping stage. Jonson too
aspired to an elevated position, somewhere remotely above 'our
Daintie age': 'high and aloofe, / Safe from the wolves black jaw, and
the dull Asses hoofe' (*The Underwood*, 23. 31, 35–6, 58).

'*Good men* are the Stars, the Planets of the Ages wherein they
live, and illustrate the times', wrote Jonson in *Discoveries*. 'These,
sensuall men thought mad, because they would not be partakers, or

---

[26] *An Essay on English Tragedy*, quoted in Vickers, *Shakespeare*, iii. 193.

practisers of their madnesse. But they, plac'd high on the top of all virtue, look'd downe on the Stage of the world, and contemned the Play of *Fortune*' (1100–1, 1104–8). The *stars*, the great figures who illustrate the age—illuminate it, make it illustrious—are paradoxically detached from it, placed high above like divine spectators of the play of human folly. It is as a star that Jonson depicts those great figures of his age whom he most admires: Lucy, Countess of Bedford, Elizabeth, Countess of Rutland, Henry, Lord La Warr, and the dead Sir Henry Morison, who

> leap'd the present age,
> Possest with holy rage,
> To see that bright eternal Day:
> Of which we *Priests*, and *Poets* say
> Such truths, as we expect for happy men,
> And there he lives with memory; and *Ben*
>
> *Jonson*, who sung this of him, e're he went
> Himselfe to rest . . .
>
> (*The Underwood*, 70. 79–86)[27]

Jonson in this arresting figure pictures himself too as having 'leap'd the present age', already living mentally 'there', in the elevated, priest-like region above his society where the dead Morison will find him.

Jonson returned repeatedly in his writings to the question of poetic survival. 'The common Rymers powre forth Verses, such as they are, (*ex tempore*) but there never comes from them one Sense, worth the life of a Day', Jonson wrote in *Discoveries* (2445–8); 'They had their humme; and, no more. Indeed, things, wrote with labour, deserve to be so read, and will last their Age' (2464–6). Jonson's tribute to Shakespeare, 'He was not of an age, but for all time!', encapsulated his own most powerful ambitions: to live beyond his age, to be matched against the great writers of the past, to be admired by the unknown readers of the future. For Jonson, great poets lived in effect out of time, or equally in all times, Horace and Virgil and Homer inhabiting the present as though they were contemporaries. As Oscar Wilde aptly remarked of Jonson, 'He made the poets of Greece and Rome terribly modern.'[28]

---

[27] *Epigrams*, 94; *The Forest*, 12. 65; *The Underwood*, 60. 14.
[28] *The Artist as Critic: Critical Writings of Oscar Wilde*, ed. Richard Ellmann (New York, 1969), 34–5.

❧

Jonson was taught by one of the great historians of his day (William Camden), admired and befriended others (Selden, Savile, Bacon, Ralegh), and was deeply interested in the function and methodologies of history.[29] But what kind of 'historian' was Jonson himself? What kind of 'mirror' do his imaginative writings hold to the age—what sort of 'image of the times' do they present? Does Jonson deserve the reputation which overtook him so disablingly in the eighteenth century and which lingers in some form to the present day: the reputation of a faithful chronicler whose work is locked irretrievably within the confines of the age in which he lived and about which he wrote; a writer routinely contrasted with the free-floating Shakespeare, whom Jan Kott a quarter of a century ago styled 'our contemporary'?

These are questions which can be addressed here only in the most preliminary and partial way. To approach them, I want to look at one form of historical representation which Jonson practised, and examine the way in which he chose to describe a celebrated contemporary: his patron William Herbert, third Earl of Pembroke. This case study is not chosen entirely at random, for Jonson's account of Pembroke has been thought by one scholar, Dick Taylor Junior, to be historically more trustworthy than the description of Pembroke offered by the Earl of Clarendon in his *History of the Rebellion*, constituting a characteristically dependable, characteristically Jonsonian 'image of the times'.[30] Yet it seems worth asking what kind of mirror Jonson holds up to Pembroke, and how truly he depicts both the man and the age in which he lived.

[29] Blair Worden, 'Ben Jonson among the Historians', in Kevin Sharpe and Peter Lake (eds.), *Culture and Politics in Early Stuart England* (1994), 67–89.

[30] Dick Taylor, Jun., 'Clarendon and Jonson as Witnesses for the Earl of Pembroke's Character', in Josephine W. Bennett, Oscar Carghil, and Vernon Hall, Jun. (eds.), *Studies in the English Renaissance Drama* (New York, 1959), 322–44. On Pembroke, see also Taylor's essay 'The Third Earl of Pembroke as a Patron of Poetry', *Tulane Studies in English*, 5 (1950), 41–67; Margot Heinemann, *Puritanism and Theatre* (Cambridge, 1980); Michael G. Brennan, *Literary Patronage in the English Renaissance: The Pembroke Family* (1988); Brian O'Farrell, *Politician, Patron, Poet: William Herbert, Third Earl of Pembroke, 1580–1630* (University Microfilms, Ann Arbor, 1966); David Riggs, *Ben Jonson: A Life* (Cambridge, Mass., 1989); Robert C. Evans, *Ben Jonson and the Poetics of Patronage* (Lewisburg, Pa., 1989).

Clarendon's account of Pembroke in *The History of the Rebellion* begins eulogistically. Pembroke, he declares, was well bred, learned, witty, affable, generous, magnificent, pious, patriotic, just, and courtly. As if to give credibility to this warmly admiring account, Clarendon then adds a few more stringent words about the man:

Yet his memory must not be so flattered that his virtues and good inclinations may be believed without some allay of vice, and without being clouded with great infirmities, which he had in too exorbitant proportion. He indulged to himself the pleasures of all kinds, almost in all excesses. Whether out of his natural constitution, or for want of his domestic content and delight, (for which he was most unhappy, for he paid much too dear for his wife's fortune by taking her person into the bargain) he was immoderately given up to women. But therein he likewise retained such a power and jurisdiction over his very appetite, that he was not so much transported with beauty and outward allurements, as with those advantages of the mind as manifested an extraordinary wit and spirit and knowledge, and administered great pleasure in the conversation. To these he sacrificed himself, his precious time, and much of his fortune.[31]

This part of Clarendon's account, as Taylor points out, was later seized upon by scholars keen to establish Pembroke as the young man celebrated in Shakespeare's sonnets. But how reliable a witness, Taylor asks, was Clarendon, and is his testimony really to be believed? Taylor notes that Clarendon was only 23 when Pembroke died in 1630, and that he had never been closely associated with Pembroke either socially or politically, nor with any of his colleagues. His account was (moreover) put together forty years after Pembroke's death. It is possible, Taylor suggests, that at this distance of time Clarendon may have confused William Herbert with his less admirable brother Philip.

As a better witness to the nature of Pembroke's character, Taylor summons Ben Jonson, who (he points out) was a close acquaintance of Pembroke and his family, had visited their various houses, associated with their friends, and would have been alert to court gossip and scandal. And Jonson, Taylor adds, was a man of 'sturdy integrity' who would not be likely to suppress the truth. The testimony that Taylor chooses to examine is Jonson's popular masque *The Gypsies Metamorphosed* that was performed before King James on three

---

[31] Edward Hyde, Earl of Clarendon, *The History of the Rebellion*, ed. W. Dunn Macreay, 6 vols. (Oxford, 1888), ii. 71–4.

separate occasions in 1621. Pembroke is in fact addressed only briefly in this long, skittish, and lively masque, but the Jackman's speech of salutation is the evidence on which Taylor chooses to rest his case:

> Though you, S[i]r, be Chamberlaine, I have a key
> To open yo[u]r fortune a little by the way:
>> You are a good Man,
>>> Denie it that can;
>> And faithfull you are,
>>> Denie it that dare.
> You knowe how to use yo[u]r sword and yo[u]r pen,
> And you love not alone the Arts, but the Men.
> The Graces and Muses everie where followe
> You, as you were theire second *Apollo*.
> Onelie yo[u]r hand here tells you to yo[u]r face,
>> You have wanted one grace
> To performe what hath beene a right of your place,
> ffor by this line, w[hi]ch is *Mars* his trenche,
> You never yet help'd yo[u]r Master to a wenche.
>> 'Tis well for yo[u]r honor, hee's pious and chaste,
>> Or you had most certainlie beene displac't. (681–97)

How does one interpret these lines? There is, to begin with, the problem of tone. The masquing occasions are festive, and the Jackman's lines are in some sense bantering. As James was not best known for his chastity—or, for that matter, his love of wenches—the final couplet is more lighthearted than Taylor appears to recognize. Yet the speech is uttered in the king's presence, and in Pembroke's, and some caution is needed in the midst of merriment. In such circumstances, Jonson's silence concerning the alleged weaknesses of Pembroke's character cannot really be taken as evidence that these weaknesses did not exist. Jonson cannot have been ignorant, for example, of the fact that Pembroke had fathered the two illegitimate children of Sir Robert Sidney's daughter, Lady Mary Wroth, whom Jonson also celebrates repeatedly as a lady of exemplary virtue.[32]

To test Jonson's reliability as a witness, to understand the manner in which he chooses to depict his patron and his age, it would be necessary to think more carefully about the kind of relationship that probably subsisted between the two men. Jonson had known

---

[32] *The Poems of Lady Mary Wroth*, ed. Josephine A. Roberts (Baton Rouge, 1983), introduction, 24–5. See *The Alchemist* (folio), Dedication; *Epigrams*, 103, 105; *The Underwood*, 28; *Conversations with Drummond*, 355–6.

Pembroke since the early years of the century, and was beholden to him for many acts of protection and patronage. His 1605 letter of appeal to Pembroke from prison where Jonson had been confined for making fun of King James in the comedy *Eastward Ho!* already suggests the existence of past favours.[33] Later Jonson was to tell William Drummond that Pembroke paid him twenty pounds every New Year's Day to buy books: a vital commodity for the impoverished poet (*Conversations with Drummond*, 312–13). It was to the protection of Pembroke that Jonson committed his tragedy *Catiline* after its disastrous performance in 1611, and it was to Pembroke (recently appointed Lord Chamberlain) that Jonson in 1616 strategically dedicated his *Epigrams*, 'the ripest of my studies', which carried 'danger in the sound' (Dedication, 4, 5). It was Pembroke who in 1619 recommended Jonson for an honorary degree at the University of Oxford, of which he was now Chancellor.[34] By the time Jonson came to write *The Gypsies Metamorphosed* then, a complex relationship had developed between the two men; a relationship of patronage on the one side, and dependency on the other. It is a relationship which places Jonson's 'sturdy integrity' in a particular light, by which both his utterances and his silences need to be read.

If one were searching through Jonson's writings for a more positive tribute to Pembroke's character, the obvious text to examine would be the one that Taylor oddly ignores: Epigram 102, 'To William, Earl of Pembroke', published in Jonson's folio in 1616. Jonson's rehearsal of Pembroke's virtues in this poem, as it happens, closely resembles and endorses Clarendon's account. That Jonson says nothing here about Pembroke's amorous adventures is scarcely surprising in a poem addressed directly *to* Pembroke in a collection that is also dedicated to him. What Jonson offers in this poem is not a balanced assessment of moral character of the kind favoured by Clarendon, but a starkly simplified and generalized vision of the age.

> I doe but name thee PEMBROKE, and I find
>   It is an *Epigramme*, on all man-kind;
> Against the bad, but of, and to the good:
>   Both which are ask'd, to have thee understood.
> Nor could the age have mist thee, in this strife
>   Of vice and vertue; wherein all great life

---

[33] Herford and Simpson, i. 199–200.
[34] See *The Poems of George Chapman*, ed. P. B. Bartlett (New York, 1941), 478, Chapman's marginal note.

>Almost, is exercis'd: and scarse one knowes
>>To which, yet, of the sides himselfe he owes.
>They follow vertue, for reward, to day;
>>To morrow vice, if shee give better pay:
>And are so good, and bad, just at a price,
>>As nothing else discernes the vertue' or vice.   (1–12)

'Bad', 'good', 'vice', 'vertue': the moral 'strife' which Jonson describes here is as sharply and clearly divided as the worlds of court masque and antimasque. Though struggle and doubt are mentioned, Pembroke himself is depicted in an unwavering stance, pitted 'Against the bad, but of, and to the good'. Though Pembroke is named in the poem's opening line, though his character is generally invoked, he is never particularly described; and the poem concludes with an appeal to examine a life that is lived, so to speak, outside the poem's rhetorical limits: 'and they, that hope to see / The commonwealth still safe, must studie thee' (19–20).

One might almost say that this poem is scarcely about Pembroke at all, sketching instead a timeless and generalized figure of virtue, a type equally familiar to the poets of antiquity as to those of the seventeenth century; a type to which the real life William Herbert, by various rhetorical manœuvres, is brought to conform.[35] 'The age' referred to in this poem is not uniquely and specifically the age of King James. It is a perennial and recurrent state, the times whose condition Cicero deplored, and which, like the poor, are always with us.[36] Jonson effortlessly reworks various passages from Seneca in order to construct a vision of the age in which he too happened to live.[37] Jonson's laments on the present age frequently derive in this way from classical sources, which in turn frequently posit the notion of an earlier age, when manners and morals were exemplary. The very ease with which this trope was deployed is indicative of Jonson's view of history, which he perceived not as a succession of entirely individual and unrepeatable experiences, events, personalities, and

[35] That the poem has none the less a precise historical context is ably demonstrated in Robert C. Evans's analysis, *Ben Jonson and the Poetics of Patronage*, 107–18. See also Ch. 4 above.

[36] On Jonson's fondness for Cicero's famous lament, 'O tempora, O mores' (*In Catilinam*, 1. 1. 2), see Ian Donaldson, 'Jonson and the Moralists', in Alvin B. Kernan (ed.), *Two Renaissance Mythmakers* (Baltimore, 1977), 146–64.

[37] See e.g. G. B. Jackson's annotation of the Elder Knowell's complaint against the times in *Every Man In His Humour* (folio), II. v. 1ff., in her Yale edition of the play (New Haven, 1969), 196–8, tracing sources in Juvenal, Ovid, Horace, and Quintilian.

dilemmas, but as a recurrent and in part predictable process, presenting similar terrors, similar declines from innocence, similar threats to public order, similar exemplars of public virtue, over and over again.

The methods of modern historical scholarship illuminate the work of Ben Jonson only to a certain point. Turn the light higher, peer more closely, and what you find are not, after all, local and topical quiddities and particularities, the grainy texture of actual characters and events, but something more closely akin to what Samuel Johnson believed he had found in the works of Shakespeare: 'those general passions and principles by which all minds are agitated, and the whole system of life is continued in motion'; the portrait not of an age, but of 'common humanity'.[38]

[38] Analysing Jonson's procedures in his Roman tragedies, Philip Ayres reaches a similar conclusion: 'The truth . . . is that to the materials of history he has so carefully sifted and assembled Jonson brings not the subtly discriminating mind of a historian but that same critical, simplifying eye of the moralist that critics have detected in his handling of the central "tragic" characters, especially Tiberius and Sejanus. His Roman plays may be "archaeologically" unexceptionable, but in the final analysis they are not, by Roman or for that matter Elizabethan standards, good history.' *Sejanus His Fall*, ed. Philip Ayres, The Revels Plays (Manchester, 1990), 30.

12

Jonson, Shakespeare, and the
Destruction of the Book

ONE of the astonishing aspects of Shakespeare's genius, so eighteenth-century readers believed, was his seeming indifference to the world of books. Shakespeare was the supreme example of the un-tutored artist, whose work sprang directly from his observation of nature and humankind, and from the inner recesses of the heart. 'Perhaps he was as learned as his dramatic province required', wrote Edward Young in his *Conjectures on Original Composition* in 1759, for

whatever other learning he wanted, he was master of two books, unknown to many of the profoundly read, though books, which the last conflagration alone can destroy; the book of nature, and that of man. These he had by heart, and transcribed many admirable pages of them, into his immortal works.

Ben Jonson, alas, was otherwise; for Jonson loved books to excess, and that was his undoing.

Johnson, in the serious drama, is as much an imitator, as *Shakespeare* is an original. He was very learned, as *Sampson* was very strong, to his own hurt: Blind to the nature of tragedy, he pulled down all antiquity on his head, and buried himself under it; we see nothing of *Johnson*, nor indeed, of his ad-mired (but also murdered) antients; for what shone in the historian is a cloud on the poet; and *Cataline* might have been a good play, if *Salust* had never writ.[1]

This contrast between the learned Jonson and the naturally gifted Shakespeare is (as we now know) largely fallacious. Shakespeare was

[1] Edward Young, *Conjectures on Original Composition*, ed. Edith J. Morley (Manchester, 1918), 36, 35. Young's views were characteristic of his time: see e.g. Edward Cappell's *Reflections on Originality in Authors* (1766), and Philip Neve, *Cursory Remarks on Some of the Ancient English Poets* (1789), in D. H. Craig (ed.), *Ben Jonson: The Critical Heritage* (1990), 499–502, 572–4. For other eighteenth-century ideas about the contrasting abilities of Shakespeare and Jonson, see Chs. 2 and 11 above.

altogether more widely and deeply read than his eighteenth-century admirers supposed, and a notorious plunderer of the books of others, while Jonson was a less prodigious scholar than was once imagined.[2] But in trying to explain why certain reputations endure from age to age and others do not, Young lights on the disabling effects of learning on the creative imagination, and the vulnerability of books themselves as material objects. As Young may possibly have remembered, Jonson's own library had been consumed by fire in 1623, an event that Jonson had wryly commemorated in his 'Execration upon Vulcan' (*The Underwood*, 43). Shakespeare, on the other hand, relied upon those 'books' of nature and of man which 'the last conflagration alone can destroy', and his writings, like his sources, had endured.[3]

The burning of his library, as I hope to show, was indeed a suggestive event within Jonson's career, epitomizing, in a more complex way than Edward Young and his contemporaries recognized, Jonson's deeply ambivalent attitude towards the print culture of his day. It ironically answered and fulfilled some of Jonson's own earliest fears, threats, and predictions about the ultimate fate of his own writing and that of his contemporaries. By a curious coincidence, it occured furthermore at a crucial historical moment in the development of Shakespeare's literary reputation—and thus, of necessity, the reputation of Jonson himself.

⁓⁂⁓

Jonson was indeed a lover of books. He bought avidly, but lacked the means to maintain a stable collection. Though his patron Pembroke sent him twenty pounds each New Year's day to purchase books, Jonson was often obliged through hardship to re-sell them subsequently. 'Sundry tymes he heth devoured his bookes', noted William Drummond, himself a great collector, 'i.[e]., sold th[em] all

---

[2] See Ch. 2 n. 40.

[3] Young was strangely taken by the thought of book-burning. 'So few are our *Originals*, that, if all other books were to be burnt, the letter'd world would resemble some metropolis in flames, where a few incombustible buildings, a fortress, temple, or tower, lift their heads, in melancholy grandeur, amid the mighty ruin. Compared with this conflagration, old *Omar* lighted up but a small bonfire, when he heated the baths of the Barbarians, for eight months together, with the famed *Alexandrian* library's inestimable spoils, that no prophane book might obstruct the triumphant progress of his holy *Alcoran* round the globe': *Conjectures*, 9.

for Necessity'.[4] To *devour* books already meant at this time to read them with passion: Jonson no doubt devoured his books in this sense, but then, in a more literal redaction of the term, was obliged to sell them in order to eat and drink, converting them (as it were) into liquid assets. Jonson's love of books, like his praise of settled living, must have derived in part from what he lacked. He often drew on the collections of his friends, periodically visiting in particular the great library of Sir Robert Cotton at Conington; some of Cotton's books, borrowed apparently on extended loan, perished in Jonson's fire in 1623. No doubt Jonson was curious to inspect the remarkable library of William Drummond when he visited Hawthornden over the winter of 1618/19. Many of Jonson's reported comments on that occasion were about books in Drummond's possession, that might have been pulled from the shelves in the course of an evening's discussion.[5]

Jonson was also attracted to an unusual degree by the lure of the printing house. While many of his poems circulated in manuscript and were read or recited amongst friends in the manner of the day, he had no wish to remain merely a 'coterie' poet like Donne and so many of his contemporaries, seeking instead to give his poems the dignity and seeming security of print. Print seemed capable also of endowing his plays and masques with a stability and significance that performance, even at Whitehall, could never afford. Jonson therefore boldly reappropriated texts of his plays that technically still belonged to the companies that had performed them, and published them with authorial pride.[6] He commended colleagues who

---

[4] *Conversations with Drummond*, 312–13, 328–9. David McPherson has studied Jonson's habits of collection and annotation in 'Ben Jonson's Library and Marginalia: An Annotated Catalogue', *Studies in Philology*, 71 (1974), pp. i–xii, 1–100.

[5] See Robert H. MacDonald (ed.), *The Library of Drummond of Hawthornden* (Edinburgh, 1971). On Jonson's use of Cotton's library, see Herford and Simpson, i. 215, xi. 78–9, and (more generally) Kevin Sharpe, *Sir Robert Cotton 1586–1631: History and Politics in Early Modern England* (Oxford, 1978), and Colin G. C. Tite, *The Manuscript Library of Sir Robert Cotton*, The Panizzi Lectures, 1993 (1994).

[6] Joseph Lowenstein, 'The Script in the Marketplace', in Stephen Greenblatt (ed.), *Representing the English Renaissance* (Berkeley, 1988), 265–78. Lowenstein's paper, 'Personal Material: Jonson and Book-Burning' (presented in July 1995 at the Leeds conference 'Ben Jonson: Text, History, Performance'), explores similar territory to the present chapter. On 'coterie' writing in the period, see Arthur F. Marotti, *John Donne, Coterie Poet* (Madison, Wis., 1986). For Jonson's trust in the printed word, see in particular Richard C. Newton, 'Jonson and the (Re-)Invention of the Book', in Claude J. Summers and Ted-Larry Pebworthy (eds.), *Classic and Cavalier: Essays on Jonson and the Sons of Ben* (Pittsburgh, 1982), 31–55; on the 1616 folio, see Jennifer Brady and W. H. Herendeen (eds.), *Ben Jonson's 1616 Folio* (Newark, NJ, 1991).

did likewise. When John Fletcher published *The Faithful Shepherd-ess* in 1610 after its rough reception in the theatre, Jonson applauded

> thy murdred *Poeme*: which shall rise
> A glorified worke to Time, when Fire,
> Or moathes shall eate, what all these Fooles admire.

(Ungathered Verse, 8. 14–16)

As a printed book, Fletcher's play would endure, safe from the moths and fire which seemed to endanger the now-favoured pieces of the playhouse. It was the step that Jonson himself had taken with *Sejanus*, and would repeat with other theatrical failures in the years to come.

Yet despite this powerful affection for books and confidence in their enduring power, Jonson retained certain doubts. Books, like the manuscripts from which they derived, might perhaps after all be vulnerable to moth and fire, and to other hazards besides. Alongside Jonson's firm declarations about the lasting nature of his writings is a recurrent lament on the chanciness of fame, the vulnerability of the writer, and the destructibility of the book. And as he confronted these topics, Jonson from the earliest stage of his career seems to have thought in particular about the complex significance of fire.

⁓❧⁓

Throughout Jonson's work fire is a powerful emblem of poetic life and energy. '*Pindares* fire', '*Delphick* fire', 'the Muses fire', 'my owne true fire' are repeatedly figured as the sources of true poetry, which is born in the forge and hammered upon 'the *Muses* anvile'. In his 'Ode: To Himself' Jonson seeks 'new fire, / To give the world againe', while 'Rapt with holy fire' he writes to his patroness Lucy, Countess of Bedford. In poetry, as in fencing, he praises 'metall'd fire'.[7]

Fire is a symbol for Jonson not only of artistic life and energy, however, but also of their opposite: of the meretricious, the self-con-suming, the transitory, of things that vanish in a sudden 'blaze'. Thus spies, in one of his favourite conceits, burn themselves out like tapers made of 'base stuffe', leaving a foul smell behind, and 'Clownishe

---

7 'Come leave the lothed stage' (Herford and Simpson, vi. 493); *The Underwood*, 25. 12; *Horace*, 1; *The Forest*, 10. 29; *Ungathered Verse*, 26. 61; *Discoveries*, 244–2; *Epigrams*, 76. 1; *The Underwood*, 59. 7.

pride' likewise flares out 'lyke a blaze of strawe', dying with 'an Ill sent'. 'All's but blaze, / Flashes, and smoke', remarks Arruntius disdainfully in *Sejanus*, contrasting the followers of Tiberius with the great figures of the Roman past. Without the enduring text of Jonson himself, the court entertainments of Inigo Jones 'had perish'd like a blaze, and gone out, in the *beholders* eyes', he declares in *Hymenaei*. When the Banqueting House burnt to ashes, Jonson remarked that Jones might appropriately follow suit.[8]

These various quasi-symbolic connotations are wittily remembered in a moment of stage action at the end of *Every Man In His Humour*, when Justice Clement, having listened to the plagiarized verses of the would-be poet Matheo, declares that this nonsense must immediately be burnt. 'Election is now governed altogether by the influence of humor', he says, calling for torches,

come lay this stuffe together. So, give fire! there, see, see, how our Poets glory shines brighter, and brighter, still, still it increaseth, oh now its at the highest, and now it declines as fast: you may see gallants, *Sic transit gloria mundi*. (quarto, V. [iii]. 344–5, 351–4)

'There's an *embleme* for you, sonne, and your studies!', says the elder Knowell, as he gazes at the flames (folio, V. v. 35–6). Though Clement reminds him that not all studies and not all verses deserve such a fate, the fire of *Every Man In His Humour* remains a vivid emblem of the ambiguity of poetic fame, which may burn out in a sudden blaze or endure as a steady fire from one age to the next.

To contemporary audiences, the burning of Matheo's papers might well have had an immediate social significance, for Clement's judicial condemnation of Matheo's writings and his chosen method of destroying them mirror a common legal practice of the day. Bookburning was regularly carried out in the 1590s. Elizabeth's bishops had been entrusted with the authorization of printing and publishing throughout the kingdom, and kept a vigilant eye on seditious, libellous, and immoral works, which they periodically ordered to be burnt. Pro-Catholic writings, the principal target of government vigilance and suspicion, were from time to time burnt in the hall of

---

[8] *Epigrams*, 59; *The Underwood*, 43. 187; *Ungathered Verse*, 48. 15–18; *Sejanus*, I, 100–1; *Hymenaei*, 5–6; *Ungathered Verse*, 34. 101–4. In a more romantic mode, lovers are imagined expiring in each other's flames, and reduced to amorous dust: *The Forest*, 2. 16; cf. *The Underwood*, 8. 6–10.

the Stationers' Company.[9] On 4 June 1599, just a few months after
the first performance of *Every Man In His Humour*, John Whitgift,
Archbishop of Canterbury, and Richard Bancroft, Bishop of
London, burnt a number of books, including works by Gabriel
Harvey, John Marston, Thomas Nashe, Sir John Davies,
Christopher Marlowe, and Joseph Hall (himself destined to become
a bishop in later life). In a well-known decree, the bishops also declared in 1599 'that no Satyres or Epigrams be printed hereafter',
'that no English historyes be printed excepte they bee allowed by
some of her majesties privie Counsell', and 'that no playes be printed
except they bee allowed by such as have aucthorytie'.[10]

In the fire scene in *Every Man In His Humour* Jonson seems to
allude quite deliberately to the well-known methods of Elizabethan
censorship. Certain writings deserve to be burnt (the scene implies)
not because they are dangerous, heretical, or immoral—qualities
that might arouse the suspicion of the bishops—but because, more
damningly, they are inferior as literature, and pilfered from the
books of others. Matheo's verses, in what is the first recorded usage
of the term in English, are said to 'parody' the writings of his betters.
In a further and more serious sense of the term, Clement's burning of
those verses might be thought itself to parody the bishops' bonfires,
comically varying the familiar processes of the law in order to
achieve a true act of poetic justice.[11] The mood of the scene is light-
hearted and even exuberant: the law is presented as a flexible instrument that a witty magistrate, playing the role of literary critic, may
wield to good purpose, distinguishing true poetry from false, en-
couraging the one and committing the other to the flames.[12]

[9] W. W. Greg and E. Boswell, *Records of the Court of the Stationers' Company 1576 to
1602* (1930), 27–8; W. W. Greg (ed.), *A Companion to Arber* (Oxford, 1967), 31; cf.
William A. Jackson (ed.), *Records of the Court of the Stationers' Company 1602–1640*
(1957), 352, 408, 446; H. S. Bennett, *English Books and Readers 1558–1603* (Cambridge,
1965), 56.

[10] E. Arber (ed.), *A Transcript of the Registers of the Company of Stationers of
London*, 5 vols. (1876), iii. 316.

[11] 'A *Parodie*! a *parodie*! with a kind of miraculous gift, to make it absurder then it was':
Elder Knowell, V. v. 26–7. The passage occurs only in the 1616 folio text, and is therefore
misdated to 1598 in the *OED*. John Florio in *Queen Anna's New World of Words* (1611)
glosses *Parodia* 'A turning of a verse by altering some wordes'.

[12] Jonson develops the analogy between the role of the critic and that of the magistrate
again in *Epigrams*, 17, 'To the Learned Critic', and the dedication of *Catiline* to the Earl of
Pembroke. In *Epigrams*, 79, 'To Elizabeth, Countess of Rutland', Jonson imagines Sir
Philip Sidney burning his own verses after reading those of his daughter: 'He should those
rare, and absolute numbers view, / As he would burne, or better farre his booke' (11–12).

Through Clement, Jonson is himself acting as a kind of comic censor, setting the torch to the kind of poetry he despises, performing the ultimate deed of literary adjudication.

But censorship was not always conducted so judiciously. In his depiction of the trial of the Roman historian Cremutius Cordus and the enforced burning of his books in the third act of *Sejanus*, Jonson glances in a very different fashion at contemporary censorship practices, of which he had now had immediate personal experience. At the Earl of Northampton's instigation (as he reported to William Drummond), Jonson was brought before the Privy Council to answer charges of 'both of popperie and treason' arising from the stage presentation of *Sejanus*.[13] In the much-revised 1605 quarto version of the play, the position of Cordus, whose account of late Republican history was thought to reflect upon the present regime of Tiberius, can be seen to resemble the position of Jonson himself, whose account of events in Imperial Rome was evidently thought to reflect upon the present regime of James, and to invite, as Cordus' writings had done, 'parallels' between 'The times, the governments' (II. 310–11). Cordus' collision with the authorities is thus presented as a kind of replay or pre-play of Jonson's own troubles with the Privy Council, and the burning of his writings as an event that will paradoxically immortalize what the censors most hope to suppress.

LATIARIS Let 'hem be burnt.

GALLUS   All sought, and burnt, to day. . . .

ARRUNTIUS Let 'hem be burnt! o, how ridiculous
   Appears the *Senates* brainlesse diligence,
   Who thinke they can, with present power, extinguish
   The memorie of all succeeding times!
SABINUS 'Tis true, when (contrarie) the punishment
   Of wit, doth make th'authoritie increase
   Nor doe they ought, that use this crueltie
   Of interdiction, and this rage of burning;
   But purchase to themselves rebuke, and shame,
   And to the writers an eternall name.

(III. 469, 471–80)

[13] *Conversations with Drummond*, 325–7; *Sejanus His Fall*, ed. Philip Ayres, The Revels Plays (Manchester, 1990), introduction; Annabel Patterson, *Censorship and Interpretation: The Conditions of Writing and Reading in Early Modern England* (Madison, Wis., 1984), ch. 2; Richard Burt, *Licensed by Authority: Ben Jonson and the Discourses of Censorship* (Ithaca, 1993); Richard Dutton, *Mastering the Revels: The Regulation and Censorship of English Renaissance Drama* (Basingstoke, 1991).

'Posteritie payes everie man his honour', says Cordus, as his works
are condemned (III. 456). Jonson is clearly thinking of his own situation as well as that of Cordus. Through this very play, *Sejanus*, now
safely printed as a quarto volume and prudently dedicated to Esmé
Stuart, Seigneur d'Aubigny, Jonson pays Cordus his due honour,
trusting that another posterity will honour in turn the name of its
author. His book would endure. Inscribing copies of the quarto edition of *Sejanus* for presentation to his friends, Jonson quietly noted
that it would 'last beyond Marble', serving as an 'eternall Witnesse'
to his affection for them—and to his qualities as a writer.[14]

Jonson's own situation both as a writer and as a private citizen had
become noticeably more imperilled since the first performance of
Every Man In His Humour in September 1598, as the contrast between these two scenes of book-burning may suggest. When his fatal
scuffle with Gabriel Spencer a few days after the first presentation of
Every Man In His Humour had led to Jonson's trial on a charge of
manslaughter, he escaped the gallows through the legal device
known as 'benefit of clergy', having demonstrated his ability to read
a verse from the Bible: thus being, in the common phrase of the day,
'saved by the book'.[15] In the Induction to *Cynthia's Revels* (1600)
Jonson makes a glancing reference to this episode, and to other judicial punishments to which both books and persons were currently
subject. 'First the title of his play is CYNTHIAS *Revels*, as any man
(that hath hope to bee saved by his booke) can witnesse', says one of
the children, describing the piece about to be performed; 'take anie
of our play-bookes without a CUPID, or a MERCURIE in it, and burne
it for an heretique in *Poetrie*' (41–2, 47–9). Through a book, as
Jonson now had cause to know, one might be either saved or damned,
and books and bodies could be destroyed with equal ease. Having
converted to Catholicism during his recent stay in prison, Jonson
was now sharply aware of the penalties attendant upon religious

[14] Herford and Simpson, viii. 665, inscriptions to Sir Robert Townshend and Francis
Crane. In the first act of *Sejanus* Tiberius declares that he wishes posterity to remember
him not from monuments and buildings erected to his honour, but knowledge of his personal qualities as an emperor. Tiberius' speech ironically invokes, and varies, celebrated
passages in Horace and Ovid (discussed below), counterpointing the later assertions of
Arruntius and Sabinus about the manner in which Cordus will be remembered: 'These
things shall be to us / Temples, and statues, reared in your mindes, / The fairest, and most
during imag'rie: / For those of stone, or brasse, if they become / Odious in judgement of
posteritie, / Are more contemn'd, as dying sepulchres, / Then tane for living monuments'
(I. 484–90).

[15] See p. 141 above.

nonconformity, and the treatment of 'heretics' in Elizabethan England.[16] The passing jokes mark his growing insecurity as a writer whose work might be damned theatrically for lack of conformity with current fashion; as a convicted felon, whose fatal brawl with Spencer was attracting public comment from fellow dramatists;[17] and as a new member of a religion now subject to increasing persecution in England.

It is not surprising that *Poetaster*, performed in 1601, should open with a poet's meditation on the theme of personal and literary survival. Ovid is discovered at his desk, revising the final lines of his *Amores*, I. xv:

> *Then, when this bodie falls in funerall fire,*
> *My name shall live, and my best part aspire*
> It shall goe so.
>
> (I. i. 1–3)

Jonson takes these lines from a translation published in Christopher Marlowe's *All Ovid's Elegies* in 1595, that had itself been banned and burnt in the bishops' fire of 1599.[18] By reprinting them so prominently at the very opening of his play Jonson pays homage to the recently dead Marlowe and his recently burnt book, openly defies the censors, and gives a new and highly specific significance to the Ovidian assertion about poetry's tenacious powers of survival.

It is a brave gesture, but *Poetaster* itself did not wholly escape the attention of the censors. At the end of the play Jonson had added an authorial 'Apology' which, though evidently spoken on stage, was 'restrain'd . . . by Authoritie' from appearing in the 1602 quarto. It is thought to have borne a general resemblance to the 'Apologetical Dialogue' that is found in the 1616 folio, in which Jonson responds to recent attacks and reflects more generally on the way in which

---

[16] See Ch. 4 above.

[17] 'Art not famous enough yet, my mad Horastratus, for killing a player, but thou must eate men alive?' etc.: Tucca to Horace in Dekker's *Satiromastix*, IV. ii. 84 ff. 'Horastratus' is 'A combination of the names of Horace and Herostratus, who made himself notorious by setting fire to the Temple of Diana at Ephesus in order "to purchase himselfe an everlasting fame" ': *Introductions, Notes, and Commentaries to texts in Fredson Bowers' Edition of 'The Dramatic Works of Thomas Dekker'*, ed. Cyrus Hoy, 4 vols. (Cambridge, 1980), i. 277.

[18] Whether the second version of *Amores* I. xv ('*The same by* B. I.') from this edition which Jonson quotes in *Poetaster* is in fact by Jonson or Marlowe is not certain: for discussion of the issues, see Tom Cain's edition of *Poetaster*, The Revels Plays (Manchester, 1995), introduction, 19 and nn. 40 and 41, and annotation to Act I, Scene i.

literary works and reputations survive and perish. It is a curiously contorted piece of writing, in which Jonson presents himself as a model of restraint, while publicly rehearsing at some length what he *might* say about his detractors if ever he should choose to speak his mind.[19] His writings, he declares, would outlive their calumnies, being stamped as 'deepe, and publike brands' into their foreheads,

> That the whole company of *Barber-Surgeons*
> Should not take off, with all their art, and playsters.
> And these my prints should last, still to be read
> In their pale fronts: when, what they write 'gainst me,
> Shall like a figure, drawne in water, fleete,
> And the poore wretched papers be employ'd
> To cloth *tobacco*, or some cheaper drug.
> This I could doe, and make them infamous.   (165–73)

Jonson's 'prints' would endure, like brands burnt into human flesh, while the writings of his enemies would be used as tobacco-paper or for wrapping drugs. Classical satirists sometimes spoke of *branding* their adversaries, but in Jonson's England branding was a still current form of legal punishment which Jonson himself had recently suffered, having had the letter T (for Tyburn) burnt into his thumb to indicate his status as a convicted felon. His satirical threat redirects a recent humiliation.[20] Even as he emphasizes the lasting nature of these (still unwritten) ripostes, however, Jonson simultaneously threatens to toss his work into the fire:

> O, this would make a learn'd, and liberall soule,
> To rive his stayned quill, up to the back,
> And damne his long-watch'd labours to the fire;
> Things, that were borne, when none but the still night,
> And his dumbe candle saw his pinching throes . . .   (209–13)

If there is something paradoxical about a threat to destroy one's manuscripts appearing within a carefully printed book, it is

[19] *Poetaster*, ed. Cain, 261 and n.; Dutton, *Mastering the Revels*, 139. Jonson's contortions are partly explained by the tactics of the opponents to whom he is (guardedly) responding. In the Epilogue to *Satiromastix*, Tucca declares that Horace will respond only if he thinks the present play is a success: '*if you set your hands and seales to this, Horace will write against it, and you may have more sport. He will not loose his labour, he shall not turne his blanke verses into wast paper*'.

[20] For branding, cf. *Volpone*, Epistle Dedicatory, 141–5, and III. viii. 17; *Ungathered Verse*, 36. 14; Martial vi. 64; Horace, *Satires*, i. iv. 1–3. Runaway slaves were treated in this manner: see Petronius, *Satyricon*, 103. For Jonson's own branding, see David Riggs, *Ben Jonson: A Life*, (Cambridge, Mass., 1989), 52–3.

symptomatic of a larger irresolution within these various assertions which testify to Jonson's general anxiety on the subject of literary survival. Like Ovid, Jonson thinks of his name, his 'best part', living on after his body falls 'in funeral fire'. Yet he also considers the possibility that his writings might themselves be consumed by fire—the censor's fire, or his own—and vanish for ever. This ambivalence is not in itself unique to Jonson, being also found in a more general form in the classical authors he chooses to imitate. It acquires particular interest, however, on account of Jonson's peculiar aspirations as an author at a critical moment in the history of literary publishing.[21]

⁓⊱

The best-known classical statements about the enduring power of poetry are Ovid's great peroration at the end of the final book of the *Metamorphoses*, 'Iamque opus exegi, quod nec Iovis ira, nec ignis / Regalique situ pyramidum altius . . .' ('my work is complete: a work which neither Jove's anger, nor fire nor sword shall destroy, nor yet the gnawing tooth of time . . .') and Horace's ode 'Exegi monumentum aere perennius' ('More durable than bronze, higher than Pharaoh's / Pyramids is the monument I have made . . .', iii. 30), to which Ovid's passage alludes. These passages of apparently immense confidence in the survival of poetry must be balanced against others in the work of both poets and elsewhere in classical literature which more gloomily survey the prospects of fame. Ovid's declaration about his undying reputation is curiously at variance with the central vision of the *Metamorphoses* of a world entirely governed by flux and change, in which nothing endures in the same form for ever. Horace's statement that his poems will outlast bronze and the Pharoahs' monuments needs to be read alongside other poems in which he imagines his writings being casually dismembered and reused to wrap frankincense, perfumes, and pepper. The idea is a common one in classical literature: Martial and Catullus likewise repeatedly contemplate the possibility that their poems may be destined merely to wrap spices or mackerel.[22]

[21] I explore this ambivalence further in 'The Destruction of the Book', in Bill Bell and Simon Eliot (eds.), *The Versatile Text: Studies in the History of the Book*, (forthcoming, Pennsylvania, 1996). See also E. R. Curtius, 'Poetry as Perpetuation', in id., *European Literature and the Latin Middle Ages*, trans. W. R. Trask (1953), 476–7.

[22] Horace, *Epistles*, II. i. 269–70; Martial, III. ii, IV. lxxxvi, III. i; Catullus, xcv.

Ovid's grand statement about the enduring power of poetry evidently had a strong appeal for Jonson. James Howell, writing to Sir Thomas Hawkins about a supper party at which Jonson had talked excessively about his own poetic abilities, adds humorously:

But for my part I am content to dispense with this *Roman* infirmity of *B.* now that time hath snowed upon his pericranium. You know Ovid, and (your) *Horace* were subject to this humour, the first bursting out into

Jamq; opus exegi quod nec Iovis ira, nec ignis, &c.

The other into *Exegi monumentum aere perennius* &c. . . .[23]

But Jonson was equally fascinated by the opposing idea, of the ephemerality of most literary work. Much highly praised writing of the day could barely be reckoned fit to serve as waste paper.

Nothing in our Age, I have observ'd, is more preposterous, then the *running Judgements* upon *Poetry*, and *Poets*; when we shall heare those things commended, and cry'd up for the best writings, which a man would scarce vouchsafe, to wrap any wholsome drug in; hee would never light his *Tobacco* with them. (*Discoveries*, 587–92)

To William Drummond he told this unsmiling joke: 'one who fired a Tobacco pipe with a ballet the next day having a sore head, swoare he had a great singing in his heade & he thought it was the ballet. a Poet should detest a Ballet maker' (*Conversations with Drummond*, 473–5).

At times Jonson realized that his own writings, too, might end their days in this ignominious fashion. Near the head of his *Epigrams* in the 1616 folio he placed a poem which eloquently reveals his conflicting hopes and fears in regard to publication, and his strongly ambivalent view of the prevailing methods of the literary market-place: 'To My Bookseller'.

---

[23] Herford and Simpson, xi. 420. 'If I can, with this day's travail and all my policy, but rescue this youth here out of the hands of the lewd man and the strange woman', says Justice Adam Overdo in *Bartholomew Fair* as he prepares to commit yet another quixotic error, 'I will sit downe at night and say with my friend *Ovid, Iamqu; opus exegi, quod nec Iovis ira, nec ignis, &c.*' (II. iv. 66–8). When he does finally sit down at night, Overdo will attempt to 'drowne the memory of all enormity' in his 'bigg'st bowle at home', and forget his Ovidian aspirations (V. vi. 99–100). John Taylor the Water Poet remembers the Ovidian passage in his poem on Jonson's death: 'As *Ovid* saith, *Sword, fire*, cannot deprive, / *Age, Death*, [n]or *Time*, can put him out of mind': Herford and Simpson, xi. 421.

Thou, that mak'st gaine thy end, and wisely well,
   Call'st a booke good, or bad, as it doth sell,
Use mine so, too: I give thee leave. But crave
   For the lucks sake, it thus much favour have,
To lye upon thy stall, till it be sought;
   Not offer'd, as it made sute to be bought;
Nor have my title-leafe on posts, or walls,
   Or in cleft-sticks, advanced to make calls
For termers, or some clarke-like serving-man,
   Who scarse can spell th'hard names: whose knight lesse can.
If, without these vile arts, it will not sell,
   Send it to *Bucklers-bury*, there 'twill, well.

(Epigrams, 3)

Bucklersbury was a street near Cheapside inhabited by grocers and apothecaries. Jonson imagines his great folio, painstakingly printed by William Stansby, now casually reused for wrapping-paper. Yet with a strategic counter-movement Jonson dedicates the collection to the Earl of Pembroke, now Lord Chamberlain, inviting him to lead '*so many good, and great names (as my verses mention on the better part) to their remembrance with posteritie*'; and follows 'To My Bookseller' immediately with a poem 'To King James'. Such a book was not to be dismembered lightly.

The publishing history of 'To My Bookseller' is nevertheless curious, for there is some evidence that the poem may originally have been published in a 1612 volume of the *Epigrams* of which no copies now remain.[24] Books were indeed regularly recycled in the manner

---

[24] 'A Booke called, Ben Johnson his Epigrams' was entered in the Stationers' Register on 15 May 1612 by Jonson's bookseller John Stepneth, to whom the present poem is evidently addressed. Stepneth died in the same year, and in the absence of any surviving copies it is often assumed that the book was never published. Yet William Drummond notes 'Ben Jonsons epigrams' amongst the 'books read by me anno 1612', and some verses by 'R. C.' support the possibility that the *Epigrams* had been published as a separate 'book' or 'pamphlet': see Herford and Simpson, viii. 16 and xi. 356. Throughout the *Epigrams* Jonson constantly refers to the poems as though they constituted a separately printed 'book' (title-page, *Epigrams*, 1, 2, 3, 49. 6, 77. 2, 83. 2, etc.). I am grateful to Ian Gadd for drawing my attention to the following verses from Henry Parrot's *The Mastive, or Young-Whelpe of the Olde Dogge. Epigrams and Satyrs*, which were published in 1615 and seem to suggest a familiarity with Jonson's poem (i/j, u/v spellings normalized):

Ad Bibliopolam

Printer or Stationer, or what thou proove,
Shalt mee record to Times posteritie:
Ile not enjoyne thee, but request in love,
Thou so much deigne my Book to dignifie;

Jonson describes in this epigram, and it is tempting to wonder what actually happened to the 1612 printing of the *Epigrams*, if it ever existed. Certainly the threat of Bucklersbury continued to loom in Jonson's later life. After the failure of *The Magnetic Lady* in 1632, Alexander Gill warned Jonson in scornful verses not to think of publishing the play; or, if he must do so, to publish on inferior cap-paper, so that the book could be quickly and conveniently reused for wrapping goods.

> And lett ytt bee so Apocriphall
> As nott to dare to venture on A stall
> Exceppt ytt bee of Druggers Grocers Cookes
> Victuallers Tobackoe men and suchlike Rookes
> From Bucklers Burye lett ytt not be barde
> But thincke nott of Ducke lane or Paules Churchyarde[25]

In an angry riposte, Jonson noted that Gill's body was more vulnerable than the books he ridiculed, and had already suffered a worse humiliation than any he currently threatened: 'A Rogue by Statute, censur'd to be whipt, / Cropt, branded, slit, neck-stockt; go, you are stript' (*Ungathered Verse*, 39. 15–16).

Jonson regarded books as vehicles of fame, couriers to posterity, monuments to art. But he could not quite avoid seeing them also in another light: as mere commodities, easily 'devoured' and dismembered, used to wrap spices, line pie-dishes, and clothe tobacco; as material objects that were as vulnerable as the authors who created them. Despite his hopeful statements to the contrary, Jonson knew very well that books, like their makers, were susceptible to Jove's anger, to fire, sword, and the gnawing tooth of time.

> As first it bee not with your Ballads mixt,
> Next, not at Play-houses, mongst Pippins solde:
> Then that on Posts, by th'Eares it stand not fixt,
> For every dull-Mechanicke to beholde.
> Last, that it come not brought in Pedlers packs,
> To common Fayres, or Countrey, Towne, or Cittie:
> Solde at a Booth mongst Pinnes and Almanacks;
> Yet on thy hands to lye, thou'lt say tw'er pittie;
>   Let it rather for Tobacco rent,
>   Or Butchers-Wives, next Clensing-week in Lent.

[25] Herford and Simpson, xi. 347–8.

Shakespeare's comparative indifference to the publication of his writing did not stem from professional naïvety or a romantic pre-occupation with the natural and human worlds; he simply worked a different market-place. By *not* publishing his plays, Shakespeare ensured that they remained the collective property of the King's Men, and could be acted repeatedly, thus providing a steady income for as long as they were well received.[26] But even after his retirement to Stratford, Shakespeare made no apparent attempt to revise and order his works for collected publication. In the play that Victorian critics liked to see as Shakespeare's farewell to the stage, Prospero had vowed to break his staff and drown his book 'deeper than did ever plummet sound', and it was attractive to imagine that Shakespeare had made a similar resolution, 'drowning' all thoughts of a fame achieved through the means of some great book. Jonson's ambitions at this time were entirely contrary, for during these years he was busy in London preparing his great folio edition of *The Workes of Benjamin Jonson* that would be published in 1616, the year of Shakespeare's death.

When his former colleagues John Heminge and Henry Condell began at last to collect most of Shakespeare's own plays for publication some years later, they may well have been advised by Jonson himself, whose own edition had established an important model and precedent.[27] The 1623 folio was prefaced by an editorial address 'To the great variety of readers', which Jonson himself conceivably helped to draft, or personally influenced. Certainly the vision of authorship and rationale of publication which it formulates are characteristically Jonsonian.[28]

It had bene a thing, we confesse, worthie to have bene wished, that the Author himselfe had liv'd to have set forth, and overseen his owne writings; But since it hath bin ordain'd otherwise, and he by death departed from that right, we pray you do not envie his Friends, the office of their care, and paine, to have collected & publish'd them; and so to have publish'd them, as where (before) you were abus'd with diverse stolne, and surreptitious copies, maimed, and deformed by the frauds and stealthes of injurious imposters,

---

[26] For fuller discussion of this topic see G. E. Bentley, *The Profession of Dramatist in Shakespeare's Time 1590–1642* (Princeton, 1971), and Peter Thomson, *Shakespeare's Professional Career* (Cambridge, 1992).

[27] Anne Barton, *Ben Jonson: Dramatist* (Cambridge, 1984), ch. 12. Quotations from *The First Folio of Shakespeare*, The Norton Facsimile, prepared by Charlton Hinman (New York, 1968).

[28] See above, Ch. 2 n. 34.

that expos'd them: even those, are now offer'd to your view cur'd, and perfect of their limbes; and all the rest, absolute in their numbers, as he conceived the[m], Who, as he was a happie imitator of Nature, was a most gentle expresser of it.

The writings that once were maimed and deformed are now 'cur'd, and perfect of their limbes', put together like the once dismembered Sejanus; what was almost destroyed has been preserved, and committed to the judgement of posterity as a printed book. For *as* and *in* a book, as Jonson confidently declared in the poem to his memory, Shakespeare would continue to live.

> Thou art a Moniment, without a tombe,
> And art alive still, while thy Booke doth live,
> And we have wits to read, and praise to give.
>
> (*Ungathered Verse*, 26. 22–4)

Shakespeare's folio was probably published in November 1623.[29] By a curious stroke of fate, it was in the same month that the fire in Jonson's lodgings destroyed his books and many of his unpublished writings, which Jonson lists ruefully in the 'Execration upon Vulcan': a translation of the *Ars Poetica*, an English grammar, a verse account of his journey by foot to Scotland, a history of the reign of Henry V, some commonplace books.[30] Jonson recalls in the 'Execration' other famous fires: the burning of Don Quixote's collection of romances, of the great library of Alexandria, and of the Globe Theatre itself, 'the glory of the Bank', during a performance of Shakespeare's *Henry VIII* in 1613, after a negligent discharge of cannon had sent sparks into the thatched roof. None of these fires seemed as devastating as the one he had just endured. Why had this happened to him?

> Had I wrote treason there, or heresie,
> Imposture, witchcraft, charmes, or blasphemie,
> I had deserv'd, then, thy consuming lookes,
> Perhaps, to have been burned with my bookes.
>
> (*The Underwood*, 43. 15–18)

---

[29] W. W. Greg, *Shakespeare's First Folio* (Oxford, 1935), 452–4; Charlton Hinman, *The Printing and Proof-Reading of the First Folio of Shakespeare*, 2 vols. (Oxford, 1963), i. 360–5.

[30] The precise date is unknown. The Oxford editors at first placed the fire 'probably in or about the month of October, 1623', but later accepted Fleay's dating 'say, in November': Herford and Simpson, i. 261, xi. 73.

Books of treason, heresy, imposture, witchcraft, and blasphemy were indeed being burnt at this time, as were some of their authors; Reginald Scot's *Discoverie of Witchcraft*, arguing that witches should not necessarily be burnt, was itself burnt by King James early in his reign, though later James had second thoughts on this matter. But, Jonson asks Vulcan, were his own manuscripts really worthy of burning?

> thou'lt say,
> There were some pieces of as base allay,
> And as false stampe there; parcels of a Play,
> Fitter to see the fire-light, then the day;
> Adulterate moneys, such as might not goe;
> Thou should'st have stay'd, till publike fame said so.
> Shee is the Judge, Thou Executioner:
> Or if thou needs would'st trench upon her power,
> Thou mightst have yet enjoy'd thy crueltie
> With some more thrift, and more varietie:
> Thou mightst have had me perish, piece, by piece,
> To light Tobacco, or save roasted Geese,
> Sindge Capons, or poore Pigges, dropping their eyes;
> Condemn'd me to the Ovens with the pies;
> And so, have kept me dying a whole age,
> Not ravish'd all hence in a minutes rage.

(*The Underwood*, 43. 41–56)

Jonson had never in fact regarded 'publike fame' as the true judge and arbiter of literary survival, and there is something curious about his invocation of 'her power' at this moment. The poem as a whole is indeed concerned in a complex and ironical way with the subject of power and powerlessness, but it is not the power (or impotence) of the public that concerns Jonson so much as that of the author himself. 'An Execration upon Vulcan' marks Jonson's attempt to assert, through the printed word, his capacity for survival when faced with the ultimate test, the destruction of his writings: with the very fate that he had imaginatively inflicted years ago on the unfortunate poetaster Matheo in *Every Man In His Humour*, and had often briefly entertained in other writings. In the 'Execration' Jonson characteristically attempts to turn the tables, to summon, berate, and condemn his own 'Executioner', performing his own acts of judgement, trenchantly declaring which works might ideally have been worth preserving and which might not, kindling his own imaginary bonfires.

George Chapman was led unkindly to wonder whether all of the writings which Jonson lamented as lost in the fire had in fact ever been written.[31] In a larger sense, it is impossible to this day to know for sure which of Jonson's so-called 'lost' works disappeared by accident, and which by authorial design; when Vulcan played the master, and when he was the slave.[32] Fire was an everyday occurrence in Jacobean London, with its houses of thatch and weatherboard, illuminated by torches and candles and heated by open fires. It is not surprising that ten years after the fire that destroyed his library Jonson should nearly have suffered another such calamity, but on this occasion his '*Son, and contiguous neighbour*' James Howell came to the rescue. After the event, Howell wrote with teasing solicitude to his '*Father Mr* Ben: Johnson',

desiring you to look better hereafter to your charcole fyre and chymney, which I am glad to be one that preservd from burning, this being the second time that *Vulcan* hath threatned you, it may be because you have spoken ill of his wife and bin too busy with his hornes . . .[33]

The coincidence of events in November 1623 is striking. As Jonson's books and writings were consumed by fire, the First Folio was published, conferring upon the plays of Shakespeare the permanence and dignity that Jonson well knew they deserved. Reading this book, posterity would in time pay Shakespeare his honour, judging

[31] 'Invective written against Mr Ben Johnson', in *The Poems of George Chapman*, ed. P. B. Bartlett (New York, 1941); R. B. Sharpe, 'Jonson's "Execration" and Chapman's "Invective": Their Place in their Authors' Rivalry', *Studies in Philology*, 42 (1945), 555–63; Herford and Simpson, x. 692–7.

[32] The formula 'The rest is lost', invoked after l. 93 of Jonson's 'Epistle to Elizabeth, Countess of Rutland', for example (*The Forest*, 12), clearly suggests an act of authorial self-editing, after Jonson had discovered that the Rutland marriage had not been consummated, and that his lines hoping for the birth of an heir were consequently inappropriate. The cancelled lines are not lost, but survive in manuscript. The full title of *The Underwood*, 25, 'An Ode to James, Earl of Desmond, writ in Queen Elizabeth's time, since lost, and recovered', is equally suspicious, as there were good prudential reasons for not publishing this poem at an earlier date. 'Here, something is wanting' in *The Underwood*, 20, may indicate a deliberate editorial excision, performed perhaps on grounds of taste by Jonson's executor, Sir Kenelm Digby. '*The rest of this Song is lost*' in *Eupheme* (*The Underwood*, 84. ii. 18) may possibly indicate Jonson's abandonment of a difficult task, a versified account of Venetia Digby's family tree. There were clearly good reasons for 'losing' troublesome plays such as *The Isle of Dogs*, and other plays with which Jonson was for some reason dissatisfied; but it is not clear whether it was entirely through authorial decision or partly through accident 'that the half of his comedies were not in Print' (*Conversations with Drummond*, 393).

[33] James Howell, *Epistola Ho-Elianae* (1645), sect, 5, xvii, pp. 22–3: cit. Herford and Simpson, i. 261.

him, by a landslide verdict, the greatest writer of this, and perhaps of
any, age. Jonson would be otherwise rated: as a writer destroyed by
his own learning, his excessive devotion to books. But books, as John
Milton was eloquently to declare, 'are not absolutely dead things',
and it was through the great book to which Jonson himself had contributed that Shakespeare was to find in the fullness of time his 'live-
long Monument'.[34]

[34] Milton, *Areopagitica*, in *Complete Poems and Major Prose*, ed. Merritt Y. Hughes
(New York, 1957), 720; 'On Shakespeare, 1630', l. 8, p. 63.

Works Cited

Where not otherwise specified, the place of publication is London.

ALSSID, MICHAEL W., 'Shadwell's *Mac Flecknoe*', *SEL: Studies in English Literature 1500–1900*, 7 (1967), 387–402.

ANON., *Memoirs of the Life of Robert Wilks, Esq.* (1732).

ARBER, E. (ed.), *A Transcript of the Registers of the Company of Stationers of London*, 5 vols. (1886).

ARMSTRONG, W. A., 'Ben Jonson and Jacobean Stagecraft', in John Russell Brown and Bernard Harris (eds.), *Jacobean Theatre*, Stratford-upon-Avon Studies, 1 (1960), 43–61.

ARNOLD, MATTHEW, *The Poems*, ed. Kenneth Allott (1965).

AUBREY, JOHN, *Aubrey's Brief Lives*, ed. O. L. Dick (Harmondsworth, 1962).

A'WOOD, ANTONY, *The Life and Times of Antony a'Wood* (1961).

AYRES, PHILIP, 'Jonson, Northampton, and the "Treason" in Sejanus', *Modern Philology*, 80 (1983), 356–63.

BABCOCK, R. W., *The Genesis of Shakespeare Idolatry, 1766–1799* (Chapel Hill, 1931).

BACON, FRANCIS, Viscount St Albans, *Works*, ed. J. Spedding, R. L. Ellis, and D. D. Heath, 14 vols. (1857–74).

BAIR, DEIRDRE, *Samuel Beckett: A Biography* (New York, 1980).

BALD, R. C., *John Donne: A Life* (Oxford, 1970).

BALDWIN, T. W., *Shakespere's Small Latine and Lesse Greeke*, 2 vols. (Urbana, Ill., 1944).

BARISH, JONAS A., *Ben Jonson and the Language of Prose Comedy* (Cambridge, Mass., 1960).

—— *The Antitheatrical Prejudice* (Berkeley, 1981).

—— (ed.), *Ben Johnson: A Collection of Critical Essays* (Englewood) Cliffs, NJ, 1963).

—— '*Volpone*': A Casebook (1972).

BARTON, ANNE, *Ben Jonson: Dramatist* (Cambridge, 1984).

BATE, JONATHAN, *Shakespearean Constitutions* (Oxford, 1989).

BATE, W. JACKSON, *The Burden of the Past and the English Poet* (1971).

BEAURLINE, LESTER, *Jonson and Elizabethan Comedy* (San Marino, Ca., 1978).

BENNETT, H. S., *English Books and Readers 1558–1603* (Cambridge, 1965).

BENTLEY, G. E., *Shakespeare and Jonson: Their Reputations in the Seventeenth Century Compared*, 2 vols. (Chicago, 1945).

—— *The Profession of Dramatist in Shakespeare's Time 1590–1642* (Princeton, 1986).

BERRY, FRANCIS, 'Stage Perspective and Elevation in *Coriolanus* and *Sejanus*', in Ian Donaldson (ed.), *Jonson and Shakespeare* (1983), 163–78.

BINGHAM, CAROLINE, *James I of England* (1981).

BLAIN, VIRGINIA, ' "Thinking Back Through our Aunts": Harriet Martineau and the Female Tradition', *Women: A Cultural Review*, 1 (1990), 223–39.

BLOOM, HAROLD, *The Anxiety of Influence: A Theory of Poetry* (New York, 1973).

BOSSY, JOHN, *The English Catholic Community, 1570–1850* (1975).

BRADLEY, J. F., and ADAMS, J. Q., *The Jonson Allusion-Book* (New Haven, 1922; repr. New York, 1971).

BRADSHAW, GRAHAM, *Misrepresentations: Shakespeare and the Materialists* (1993).

BRADY, JENNIFER, 'Collaborating with the Forebear: Dryden's Reception of Ben Jonson', *Modern Language Quarterly*, 54 (1993), 345–69.

—— 'Dryden and Negotiations of Literary Succession and Precession', in Earl Miner and Jennifer Brady (eds.), *Literary Transmission and Authority: Dryden and Other Writers* (Cambridge, 1993), 27–54.

—— and HERENDEEN, W. H. (eds.), *Ben Jonson's 1616 Folio* (Newark, NJ, 1991).

BRAUNMULLER, A. R. (ed.), *A Seventeenth-Century Letter-Book: A Facsimile Edition of Folger MS. V.a.321* (Newark, NJ, 1983).

BRENNAN, MICHAEL G., *Literary Patronage in the English Renaissance: The Pembroke Family* (1988).

BROOKS, ALDEN, *This Side of Shakespear* (New York, 1964).

BROWNING, ELIZABETH BARRETT, *Aurora Leigh*, ed. Margaret Reynolds (Athens, Oh., 1992).

BURKE, SEAN, *The Death and Return of the Author: Criticism and Subjectivity in Barthes, Foucault, and Derrida* (Edinburgh, 1992).

BURROW, JOHN (ed.), *Geoffrey Chaucer: A Critical Anthology* (Harmondsworth, 1969).

BURT, RICHARD, *Licensed by Authority: Ben Jonson and the Discourses of Censorship* (Ithaca, 1993).

BUTLER, MARTIN, *Theatre and Crisis 1632–1642* (Cambridge, 1984).

—— *Ben Jonson, 'Volpone': A Critical Study* (Harmondsworth, 1987).

CALVIN, JOHN, *Institutes of the Christian Religion*, ed. John T. McNeill, trans. Ford Lewis Battles, 2 vols., The Library of Christian Classics (Philadelphia, 1960).

CAPP, B. S., *The Fifth Monarchy Men: A Study in Seventeenth-Century English Millenarianism* (1972).

CAPPELL, EDWARD, *Reflections on Originality in Authors* (1766).

CAREW, THOMAS, *The Poems*, ed. Rhodes Dunlap (Oxford, 1949).

CARLYLE, THOMAS, *Historical Sketches of Notable Persons and Events in the Reigns of James I and Charles I* (1898).

[CARTWRIGHT, ROBERT], *Shakespere and Jonson: Dramatic, versus Wit-Combats* (1864).

CASSAVETTI, EILEEN, *The Lion and the Lilies: The Stuarts and France* (1977).

CHAMBERS, E. K., *The Elizabethan Stage*, 4 vols. (Oxford, 1923).

—— *William Shakespeare: A Study of Facts and Problems*, 2 vols. (Oxford, 1930).

CHAPMAN, GEORGE, *The Poems*, ed. P. B. Bartlett (New York, 1941).

[CHETWOOD, W. R.], *The British Theatre* (Dublin, 1750).

CIBBER, Theophilus [Robert Shiels], *The Lives of the Poets of Great Britain and Ireland*, 5 vols. (1753).

CICERO, *Brutus*, trans. G. L. Hendrickson, and *Orator*, trans. H. M. Hubbell, Loeb Classical Library (1962).

—— *De Oratore*, trans. E. W. Sutton and H. Rackham, Loeb Classical Library, 3 vols. (1967–8).

—— *De Re Publica* and *De Legibus* trans. C. W. Keyes, Loeb Classical Library (1970).

CLARE, JANET, *'Art Made Tongue-Tied by Authority': Elizabethan and Jacobean Dramatic Censorship* (Manchester, 1990).

CLARKE, CHARLES COWDEN, 'On the Comic Writers of England: II—Ben Jonson', *The Gentleman's Magazine* (May 1871), 630–50.

CLAYTON, MARGARET [Tudeau], 'Ben Jonson, "In Travaile with Expression of Another": His Use of John of Salisbury's Policratus in Timber', *The Review of English Studies*, NS 30 (1979), 397–408.

COLERIDGE, SAMUEL TAYLOR, *Biographia Literaria* (1817; Everyman edn. 1906).

—— *Literary Remains* (1836).

—— *Shakespearean Criticism*, ed. T. M. Raysor, 2 vols. (1960).

—— *Table Talk* (1835), in James Thornton (ed.), *Table Talk from Ben Jonson to Leigh Hunt* (1934).

COLLIER, JEREMY, *A Short View of the Immorality and Profaneness of the English Stage* (1698).

CORBIN, ALAIN, *The Foul and the Fragrant: Odor and the French Social Imagination* (Cambridge, Mass., 1986): trans. of *Le Miasme et la jonquille* (1982).

'CORNWALL, BARRY' [B. W. Procter], *Memoir of the Life and Writing of Ben Jonson* (1838).

CRAIG, D. H. (ed.), *Ben Jonson: The Critical Heritage* (1990).

CREASER, JOHN W., 'The Popularity of Jonson's Tortoise', *The Review of English Studies*, NS 27 (1976), 38–46.

CUBETA, PAUL M., ' "A Celebration of Charis": An Evaluation of Jonsonian Poetic Strategy', *ELH: A Journal of English Literary History*, 25 (1958), 163–80.

CUDDY, NEIL, 'The Revival of the Entourage: The Bedchamber of James I, 1603–1625', in David Starkey et al. (eds.), *The English Court: From the Wars of the Roses to the Civil War* (1987), 173–225.

CURTIUS, E. R., *European Literature and the Latin Middle Ages*, trans. W. T. Trask (1953).

CUST, LADY ELIZABETH, *Some Account of the Stuarts of Aubigny in France [1422–1672]*, privately printed (1891).

DANSON, LAWRENCE, 'Jonsonian Comedy and the Discovery of the Social Self', *PMLA: Publications of the Modern Language Association*, 99 (1984), 179–93.

DAVENANT, SIR WILLIAM, *The Shorter Poems and Songs From the Plays and Masques*, ed. A. M. Gibbs (Oxford, 1972).

DAVIES, THOMAS, *Dramatic Miscellanies*, 2 vols. (1784).

DE GRAZIA, MARGRETA, *Shakespeare Verbatim* (Oxford, 1991).

DEKKER, THOMAS, *The Dramatic Works of Thomas Dekker*, ed. Fredson Bowers, 4 vols. (Cambridge, 1953).

—— *Introductions, Notes, and Commentaries to Texts in Fredson Bowers' edition of 'The Dramatic Works of Thomas Dekker'*, ed. Cyrus Hoy, 4 vols. (Cambridge, 1982).

DE LUNA, B. N., *Jonson's Romish Plot: A Study of 'Catiline' and its Historical Context* (Oxford, 1967).

DENNIS, JOHN, *The Critical Works*, ed. E. N. Hooker, 2 vols. (Baltimore, 1943).

DEVLIN, CHRISTOPHER, *The Life of Robert Southwell, Poet and Martyr* (New York, 1956).

DE WITT, N. W., *Epicurus and his Philosophy* (Minneapolis, 1954).

DIANO, CARLO, 'Epicureanism', *Encyclopaedia Britannica*, 15th edn. (Chicago, 1983), vi. 911–14.

DONALDSON, IAN, 'Jonson's Tortoise', *The Review of English Studies*, NS 19 (1968), 162–6.

—— 'The Clockwork Novel: Three Notes on an Eighteenth-Century Analogy', *The Review of English Studies*, NS 21/81 (1970), 14–22.

—— 'Language, Noise, and Nonsense: *The Alchemist*', in Earl Miner (ed.), *Seventeenth-Century Imagery* (Berkeley, 1971), 69–82.

—— 'Damned by Analogies: Or, How to Get Rid of Ben Jonson', *Gambit: International Theatre Review*, 6 (1972), 38–46.

—— 'Jonson's Italy: *Volpone* and Fr. Thomas Wright', *Notes and Queries*, 19 (1972), 450–2.

—— 'Jonson's Ode to Sir Lucius Cary and Sir H. Morison', *Studies in the Literary Imagination*, 6 (1973), 139–52.

—— 'Jonson and the Moralists', in Alvin B. Kernan (ed.), *Two Renaissance Mythmakers* (Baltimore, 1977), 146–64.

—— 'Jonson and Anger', in Claude Rawson (ed.), assisted by Jenny Mezciems, *English Satire and the Satiric Tradition* (Oxford, 1984), 56–71.

—— 'Life into Text', *Essays in Criticism*, 41 (July 1991), 253–61.

—— 'The Destruction of the Book', in Bill Bell and Simon Eliot (eds.), *The Versatile Text: Studies in the History of the Book* (forthcoming, Pennsylvania, 1996).

—— (ed.), *Jonson and Shakespeare* (1983).

DRAKE, NATHAN, *Shakspeare and his Times*, 2 vols. (1817).

DRUMMOND OF HAWTHORNDEN, WILLIAM, *The Works* [ed. J. Sage and T. Ruddiman] (Edinburgh, 1711).

DRYDEN, JOHN, *Notes and Observations on The Empress of Morocco Revised* (1674).

—— *Of Dramatic Poesy and Other Critical Essays*, ed. George Watson, 2 vols. (1962).

—— *The Poems*, ed. Paul Hammond, 4 vols. [in progress] (1995–   ).

—— *The Poems*, ed. James Kinsley, 4 vols. (Oxford, 1958).

—— *The Works*, ed. E. N. Hooker and H. T. Swenberg Jr. (Berkeley, 1956–   ).

DUFFY, EAMON, *The Stripping of the Altars: Traditional Religion in England 1400–1580* (New Haven, 1992).

DUTTON, RICHARD, *Ben Jonson: To the First Folio* (Cambridge, 1983).

—— *Mastering the Revels: The Regulation and Censorship of English Renaissance Drama* (Basingstoke, 1991).

ECCLES, MARK, 'Jonson's Marriage', *The Review of English Studies*, 12 (1936), 257–72.

ELIOT, T. S., *Selected Essays*, 3rd, enlarged, edn. (1951).

ENCK, JOHN, *Jonson and the Comic Truth* (Madison, Wis., 1966).

EVANS, G. BLAKEMORE, 'Dryden's *Mac Flecknoe* and Dekker's *Satiromastix*', *Modern Language Notes*, 76 (1961), 598–600.

EVANS, ROBERT C., *Ben Jonson and the Poetics of Patronage* (Lewisburg, Pa., 1989).

—— *Jonson and the Contexts of his Time* (Lewisburg, Pa., 1994).

FELPERIN, HOWARD, *The Uses of the Canon* (Oxford, 1990).

FENTON, ELIJAH, *An Epistle to Mr Southerne, From Kent* (1711).

FERRY, ANNE, *All in War With Time: Love Poetry of Shakespeare, Donne, Jonson, Marvell* (Cambridge, Mass., 1975).

FINCHAM, KENNETH, and LAKE, PETER, 'The Ecclesiastical Policies of James I and Charles I', in Kenneth Fincham (ed.), *The Early Stuart Church 1603–1642* (Basingstoke, 1993), 23–49.

FIRTH, C. H., *An English Garner* (1903).

FLEAY, F. G., *A Biographical Chronicle of the English Drama 1559–1642*, 2 vols. (1891).

FLECKNOE, RICHARD, *A Short Discourse of the English Stage*, appended to *Love's Kingdom* (1664).

FOCKE, Friedrich, 'Synkrisis', *Hermes*, 58 (1923), 327–68.

FORBES-LEITH, WILLIAM, SJ, *Narratives of Scottish Catholics under Mary Stuart and James VI* (Edinburgh, 1885).

FOWLER, ALASTAIR, *Conceitful Thought* (Edinburgh, 1975).

—— *The Country House Poem* (Edinburgh, 1994).

—— 'The Silva Tradition in Jonson's *The Forest*', in Maynard Mack and George deForest Lord (eds.), *Poetic Traditions of the English Renaissance* (New Haven, 1982), 163–80.

FRASER, SIR WILLIAM, *The Lennox*, 2 vols. (Edinburgh, 1874).

FROST, DAVID L., *The School of Shakespeare* (Cambridge, 1968).

FRYE, B. J. (ed.), *John Dryden: 'Mac Flecknoe'* (Columbus, Oh., 1970).

FULLER, THOMAS, *The History of the Worthies of England* (1662).

GARRICK, DAVID, *The Plays*, ed. H. W. Pedicord and F. L. Bergmann, 7 vols. (Carbondale, Ill., 1980–2).

GILCHRIST, OCTAVIUS, *An Examination of the Charges Maintained by Messrs Malone, Chalmers, and Others, of Ben Jonson's Enmity, &c. Towards Shakespeare* (1808).

GILDON, CHARLES, *An Essay on the Art, Rise, and Progress of the Stage in Greece, Rome, and England* (1710).

GOLDBERG, S. L., 'Folly into Crime: The Catastrophe of *Volpone*', *Modern Language Quarterly*, 20 (1959), 233–42.

GOLDSWORTHY, W. LANDSDOWN, *Ben Jonson and the First Folio* (1931).

GORDON, D. J., 'Poet and Architect: The Intellectual Setting of the Quarrel between Ben Jonson and Inigo Jones', in *The Renaissance Imagination: Essays and Lectures by D. J. Gordon*, collected and edited by Stephen Orgel (Berkeley, 1975).

GORDON OF GORDONSTOUN, SIR ROBERT, *A Genealogical History of the Earldom of Sutherland From its Origins to the Year 1630* (Edinburgh, 1813).

GOULD, ROBERT, *The Play-House: A Satyr* (1695), in *The Works* (1709).

GRAVES, THORNTON, 'Jonson in the Jest Books', in *The Manly Anniversary Studies in Language and Literature* (Chicago, 1923), 127–39.

GREENBLATT, STEPHEN, 'The False Ending in *Volpone*', *Journal of English and Germanic Philology*, 75 (1976), 90–104.

—— 'Psychoanalysis and Renaissance Culture', in Patricia Parker and David Quint (eds.), *Literary Theory/Renaissance Texts* (Baltimore, 1986), 210–24.

GREENE, THOMAS M., 'Jonson and the Centered Self', *SEL: Studies in English Literature 1500–1900*, 10 (1970), 325–48.

GREENWOOD, SIR GEORGE, *Ben Jonson and Shakespeare* (1921).

GREG, W. W., *Shakespeare's First Folio* (Oxford, 1935).

—— (ed.), *A Companion to Arber* (Oxford, 1967).

—— and BOSWELL, E., *Records of the Court of the Stationers' Company 1576 to 1602* (1930).

GREY, ZACHARY, *et al.*, Preface to *Critical, Historical, and Explanatory Notes on Shakespeare*, 2 vols. (1754).

GUINEY, L. I., *Recusant Poets* (New York, 1939).

GUTHRIE, WILLIAM, *An Essay on English Tragedy* (1747).

HANDOVER, P.M., *Arabella Stuart: Royal Lady of Hardwick and Cousin to King James* (1957).

HAZLITT, WILLIAM, *The Complete Works*, ed. P. P. Howe, after the edition of A. R. Waller and Arnold Glover, 21 vols. (1931).

HEINEMANN, MARGOT, *Puritanism and Theatre* (Cambridge, 1980).

HELGERSON, RICHARD, *Self-Crowned Laureates: Spenser, Jonson, Milton, and the Literary System* (Berkeley, 1983).

HERBERT, ROBERT L., *David, Voltaire, 'Brutus', and the French Revolution* (1972).

HIBBARD, G. R., 'The Country House Poem of the Seventeenth Century', *Journal of the Warburg and Courtauld Institutes*, 19 (1956), 159–74.

HINMAN, CHARLTON, *The Printing and Proof-Reading of the First Folio of Shakespeare*, 2 vols. (Oxford, 1963).

HOLROYD, MICHAEL, *Bernard Shaw*, 5 vols. (1988–92), vol. i, *The Search for Love* (1988).

HONIGMANN, E. A. J., *Shakespeare's Impact on his Contemporaries* (1982).

—— *John Weaver: A Biography of a Literary Associate of Shakespeare and Jonson* (Manchester, 1987).

HORACE, *Satires, Epistles, and Ars Poetica*, trans. H. R. Fairclough, Loeb Classical Library (1970).

'HORATIO', *Gentleman's Magazine*, 42 (1772), 522–3.

HOWARTH, HERBERT, 'Shakespeare's Gentleness', *Shakespeare Survey*, 14 (1961), 90–7.

HOWELL, JAMES, *Epistola Ho-Elianae* (1645).

HYDE, EDWARD, Earl of Clarendon, *The History of the Rebellion*, ed. W. Dunn Macreay, 6 vols. (Oxford, 1888).

INGLEBY, C. M., TOULMIN SMITH, L., and FURNIVALL, P. J. (comp.), and MUNRO, JOHN (ed.), *The Shakespeare Allusion-Book*, 2 vols. (1932).

JACKSON, WILLIAM A. (ed.), *Records of the Court of the Stationers' Company 1602–1640* (1957).

JAMES VI OF SCOTLAND, *The Poems*, ed. James Craigie, 2 vols., The Scottish Text Society (Edinburgh, 1955).

JOHNSON, A. W., *Ben Jonson: Poetry and Architecture* (Oxford, 1994).

JOHNSON, SAMUEL, *The Lives of the English Poets*, ed. George Birkbeck Hill, 3 vols. (Oxford, 1905).

—— *Preface to Shakespeare* (1765), in *Johnson on Shakespeare*, ed. Arthur Sherbo, vol. vii of the Yale Edition of the Works of Samuel Johnson (New Haven, 1968).

JONES, EMRYS, *The Origins of Shakespeare* (Oxford, 1977).

—— 'The First West End Comedy', *Proceedings of the British Academy*, 68 (1982), 215–58.

JONSON, BEN, *The Alchemist*, ed. F. H. Mares, The Revels Plays (1967).

—— *Ben Jonson*, ed. C. H. Herford and Percy and Evelyn Simpson, 11 vols. (Oxford, 1925–52).

—— *Ben Jonson*, ed. Ian Donaldson, The Oxford Authors (Oxford, 1986).

—— *The Complete Masques*, ed. Stephen Orgel, The Yale Ben Jonson (New Haven, 1969).

—— *Discoveries*, ed. Maurice Castelain (Paris, n.d. [1907]).

—— *Epicoene*, ed. R. V. Holdsworth, New Mermaids (1979).

—— *Every Man In His Humour*, ed. G. B. Jackson, The Yale Ben Jonson (New Haven, 1969).

—— *The Poems*, ed. G. B. Johnston, The Muses Library (1954).

—— *Poetaster*, ed. Tom Cain, The Revels Plays (Manchester, 1995).

—— *Sejanus His Fall*, ed. Philip Ayres, The Revels Plays (Manchester, 1990).

—— *Volpone*, ed. John Creaser, The London Mediaeval and Renaissance series (1978).

—— *Volpone*, ed. Alvin B. Kernan, The Yale Ben Jonson (New Haven, 1962).

—— *The Works*, ed. William Gifford, 9 vols. (1816).

—— *The Works*, ed. William Gifford and Francis Cunningham, 3 vols. (1904).

JOWETT, JOHN, ' "Fall Before this Booke": The 1605 Quarto of *Sejanus*', *TEXT: Transactions of the Society for Textual Scholarship*, 4 (1988), 279–95.

JUVENAL, *Juvenal and Persius*, trans. G. G. Ramsay, Loeb Classical Library (1930).

KAY, W. DAVID, 'The Shaping of Ben Jonson's Career', *Modern Philology*, 67 (1970), 224–37.

—— *Ben Jonson: A Literary Life* (1995).

KERMODE, FRANK, *The Sense of an Ending* (1967).

—— 'Waiting for the End', in Malcolm Bull (ed.), *Apocalypse Theory and the Ends of the World* (Oxford, 1995), ch. 11.

KERRIGAN, W., 'Ben Jonson Full of Scorn and Shame', *Studies in the Literary Imagination*, 6 (1973), 199–217.

KIERNAN, V. G., *The Duel in European History: Honour and the Reign of Aristocracy* (Oxford, 1988).

KNIGHTS, L. C., *Drama and Society in the Age of Jonson* (1937).

—— *Explorations* (1946).

KRANIDAS, THOMAS, 'Possible Revisions or Additions to Jonson's *Epicoene*', *Anglia*, 83 (1965), 451–3.

LANGBAINE, GERARD, *An Account of the English Dramatic Poets* (Oxford, 1691).

LEAVIS, F. R., *Revaluation* (1962).

LECLERCQ, R. V., 'The Reciprocal Harmony of Jonson's "A Celebration of Charis" ', *Texas Studies in Language and Literature*, 16 (1975), 627–50.

LEHMAN, DAVID, *Signs of the Times: Deconstruction and the Fall of Paul de Man* (New York, 1991).

LEISHMAN, J. B. (ed.), *The Three Parnassus Plays (1598–1601)*, (1949).

LEMPRIERE, J., *A Classical Dictionary* (Halifax, 1865).

LE STRANGE, SIR NICHOLAS, *Merry Passages and Jeasts: A Manuscript Jestbook*, ed. H. F. Lippincott (Salzburg, 1974).

LIMON, JERZY, *Dangerous Matter: English Drama and Politics in 1623/24* (Cambridge, 1986).

LINDLEY, DAVID, *The Trials of Frances Howard: Fact and Fiction at the Court of King James* (1993).

LIPKING, LAWRENCE, *The Life of the Poet: Beginning and Ending Poetic Careers* (Chicago, 1981).

—— 'Life, Death, and Other Theories', in Jerome J. McGann (ed.), *Historical Studies and Literary Criticism* (Madison, Wis., 1985), 180–98.

LONGHURST, DEREK, ' "Not for all time, but for an Age": An Approach to Shakespeare Studies', in Peter Widdowson (ed.), *Re-Reading English* (1982), 150–63.

'LONGINUS', *'Longinus' on the Sublime*, ed. D. A. Russell (Oxford, 1964).

LOOMIE, ALBERT J., 'King James I's Catholic Consort', *Huntington Library Quarterly*, 34 (1971), 303–16.

LOWENSTEIN, JOSEPH, 'The Script in the Marketplace', in Stephen Greenblatt (ed.), *Representing the English Renaissance* (Berkeley, 1988), 265–78.

—— 'Personal Material: Jonson and Book-Burning', paper presented at the Leeds conference, 'Ben Jonson: Text, History, Performance', July 1995.

MACAULAY, LORD, *Critical and Historical Essays Contributed to the Edinburgh Review* (1878).

MACDONALD, ROBERT H. (ed.), *The Library of Drummond of Hawthornden* (Edinburgh, 1971).

MCDONALD, RUSS, *Shakespeare and Jonson: Jonson and Shakespeare* (Lincoln, Nebr., 1988).

McElwee, William, *The Murder of Sir Thomas Overbury* (New York, 1952).

Macey, David, *The Lives of Michel Foucault* (1993).

McKeithan, D. M., 'The Occasion of *Mac Flecknoe*', *PMLA: Publications of the Modern Language Association*, 47 (1932), 766–71.

McPherson, David, 'Ben Jonson's Library and Marginalia: An Annotated Catalogue', *Studies in Philology*, 71 (1974), pp. i–xii, 1–100.

—— 'The Origins of Overdo', *Modern Language Quarterly*, 37 (1976), 221–33.

Manningham, John, *The Diary*, ed. R. B. Sorlien (Hanover, NH, 1976).

Marotti, Arthur F., *John Donne, Coterie Poet* (Madison, Wis., 1986).

Martial, *Epigrams*, trans. Walter C. A. Ker, Loeb Classical Library, 2 vols. (1968).

Matchett, W. H., *The Phoenix and Turtle* (The Hague, 1965).

Matthew, David, *Catholicism in England* (1955).

Miles, Rosalind, *Ben Jonson: His Life and Work* (1986).

Miller, Anthony, 'Jonson's Praise of Shakespeare and Cicero's *De Oratore*, III. vii', *Notes and Queries*, NS 38/236 (March 1991).

Milton, John, *Complete Poems and Major Prose*, ed. Merritt Y. Hughes (New York, 1957).

Montagu, Elizabeth, *An Essay on the Writings and Genius of Shakespeare* (1769).

Montagu, Lady Mary Wortley, *The Works*, ed. Robert Halsband and Isobel Grundy (Oxford, 1977).

Morris, Corbyn, *An Essay Towards Fixing the True Standards of Wit, Humour, Raillery, Satire, and Ridicule* (1744).

Moysie, David, *Memoirs of the Affairs of Scotland 1577–1603* [ed. J. Dennistoun], privately printed at the Bannatyne Club, 39 (Edinburgh, 1830).

Musgrove, S., *Shakespeare and Jonson*, The Macmillan Brown Lectures (Auckland, 1957; repr. Folcroft, Pa., 1975).

Neve, Philip, *Cursory Remarks on Some of the Ancient English Poets* (1789), in D. H. Craig (ed.), *Ben Jonson: The Critical Heritage* (1990).

Newton, Richard C., 'Jonson and the (Re-)Invention of the Book', in Claude J. Summers and Ted-Larry Pebworth (eds.), *Classic and Cavalier: Essays on Jonson and the Sons of Ben* (Pittsburgh, 1982), 31–55.

—— 'Making Books From Leaves: Poets Become Editors', in Gerald P. Tyson and Sylvia S. Wagonheim (eds.), *Print and Culture in the Renaissance* (Newark, NJ, 1986), 246–64.

Nicoll, Allardyce, *Stuart Masques and the Renaissance Stage* (1937).

Norman, Edward, *Roman Catholicism in England from the Elizabethan Settlement to the Second Vatican Council* (Oxford, 1985).

NOYES, R. G., *Ben Jonson on the English Stage, 1660–1776* (Cambridge, Mass., 1935).

OATES, WHITNEY J. (ed.), *The Stoic and Epicurean Philosophers* (New York, 1940).

O'FARRELL, BRIAN, *Politician, Patron, Poet: William Herbert, Third Earl of Pembroke 1580–1630* (University Microfilms, Ann Arbor, 1966).

OLSON, THEODORE, *Millennialism, Utopianism, and Progress* (Toronto, 1982).

ORGEL, STEPHEN, *The Jonsonian Masque* (Cambridge, Mass., 1965).

—— and STRONG, ROY, *Inigo Jones: The Theatre of the Stuart Court*, 2 vols. (1973).

PANICHAS, GEORGE A., *Epicurus* (New York, 1967).

PARROT, HENRY, *The Mastive, or Young-Whelpe of the Olde Dogge. Epigrams and Satyrs* (1615).

PARTRIDGE, EDWARD B., 'Jonson's *Epigrammes*: The Named and the Nameless', *Studies in the Literary Imagination*, 6 (1973), 153–98.

PATTERSON, ANNABEL, *Censorship and Interpretation: The Conditions of Writing and Reading in Early Modern England* (Madison, Wis., 1984).

PEARLMAN, E., 'Ben Jonson: An Anatomy', *English Literary Renaissance*, 9 (1979), 364–93.

PECK, LINDA LEVY, *Northampton: Patronage and Policy at the Court of James I* (1982).

PEPYS, SAMUEL, *The Diary*, ed. R. C. Latham and W. Matthews, 11 vols. (1971–95).

PETERSON, RICHARD S., 'Virtue Reconciled to Pleasure: Jonson's "A Celebration of Charis" ', *Studies in the Literary Imagination*, 6 (1973), 219–68.

—— *Imitation and Praise in the Poems of Ben Jonson* (New Haven, 1981).

PETERSON, R. T., *Sir Kenelm Digby* (1956).

PETRONIUS, *The Satyricon*, trans. Michael Heseltine, revised E. H. Warmington, Loeb Classical Library (1969).

PINDAR, *The Odes*, trans. Sir John Sandys, Loeb Classical Library (1937).

PLINY, *Natural History*, trans. H. Rackham *et al.*, Loeb Classical Library, 10 vols. (1949–62).

PRITCHARD, ARNOLD, *Catholic Loyalism in Elizabethan England* (Chapel Hill, 1979).

QUINTILIAN, *Institutio Oratoria*, trans. H. E. Butler, Loeb Classical Library, 4 vols. (1920–2).

RANDOLPH, THOMAS, *Poems with The Muses Looking-glass: and Amyntas* (1638).

RATHMELL, J. C. A., 'Jonson, Lord Lisle, and Penshurst', *English Literary Renaissance*, 1 (1971), 250–60.

RENDALL, GERALD H., *Ben Jonson and the First Folio Edition of Shakespeare's Plays* (Colchester, 1939).

RICKS, CHRISTOPHER, 'Allusion: The Poet as Heir', in R. F. Brissenden and J. C. Eade (eds.), *Studies in the Eighteenth Century*, vol. iii (Canberra, 1976), 209–40.

RIDDELL, JAMES A., 'The Arrangement of Ben Jonson's *Epigrammes*', *SEL: Studies in English Literature 1500–1900*, 27 (1987), 53–70.

RIGGS, DAVID, *Ben Jonson: A Life* (Cambridge, Mass., 1989).

ROGERS, P. G., *The Fifth Monarchy Men* (1966).

ROSS, CHERYL LYNN, 'The Plague of *The Alchemist*', *Renaissance Quarterly*, 41 (1988), 439–58.

ROUSSEAU, G. S. (ed.), *Organic Form: The Life of an Idea* (1972).

SACKS, OLIVER, *The Man Who Mistook his Wife for a Hat* (1985).

S[ANDYS], G[EORGE], *Ovid's Metamorphosis [sic] Englished, Mythologiz'd, and Represented in Figures* (Oxford, 1632).

SCHELLING, FELIX E., *Ben Jonson and the Classical School* (Baltimore, 1898).

SCHOENBAUM, SAMUEL, 'Shakespeare and Jonson: Fact and Myth', in David Galloway (ed.), *The Elizabethan Theatre*, vol. v (Hamden, Conn., 1970); 1–19.

—— *Shakespeare's Lives* (Oxford, 1970).

SENECA, *Ad Lucilium Epistulae Morales*, trans. Richard M. Gummere, 3 vols. (1917–25).

SHADWELL, THOMAS, *The Complete Works*, ed. Montague Summers, 5 vols. (1927).

SHAKESPEARE, WILLIAM, *The Complete Works*, ed. Peter Alexander (1951).

—— *The First Folio of Shakespeare*, The Norton Facsimile, prepared by Charlton Hinman (New York, 1968).

—— *The Works*, ed. Alexander Pope, 6 vols. (1725).

—— *The Works*, ed. Nicholas Rowe, 6 vols. (1709).

SHAPIRO, I. A., 'The Mermaid Club', *Modern Language Review*, 45 (1950), 6–17.

SHARPE, KEVIN, *Sir Robert Cotton 1586–1631: History and Politics in Early Modern England* (Oxford, 1978).

—— and LAKE, PETER (eds.), *Culture and Politics in Early Modern England* (1994).

SHARPE, R. B., 'Jonson's "Execration" and Chapman's "Invective": Their Place in their Authors' Rivalry', *Studies in Philology*, 42 (1945), 555–63.

SHAW, BERNARD, *The Complete Prefaces* (1965).

SHIRLEY, JAMES, *The Poems, &c.* (1646).

SIDNEY, SIR PHILIP, *An Apology for Poetry*, ed. Geoffrey Shepherd (1965).

SISSON, C. J., *Lost Plays of Shakespeare's Age* (Cambridge, 1936).

SLACK, PAUL, *The Impact of the Plague in Tudor and Stuart England* (1985).

SLIGHTS, WILLIAM W. E., *Ben Jonson and the Art of Secrecy* (Toronto, 1994).

SMALLWOOD, R. L., ' "Here, in the Friars": Immediacy and Theatricality in *The Alchemist*', *The Review of English Studies*, 32 (1980), 142–60.

SMITH, G. GREGORY, *Ben Jonson*, English Men of Letters (1919).

SMITH, R. JACK, 'Shadwell's Impact upon John Dryden', *The Review of English Studies*, 20 (1944), 29–44.

SPENCER, T. J. B., 'Ben Jonson on his Beloved, The Author, Mr William Shakespeare', in George Hibbard (ed.), *The Elizabethan Theatre*, vol. iv (1974), 22–40.

STARKEY, DAVID, 'Representation Through Intimacy: A Study of the Symbolism of Monarchy and Court in Early Modern England', in Joan Lewis (ed.), *Symbols and Sentiments: Cross-Cultural Studies in Symbolism* (1977).

STONE, LAWRENCE, *The Family, Sex, and Marriage in England 1500–1800* (1977).

——*The Road to Divorce: England 1530–1987* (Oxford, 1992).

STROUD, THEODORE A., 'Ben Jonson and Father Thomas Wright', *ELH: A Journal of English Literary History*, 14 (1947), 274–82.

—— 'Father Thomas Wright: A Test Case for Toleration', *Biographical Studies, 1534–1829*, 1 (1951–2), 189–219, with an 'addition' by B. Fitzgibbon, SJ, 261–80.

STUART, ANDREW, *Genealogical History of the Stewarts From the Earliest Period of their Authentic History to the Present Times* (1798).

SUCKLING, SIR JOHN, *Non-Dramatic Works*, ed. Thomas Clayton (Oxford, 1971).

SUETONIUS, *The Lives of Illustrious Men*, in *Suetonius*, trans. J. C. Rolfe, Loeb Classical Library, 2 vols. (1914).

SWINBURNE, A. C., *A Study of Ben Jonson* (1880).

TAVE, STUART, *The Amiable Humorist* (Chicago, 1960).

TAYLOR, DICK, Jun., 'The Third Earl of Pembroke as a Patron of Poetry', *Tulane Studies in English*, 5 (1950), 41–67.

—— 'Clarendon and Jonson as Witnesses for the Earl of Pembroke's Character', in Josephine W. Bennett, Oscar Carghil, and Vernon Hall, Jun. (eds.), *Studies in the English Renaissance Drama* (New York, 1959), 322–44.

TAYLOR, GARY, *Reinventing Shakespeare* (1991).

THOMSON, PETER, *Shakespeare's Professional Career* (Cambridge, 1992).

TITE, COLIN G. C., *The Manuscript Library of Sir Robert Cotton*, The Panizzi Lectures, 1993 (1994).

TRICKETT, RACHEL, *The Honest Muse* (Oxford, 1967).

TOWERS, TOM H., 'The Lineage of Shadwell: An Approach to *Mac Flecknoe*', *SEL: Studies in English Literature 1500–1900*, 3 (1963), 323–34.

TRIMPI, WESLEY, *Ben Jonson's Poems: A Study of the Plain Style* (Stanford, 1962).

TULIP, JAMES, 'Comedy as Equivocation: An Approach to the Reference of *Volpone*', *Southern Review*, 5 (1972), 91–101.

TUVESON, E. L., *Millenium and Utopia: A Study of the Background of the Idea of Progress* (Berkeley, 1949).

VAN DEN BERG, SARA, 'The Play of Wit and Love: Demetrius *On Style* and Jonson's "A Celebration of Charis" ', *ELH: A Journal of English Literary History*, 41 (1974), 26–36.

—— *The Action of Ben Jonson's Poetry* (Newark, NJ, 1987).

VEEVERS, ERICA, *Images of Love and Religion: Queen Henrietta Maria and Court Entertainments* (Cambridge, 1989).

VICKERS, BRIAN, *Shakespeare: The Critical Heritage*, 6 vols. (1974–81).

VILLIERS, GEORGE, Duke of Buckingham, *The Rehearsal*, ed. Edward Arber, The English Reprints (1868).

WADDINGTON, RAYMOND B., ' "A Celebration of Charis": Socratic Lover and Silenic Speaker', in Claude J. Summers and Ted-Larry Pebworthy (eds.), *Classic and Cavalier: Essays on Jonson and the Sons of Ben* (Pittsburgh, 1982), 121–38.

WALTERS, DEREK, *Chinese Geomancy* (Longmead, Shaftesbury, Dorset, 1989).

—— *The Feng Shui Handbook* (1991).

WAYNE, DON E., 'Drama and Society in the Age of Jonson: An Alternative View', in Leonard Barkan (ed.), *Renaissance Drama*, vol. xiii (Evanston, 1982).

—— *Penshurst: The Semiotics of Place and the Poetics of History* (1984).

WEINBERGER, G. J., 'Jonson's Mock-Encomiastic "Celebration of Charis" ', *Genre*, 4 (1971), 305–28.

WHITE, BEATRICE, *Cast of Ravens* (1965).

WILDE, OSCAR, *The Artist as Critic: Critical Writings*, ed. Richard Ellmann (New York, 1969).

WILDING, MICHAEL, 'Allusion and Innuendo in *Mac Flecknoe*', *Essays in Criticism*, 19 (1969), 355–70. Revised version in Earl Miner (ed.), *John Dryden* (1972), 191–233.

WILSON, EDMUND, 'Morose Ben Jonson', in id., *The Triple Thinkers* (1952), 240–61.

WILSON, F. P., *The Plague in Shakespeare's London* (Oxford, 1927).

WIND, EDGAR, *Pagan Mysteries in the Renaissance* (1958).

WOOLF, VIRGINIA, *A Room of One's Own* (1928).

WORDEN, BLAIR, 'Ben Jonson among the Historians', in Kevin Sharpe and

Peter Lake (eds.), *Culture and Politics in Early Stuart England* (1994), 67–89.

WRIGHT, JAMES, *Country Conversations* (1694).

WRIGHT, FR. THOMAS, *The Passions of the Mind in Generall*, ed. Thomas O. Sloan (Urbana, Ill., 1971).

—— *The Passions of the Mind in Generall*, ed. William Webster Newbold, The Renaissance Imagination, vol. xv (New York, 1986).

WROTH, LADY MARY, *The Poems*, ed. Josephine A. Roberts (Baton Rouge, 1983).

YEATS, W. B., *Letters*, ed. Allan Wade (1954).

—— *On the Boiler* (Dublin, 1939).

YOUNG, EDWARD, *Conjectures on Original Composition*, ed. Edith J. Morley (Manchester, 1918).

ZITNER, S. P., 'The Revenge on Charis', in G. R. Hibbard (ed.), *The Elizabethan Theatre*, vol. iv (1974).

Index